D1191202

FREEDOM CHALLENGE

FREEDOM CHALLENGE: AFRICAN AMERICAN HOMESCHOOLERS
Copyright © 1996 by Grace Llewellyn.

Freedom challenge : African American homeschoolers / editor, Grace Llewellyn. --
    Eugene, Or. : Lowry House Publishers, 1996.
        p. : ill. : cm.
        SUMMARY: Essays written by African American homeschoolers, parents and students, telling why and how they choose to take control of their own educations.
        Includes bibliographical references and index.
        ISBN: 0-9629591-1-1

        1. Home-schooling--United States. 2. Self-culture. 3. Afro-Americans--Education. I. Llewellyn, Grace

LC32.F   371.3'944 dc20

10 9 8 7 6 5 4 3 2 1   Printed in the U.S.A.

FREEDOM CHALLENGE

African American homeschoolers

edited and with an introduction by Grace Llewellyn

Lowry House * 1996 * Eugene, Oregon

Whenever I hear an African person in the United States equate schooling with education, I become more concerned for our future as a cultural nation....For African-Americans, individual success in schooling is often simply a matter of demonstrating one's ability to represent the interests of the European-American elite....Too many of our best and brightest have been rendered virtually inaccessible to us largely because they have experienced too much schooling and too little education.
—Mwalimu J. Shujaa, in *Too Much Schooling, Too Little Education: A Paradox of Black Life in White Societies*

I have often reflected upon the new vistas that reading opened to me. I knew right there in prison that reading had changed forever the course of my life. As I see it today, the ability to read awoke inside me some long dormant craving to be mentally alive. I certainly wasn't seeking any degree, the way a college confers a status symbol upon it students. My homemade education gave me, with every additional book that I read, a little bit more sensitivity to the deafness, dumbness, and blindness that was afflicting the black race in America. Not long ago, an English writer telephoned me from London, asking questions. One was, "What's your alma mater?" I told him, "Books."
—*The Autobiography of Malcolm X*

Contents

Acknowledgments

This book has drawn on the cooperation, support, and inspiration of many people.

The essayists thank the following for their support and help--both with the daily work of homeschooling and with the specific task of writing about it: their families, Ray and Eldean Rempel, Allah, Aqiylah Collins, Omar Acuay, Hafidha Acuay, Latif Acuay, John and Lula Lewis, the Lewis's, the Borns, the Clarks, Carol Bridwell, the Spences, Mrs. Birden and the P'cola Library staff, Miss Lazetta, the kids at Hallmark Elementary, the Dare to Dream Dance Company, Percilla White, Lenicha Bell, Elizabeth Fields, Marc Gounard, Maya Gounard, Tristan Gounard, Terry Winston, Marsha Burnett, MTunu Hood, Tunu Hood, Tiye Hood, God, Michael Pogue, Daedra McGhee, VICTORY, We Are Nuts Homeschool Support Group, New Testament Christian Church, Annie Wright, Nadine Robertson, Clinton Township Photo Center, Bryan Styble and WJR, the U.S. Marine Corps, The Bridgeton, New Jersey "Advanced Class" of 1982, Reconciliation Community Church, The Nazarios, The Alaurias, and the Okinawa Christian Home Educators Association.

For enthusiasm, support, and ideas, I (Grace Llewellyn) thank the many African American homeschoolers whose words are not directly included in this book.
For thoughtful communication regarding my role as editor: Kristin Williams.
For reading parts of the manuscript and responding with astute criticism: Susannah Sheffer and Donna E. Nichols-White.
For numerous computer emergency rescues: Ned Llewellyn.
For ideas, support, conversation, and many other forms of help: Donna E. Nichols-White.
For cheerful and intelligent typing, mailing, phoning, errand-running, and other indispensable help with the logistics of this book: Janet Taylor and Josanna Crawford.
For feeding me, massaging me, and restoring my energy at the end of so many long days: Skip Llewellyn, my true love.

INTRODUCTION

Soon after I published *The Teenage Liberation Handbook: how to quit school and get a real life and education*, I was surprised by an invitation to speak in a public high school. I walked down a locker-lined hallway for the first time since leaving my teaching career and proceeded to spend several hours discussing unschooling with a crowd of excited but skeptical teenagers. (I often use the term "unschooling." "Homeschooling" can sound like doing *school* at *home*, while the kind of homeschooling that excites me does not resemble school, and often takes place as much out in the world—museums, workplaces, riverbanks—as in the home.)

We talked of the infinite possibilities available to young people who leave school to take on the challenge of educating themselves. My audience radiated first confusion, and then amazement. I explained that unschoolers need not be controlled by the burden of soulless homework, by curriculums which seem irrelevant to their lives, by teachers who do not understand or respect them, by tests and report cards which ignore their true strengths—and even their true weaknesses. Instead, unschoolers' educations are limited only by the bounds of their own courage, resourcefulness, and imagination...and, admittedly, sometimes by the fears of their well-meaning parents.

Naturally, most teenagers get excited when they start to envision what this sort of freedom might look like in their own lives, and these kids were no exception. In self-conscious bursts of passion, they raised their hands and confessed their true loves: exploring forests, exploring city streets, reading Isaac Asimov, playing flutes and drums, programming computers, writing poetry. I tried to show them how possible their own dreams were, by describing the lives of actual unschooled teenagers. I told them of the photographer-marine-biologist-freestyle biker, of the autobiographer-weaver-dancer-singer, of the solo traveler who visited me during a four-month odyssey through the United States. I told them of dedicated gymnasts, writers, jugglers, scientists, naturalists, veterinary assistants, painters, computer experts, and musicians whose time and brains belonged to themselves.

The final bell rang, and most of the students hoisted their textbook-filled backpacks and went home. But several stayed and clustered around me, their eyes intense. Among them stood a young man whose voice wavered between resignation and longing. He told me his name was Michael. "I totally see what you're saying about school, how it's a waste of time," he said, "And I know there's a lot more I could learn and do on my own. But I can't do it, because I'm black. I walk into some business to get a job, they want to see my diploma, I tell them I educated myself according to my own interests, and it's over. They say, 'Right. Another dropped out nigger.' "

Michael's lament raised enough subjects to fill a whole book—some having to do with racial issues, some not. Of course his concerns were valid. Where prejudice and discrimination exist, it's hard enough for a young black person to prove himself worthy of opportunities—even when he has been conventionally schooled. An unconventional education may indeed, at times, add yet another strike against him in the eyes of an unimaginative personnel director or scholarship foundation. But as legitimate as Michael's concern was, I think its opposite must be equally true: those who are least served by conventional schooling stand to benefit the most from trying something different. As scary as it can be to challenge the system and risk going without formal credentials, black people may—as a group—stand to benefit more than anyone else from the opportunities homeschooling can offer. (And actually, as homeschooling becomes more widely practiced, it becomes increasingly easier for homeschoolers to earn regular high school diplomas and other credentials anyway.)

In those few moments with Michael, I offered what encouragement I could squeeze in before his bus left. I reminded him how significant it might be to have the hours of eight a.m. to three p.m.—not to mention evening homework time—back in his own control. That's far more time than unschoolers need to spend on academic work, even if they hold themselves to higher standards than the snootiest private school in town. Again and again, experienced homeschooling families come up with the statement that two to three hours daily is more than enough for academics. David and Micki Colfax—whose homeschooled boys went on to Harvard—point out in their book *Homeschooling For Excellence* that in school, children spend only about twenty percent of their time "on task," or actually engaged in academic learning. In contrast, unschoolers discover that without compromising their educations, they can also spend four or five hours each day on art, sport, job, hobby, business, volunteer work, writing letters or song lyrics, whatever—and that's *before* the dismissal bell rings at the school down the street.

Wise unschoolers use some of this time as an investment into future work that will support them financially *and* emotionally. Some work jobs, acquiring money and experience with which to later launch their own business. Some actually start tiny shoestring businesses during childhood, building gradually. Some apprentice, volunteer, or intern with experts in fields that interest them....and this experience builds a résumé and sometimes leads directly to an interesting job offer. Some unschoolers build portfolios showing off their skills. Many go to college—and their good track record makes it increasingly easy for others to follow. In fact, many colleges are particularly excited about admitting unschoolers, and of course no employer asks about your high school diploma when you wave your B.S. in his face. Indeed, it has become obvious to me that unschooling allows kids an *advantage* in preparing for their futures.

So, I pointed out to Michael that if he chose to unschool himself with the goals of both having a fantastic time and preparing himself for adult work, chances are he would never have to walk into the depressing situation he predicted.

Later I thought back to the conversation, and I wished that I had also been able to say, simply, "Well, Michael, black people homeschool too." But at the time I didn't know whether that was even true.

Now I know it is true, and that many black people homeschool to save themselves from a system which limits and destroys them, to reclaim their own lives, families, and culture, *to create for themselves something very different from conventional schooling.* I also know that the numbers of these people increase every year, and—especially when I remember my first year of teaching—I hope the numbers will continue to increase, by hundreds and thousands. I remember the horrifying smell of human energy and talent rotting in all schools, any schools, but especially in the mostly black, badly funded schools where I substitute taught in Oakland, California. I remember a Friday when the school secretary told me to plan on coming back Monday because the chemistry teacher liked to take Fridays and Mondays off. I remember walking past vice principals' offices that were bulging with young men who had been kicked out of class. I remember the soft eager eyes of preschoolers and the hard cynical eyes of high school seniors. I remember the principal who introduced me as a long-term sub for a choir teacher, telling the class it didn't matter what they thought of my teaching, the state had given me a certificate (though in English, not music) and that's all they needed to know.

Back then I didn't know enough to announce to my students that there was an altogether different and completely legal option called "homeschooling," let alone that people in their own communities were busy inventing and adapting this option to fit their own needs. Ironically, though, it was the desperation of that year in Oakland that first got me to thinking about what it would take to start a very tiny, very inexpensive private school. I wanted to keep teaching kids without squashing them the way regular schools seemed inevitably to do. That thinking led me from one publication to the next, until I had a copy of John Holt's *Instead of Education*.

With that book, I discovered the realm of unschooling, and my life changed. My mind opened to new possibilities and a deeper understanding of my own childhood and adolescence. For the first time I understood that *learning* and *being taught* are not the same thing. Although I did teach a couple more years in a private college-preparatory middle school, I eventually quit in favor of the work I do now, spreading the word that kids can learn better and grow into brighter, more competent, livelier human beings outside of school.

While I've worked on this book, people have often asked me why black people homeschool. Having only communicated with about twenty families in the process of editing this book, I'm hardly the expert. What I do know is that homeschoolers, in general, are an extremely diverse bunch. People, in general, homeschool so that children can learn more naturally and develop their unique talents. They homeschool to lessen the possibility of children being shot with a gun at school. They homeschool to maintain close family relationships. They homeschool to avoid the brutal school socialization process, which often turns thoughtful, unique children into rude conformists. They homeschool to honor their children's individual learning styles, which are not always compatible with sitting in a desk and shutting up. They homeschool to provide more challenging and thorough academic educations. They homeschool because they are tired of the racist, sexist propaganda that masquerades as truth in history textbooks. They homeschool to break down artificial barriers between life and learning. They homeschool for other reasons too, concerning health, religion, geography, and self-esteem.

As the writers in this book show, African Americans homeschool for all these reasons and then some. Some homeschool because they see that racial integration in the schools has not always worked for their benefit. (Among other things, they feel that it has disrupted community life and thrust children into hate-filled classrooms where few people encourage or hope for their success.) Some homeschool because they see that schools perpetuate institutionalized racism. Some homeschool because they are tired of curriculums emphasizing Europe and excluding Africa. Some homeschool because their children are overwhelmingly treated as problems in schools, and quickly labeled Attention Deficit Disordered or Learning Disabled. Some homeschool because black kids drop out of school at much higher rates than white kids. Some homeschool because they want to continue the Civil Rights struggle for equal educational rights, and they feel that they can best do so by reclaiming their right to help their own children develop fully—rather than by working to get them equal access to conventional schooling.

People also asked me if I noticed differences in black and white homeschooling *styles*. Again, all I can say with authority is that diversity reigns, no matter what color you're talking about. Some homeschoolers use expensive prepackaged curriculums, though many families who try this approach gradually relax into a more natural method using fewer textbooks and more "real books," exploring outdoors and in their communities as well as completing academic work at home. Some families de-emphasize books and emphasize learning through interesting volunteer positions and internships. Some very successfully allow their children to simply follow their greatest interests until they are experts in beekeeping or library science or computer programming or newsletter publishing. Some enroll in community classes and attend lectures. Some travel. Each family figures out, through trial and error, what works best for them.

Several African American homeschoolers have told me that black people are much more likely than whites to emphasize academics and maintain a structured curriculum. And their observations were indeed borne out by my contact with some of the essayists and potential essayists for this book. It seems that this state of affairs reflects, at least in part, the same concern Michael expressed to me when I spoke in his high school. If more black homeschoolers (than white) follow a structured curriculum, it's *not* necessarily because they value conformity or because they don't trust their children to acquire the skills they need to become happy, well-educated adults. Rather, for obvious reasons, they don't trust *society* to recognize their kids' intelligence without benefit of, at least, a list of textbooks completed or classes taken through an academic summer program.

I have to admit that from my position, I can't help but hope that this somewhat school-like approach to education is a temporary trend among black homeschoolers. Where a strong emphasis on conventional academics is based on fear, I hope that this fear will give way to the joyous confidence that many white unschoolers enjoy. (Largely, but not completely, what this boils down to is that I fervently hope *society* will get a lot saner and make it easier for black homeschoolers to feel that it's safe for them to give their kids more freedom.)

In my travels, correspondence, and reading I've noticed again and again that the brightest and most competent homeschooled kids are the ones who have been given the most freedom and support to pursue their own interests seriously. They may not be the most "well-rounded" in the conventional sense—they may not have absorbed equal parts of European and American literature, Eurocentrically written history, essay-writing, textbook mathematics, basic competency in a foreign language, a smattering of artistic or musical knowledge, biology, chemistry, and physics. But they do usually have a broad, relaxed, overall understanding of the world. (Graduate students often suffer from overspecialized academia; I've rarely seen that quality in an unschooler.) Furthermore, these kids often attain a serious level of expertise in the one or two areas they love best, going far beyond schools' mediocre version of "excellence." So it is my hope that *all* homeschoolers will increasingly choose to take full advantage of their potential freedom.

Is this a book just for African Americans? Absolutely not. As far as I know, it is the first collection of essays written entirely by homeschooling parents and kids of any color. (There are a few other excellent homeschooling books which *include* essays by parents and/or kids.) The essayists address a myriad of classic homeschooling issues, relevant and informative for people of any ethnic background—such as socialization, learning from experts in a specific subject instead of from schoolteachers, learning to read with and without parental instruction, doing science.

I also hope that experienced white homeschoolers by the thousands will read this book. Some of the essayists shed a bright light on race relations within the homeschooling movement, and they make it clear that we all have a lot to learn about the consequences of our attitudes and actions. If we make a sincere effort to listen and understand, certainly it will be easier for us to stop being part of the problem that homeschoolers of color face.

You may have a particular educational concern that is not discussed much in these pages—for instance, perhaps your children have been labeled dyslexic and you are wondering about the pros, cons, and possible methods of homeschooling them. Though this book doesn't address every homeschooling issue in detail, there's a good chance that some other homeschooling literature will speak to any concern you have. White people do still form the vast majority of the homeschooling movement, so perhaps it's inevitable that some of your inspiration and ideas will come from their stories. I highly recommend *Growing Without Schooling* magazine, because it offers in-depth autobiographical letters from readers on almost every imaginable aspect of homeschooling, including single parent homeschooling; homeschooling kids with various labels including ADD and ADHD; educating spouses and relatives about homeschooling; homeschooling as African Americans, Asians, and Latinos; and finding ways to give children safe access to the adult world. See the resource listing in Appendix III for more information on this and other recommended books and magazines.

One particular concern which isn't discussed much in this book is homeschooling children who have been labeled Attention Deficit Disordered. Again, *Growing Without Schooling* and other publications address this issue, but I also wanted to mention that one of the original writers for this book, Monica Satterwhite, had wonderful success removing her so-called "ADD/Future Menace to Society" son from school. Unfortunately, she felt forced by family circumstances to return him to school, and therefore, despite my pleas, felt unqualified to contribute an essay. But in an early letter, she wrote,

> When Sean was in kindergarten, I was receiving at least one call a week from his school, telling me that my five-year-old was a "menace to society." After getting through that year, we began to experience the disaster of the public school system. Two months into the school year, Sean's teacher informed us that Sean was going to fail the first grade and that he needed

special education. I felt that even if he did improve, his teacher had already made her judgment and that he would not be treated fairly. Well, I removed him from there and next came Catholic school. There, I was told that Sean had Attention Deficit Disorder and we should put him on Ritalin. He was also given an IQ test and we discovered that he had one of the highest scores in the school. Imagine that—well, we medicated our child and sent him away for the nuns to handle him. This went fairly well until about the third grade. He began to get into fights and all type of trouble as he'd walk home from school....While looking for yet another school to put him in, I came across a book by a man named Jawanza Kunjufu, called *The Conspiracy to Destroy Black Boys*. After reading that, I was convinced that no school could ever treat him fairly or teach him the way he needed to be taught.

Monica went on to explain how they decided to try homeschooling, and concluded her letter by saying, "It definitely has not been easy but God has blessed us. Sean no longer takes Ritalin, he's a self-proclaimed vegetarian, and he's doing great work." When Sean did return to school, he was stronger and better able to cope. "It was nothing like the public school situation we had before," Monica says, "I would like to think that the increased confidence and self esteem that he acquired through homschooling contributed to the change. By the way, he made honor roll twice this year! His first time ever!....I know homeschooling works, and if I could, I'd do it all over again."

The territory of unschooling is wide, welcoming, unrushed, and forgiving. Ironically, though, the entry gate may seem narrow and forbidding. Many families are able to decide to homeschool because they feel "qualified" to do so: one or both parents has a college degree and, surprisingly often, a school-teaching background. They begin in a fairly unimaginative "school at home" way, with the parent-teachers modeling their procedures after their own memories of school, buying or creating a conventional academic curriculum, giving assignments and leading daily lessons—confident that their own academic background will ensure a proper education for their kids.

The real truth dawns on them some months later: a parent's academic background is only one of many factors that influence homeschooling success. Certainly, it's less important than a determination to help their children knock on doors, make phone calls, read bulletin boards, write letters, use the library, and otherwise access learning opportunities. In fact, the more a parent clings to a sense of importance and authority due to her own academic background, the more likely she is to blindly get in her children's way, pompously cramming her own skills down their gullets and failing to see the seeds of their individual curiosities. And so, in many homeschooling families, school-at-home gives way to a more radical, exciting, and sustainable educational process, in which the parent backs off and offers support rather than heavy-handed direction. Children are encouraged to follow their own interests, in their own way, and since this often leads them out of their parents' realm of knowledge, the family quickly finds out just how unnecessary is parental academic expertise. There are always other teachers to be found, in the form of neighbors, community-based classes, library books, on-line forums, and relatives.

All a parent really needs to homeschool successfully, an African American father pointed out to me, is the motivation of love. The stronger and truer the love, the better the parents will see their children's genius, and the more enthusiastically they'll help their children find other situations where they can blossom. None of this requires full-time attention or damaging self-sacrifice. In many homeschooling families, teenagers and older children educate themselves while both parents hold regular jobs.

In fact, judging by the hundreds of letters I've received from unschooling teenagers, I would go so far as to say that when older children or teenagers want badly enough to educate themselves, they already have all they need. Even if their parents can offer no more support than to give permission to unschool, they can succeed. Even without parental help, determined kids can seek out all sorts of mentors, guides, and learning situations; and many, of course, use library books, textbooks, computers, or other resources to teach themselves. Most younger children do need somewhat more adult guidance—though, as the essays in this book demonstrate, not so much that their parents must necessarily give up their own interests or careers.

Of course it helps—not just for homeschooling, but for all of life—to have (or build) a strong community. Maya Gounard learns not only from her parents, but also from numerous other adults who live in her houseboat neighborhood. The Cloughs' neighbors built a barn for them, and Adam Clough helped; later, when those neighbors moved to Costa Rica they invited Adam to come stay with them. Sunshine Lewis and her brothers learn about astronomy, Spanish, architecture, and chess from adult friends of their family. Erin Tackoor has special lessons with her aunt once a week. Detra Rose Hood has worked with other African American homeschooling families—despite their ideological differences—to set up science classes taught by volunteer experts, which her son Tunu enjoys.

Anyway, the problem with all of this comes at the beginning: that gate into the land of homeschooling, which many people perceive as narrow and formidable. With the false confidence provided by a background of academic success, middle class college educated parents at least have the guts to walk through that gate, after which they embark on an unexpected adventure and discover *true* education. Conversely, working class families without college backgrounds often lack the confidence to walk through the gate in the first place. School officials, relatives, spouses, even children can shatter frail hopes when they accuse: "You? Homeschool your kids? Didn't you drop out of high school? Don't you remember how badly you did in history and science? You never even took algebra! Your spelling is atrocious!" Often, I believe, parents who would have no trouble with the real work of homeschooling never even consider it as an option, simply because they've been thoroughly indoctrinated by the school system to believe that A) they are stupid, and B) without academic success, they have no business homeschooling their own children. The sooner these lies are blasted and the vicious cycle halted, the smarter and happier this world will become.

I think back to my day as guest rabble-rouser at Garfield High School. Michael would be around twenty years old by now, and I wonder where he is. It's too late for him to quit high school, but many of us have learned that it's possible to unschool at any age—to detoxify your mind, soul, and self-esteem from its many years of institutionalized battering, to unlearn the lies. So I hope that he, and other adults, might still discover this book and use it as a stepping stone to greater freedom, joy, and power in the continuation of their lifelong educations.

And, of course, I pray that families, children, and teenagers of all colors and backgrounds will not just read, but *use* this book. As a caucasian committed to educational freedom and excellence, my deepest motive for editing this book is hope for a brighter world for all of us. Young people who do not have to sacrifice themselves to unimaginative busywork and a standardized educational agenda can more likely flourish, develop their unique talents and voices, and give the *gift* of themselves to the world—their poetry, their scientific discoveries, their buildings, their music, their inventions, their autobiographies. It is a blessing, each month, to receive my favorite unschooling magazines in the mail and to read letters and essays describing kids' vastly diverse, impassioned lives. Even just knowing about each of these kids makes my own world bigger and more beautiful, and as they grow up and develop further, we all reap rewards. What a much *greater* gift to the world it will be, when children of all cultural backgrounds and races grow up free from schools' narrow shaping, and instead remain true to their own unique natures. ❖

Pamela Sparks
Houston, Texas

THE DAILY
RHYTHM OF LIFE

We came to homeschooling in part by luck, in part through misfortune, and in part through philosophical choice. Keith and I began having children earlier than either of us intended. I was nineteen when I left college, got married, moved to a new state and had my first child, Whitney. My second, Brandon, came along within a year. I had to rethink all of my life's plans. But although it seemed like misfortune, the timing of my pregnancies and leaving my college path really allowed me to experience motherhood more fully than I might have if I'd waited until I was in mid-career, with a six-week maternity leave.

Keith and I moved to Austin, Texas from California in 1984 so that Keith could attend law school at the University of Texas. I was a full time mom for those three years, and I immersed myself in baby gym classes and toddler teaching programs, excited by every aspect of Whitney and Brandon's development. I got my first awareness of homeschooling during this time and was immediately attracted.

I had become involved with an organization called Renaissance Child, which conducts workshops, holds parent meetings, and offers information and materials on early childhood education. It was wonderfully stimulating.

One realization in particular that I gained at that time sticks with me because it dramatically influenced my approach to parenting and, later, my decision to homeschool. I came to see learning as a survival mechanism, as natural and as crucial as the instinct to suckle. Human beings learn. And unless this process is thwarted, we learn eagerly. During the early years, children have to amass amazing amounts of information in order to survive—and hopefully thrive—in the environment they are born into. Without formal instruction, they easily learn every-

The Sparks Family (from left):
Whitney, Kyle, Pamela, Haley, Keith, and Brandon

Gina Carroll

thing from the names and faces in their world to the language or languages in their home, to names of plants and animals, to household objects and how they work, to colors, shapes and textures. They learn about their bodies and how to crawl, walk, run, throw, catch and jump.

All of this may seem obvious to you, and not at all enlightening. But for me at that time, thinking consciously about my toddlers' busy learning allowed me to see their activities with respect and patience. Whitney's desire to pour her own juice at two, while messy and inconvenient for me, was important and educational for her. Brandon's obsession with emptying and refilling drawers or cupboards or bowls truly served some other purpose besides undoing all of my housekeeping efforts. I must relay an anecdote about a particularly patient and perceptive mother who recognized the pursuit of discovery at hand when her two year old broke a dozen eggs one by one on the floor. Upon viewing the mess, she exclaimed, "Oh darling! They're all the same inside!" Truly, I too came to take delight in my children's curiosity and daily discoveries.

The theories of Glen Doman (director of the Institutes for the Achievement of Human Potential) and Renaissance Child encourage parents to recognize the preschool years as a prime learning time neurologically, and then to take advantage of this neurological predisposition to promote greater learning. Inspired by both, I actively tried to create a stimulating learning environment in our home.

So we did lots of reading and counting, singing and listening to music. I involved the children in cooking—or just mixing and stirring— and cleaning. I showed them hundreds of picture cards of everything from birds and fish and reptiles and other animals, to flowers and trees and other plants, to seashells, planets, constellations, maps, flags, vehicles, art prints and famous artists or inventors or leaders or writers. We took outings to parks, zoos, museums, the grocery store, and ball games.

I really took my role as the parent/educator to heart and I think I enjoyed all of our activities and outings as much as the children did. So, as I looked ahead, I was already forming reservations about schooling. I wanted always to preserve the curiosity and eager learning I saw in Whitney and Brandon; and furthermore, I selfishly enjoyed teaching them and learning with them.

When Keith graduated from law school, we moved back to the Bay Area in California. We lived on campus at Stanford University so that I could finish my degree. Keith commuted to San Francisco to work at a law firm, and we arranged childcare for the first time through two dramatically different preschools.

One was the on-campus laboratory preschool, Bing, at Stanford. It was wonderful in so many ways. The children entered a large space arranged with choices everyday: playdough table, block area, painting easels, a daily prepared craft activity, an imaginative play area with dress-up, dolls and homemaking furniture, a puzzle/manipulative play area, music, a reading area, and an area with access to paper/writing/cutting/stapling/pasting materials. The yards were huge with man-made grassy, rolling hills, bridges, gazebos, animals, gardens, sand and water play, oversized blocks, playhouses, boats and trains, climbing structures, swings and slides. I still think fondly of the Bing school as an ideal form of schôoling. A rich environment with free choices and non-compulsory attendance makes a wonderful learning place at any age—kind of like a museum or library.

Unfortunately, there was space for one of our children, but the other had to go on the waitlist. And, Bing was expensive and we couldn't afford the five-day program. So we looked for another preschool.

We saw a lot of noisy, chaotic environments, cramped spaces, and frazzled teachers. So when we stumbled into the quiet, ordered, well-spaced atmosphere of a Montessori preschool, we were impressed. The teachers were calm, friendly, and certainly in control of their classrooms. The children were all quietly busy, no running or screaming or messy toys. We selected this school, and sent both children there three days each week. We also sent Whitney to the Bing school on Tuesday and Thursday mornings while a sitter came to care for Brandon.

We learned many things. Whitney loved the Bing school. At first she wanted me to stay with her so I arranged to assist in her class for one quarter. Thereafter, she felt completely happy, eager, and comfortable in that school on her own. Brandon also fully enjoyed Bing, once he got in the second quarter.

Both children hated the Montessori school. Brandon screamed and cried from the second day through the second week, each time I dropped him off. (Of course they reassured me that he ceased crying once I was gone. And they reassured me that this was "completely normal" behavior and I should not respond to it.) I felt rotten during this period. In retrospect I can't imagine why we stuck with this school for a year and a half, except that we became convinced that the children's protestations were part of life and that this school was 1) necessary while I was in school and 2) good for them.

It did get better, but it never got *good*. The children grew to calmly accept the Montessori school, but by comparison, they eagerly ran into the Bing school classrooms. At Bing they made good friends and laughter was abundant throughout their mornings. Eventually we got a clue about the Montessori school when the teachers began sending home alphabet writing practice sheets with red X's marked on them to indicate poor work. This, to a four-year-old who not only knew her alphabet but had been reading for a year—a fact they never discovered. After this episode the teachers began reporting that Whitney was on "strike" and refused to do anything but occasionally paint. We finally took the kids out and during my last year of college we sent them to the Bing school five afternoons a week.

This worked out well for a while. And actually for Brandon this school continued to be a wonderful experience. For Whitney, though, a second set of school frustrations began to reveal themselves (the first being academic scrutiny and failure grading). This time it was negative socialization. Somehow she and her peers stumbled onto cliques, pecking orders, and peer pressure—at the age of five! Whitney began to request certain dresses and dolls, sure they were crucial to fitting in and having friends. And as the only African American child in her class, she began to ask why her hair wouldn't do certain things or make certain styles. Where previously Whitney would skip into each day at Bing, making the rounds through her favorite activities and engaging with friends along the way, now she would fretfully anticipate her arrival. Upon entering the class she would make a beeline for a group of girls huddled over the important assessments of the day: who wore what, who brought what toy, who would be included, and what, en masse, they should do. Whitney began crying, and then fighting, in reaction to the fears and realities of exclusion. Keith and I were mostly ineffective in helping her cope. We ultimately took her out for a while and then found a way to finish the year as peacefully as possible.

It is interesting to think back on those dynamics in light of the recurrent question we hear as homeschoolers: "What about socialization?" There does come a time for children when friendships become important. They begin to figure out what it means to be a friend or to have a friend, and how to make friends and keep friends. It seems that Whitney and the other children in her homogeneously age-segregated class were all coming to these questions at the same time and experimenting with answers. They were all just beginning to learn, and unfortunately didn't have their parents around for more mature models of behavior or for assistance in the midst of the process. So they arrived at awkward, frustrating, and often hurtful ways of attempting to make or keep friends. And one unresolved awkward or hurtful situation seemed to build upon another until insecurities and fears and negative patterns set in.

Keith and I would talk with Whitney in the evening about some situation that had occurred, and we would all come to some resolution and good resolve for the next day. But somehow things wouldn't play themselves out for Whitney as we had anticipated, and she would flounder in her attempt to find a new solution. It was really tough on her emotionally.

If Whitney had continued in school she would have been forced to handle it. And I'm sure she would have. But I'm not sure we or she would have been happy with the results. Too many children at the mercy of their social environments develop mean or self-defensive coping mechanisms. Or they become materialistic and self-absorbed in pursuit of fitting in. Or self esteem falls, resulting in lack of confidence or false bravado and showcasing. And all of these problems are compounded when children bring into their peer relations frustrations at home or with teachers.

These are not even the worst of the effects of negative socialization. The inability of male and female adolescents, and later adults, to communicate well is, I think, directly related to the awkward and artificial social arena of the schools. Not to mention peer pressure ills like premature sexual involvement, drug use, and criminal behavior.

For children in homeschooling families, there can be plenty of socializing, but they are not isolated from a larger community context, individual assistance, and mature models of behavior. And rarely do they feel *at the mercy* of their social environments. My son encountered a real bully on his little league team last year. But he did not have to deal with this child beyond that arena, in which he *chose* to participate. Further, he knew other kids in separate settings, so his whole social identity was not on the line. He was psychologically free to decide for himself how to handle the situation. And he handled it well. However, *had* he "failed" in this particular encounter, it would have been a passing reality to learn and grow from, not to be doomed by for the whole school year—or even for years as reputations linger.

Some argue that social Darwinism is a reality, and children need the training ground that schools provide. Perhaps, but I think what happens more often is that in adulthood we have to shake off those childhood insecurities and unhealthy coping mechanisms in pursuit of better relationships and greater self esteem. Insecurities and bad habits *don't* make us better or stronger as adults. Dealing with adversity does, sure, when one can learn and grow from it. And good friendships make us better and stronger as adults. With freedom from the social constraints of school, successful social connections can be maximized. Friendships can develop based upon mutual interest rather than on shared confinement.

Whitney, Brandon, and I completed our formal education at the same time. I graduated from Stanford pregnant with our third child in 1990. I had the perfect excuse for not going to work and doing instead what I by now was convinced we needed to do: homeschool.

Our first year I was very structured with the children and planned elaborate "lessons" for every morning. I wanted the children to learn a lot about a lot of different things, and I wanted them to be busy and doing great creative projects all the time. I didn't want to bore them or to force them, though. So I had this idea that if I had lots of great projects and activities prepared and displayed every morning, they would naturally gravitate to them, learn by doing these great things, and I wouldn't have to play the heavy "teacher" too much. So that's what I did.

In different sections of our dining room, I set up separate projects for math, science, history, art, and language arts. I insisted that the mornings be spent on these activities. Although the children didn't have to do everything everyday, they had to eventually make the rounds. They seemed to enjoy these morning lessons and I did take pains to prepare fun, interesting projects. But they also questioned me periodically—"Do we have to do these morning lessons?"

Initially I did feel pressure to prove that homeschooling would work. I also had the notion that the children should amass as much information as possible as quickly as possible. That was a holdover from my Renaissance Child activities and the theory that young children are neurological "sponges." So I tried to stuff them full of knowledge.

I think the failure of this approach is obvious from the cram, test, and forget syndrome that many children in school adopt in response to teachers' attempts to stuff them full of knowledge. David Guterson illustrates this point well in his book *Family Matters: Why Homeschooling Makes Sense,* Guterson and his wife homeschool their four children but he also teaches high school English, and he tells about running a little experiment with his students. In addition to regular Friday quizzes which were a standard part of the curriculum, he began to repeat the same quizzes on Mondays. The Monday quiz was the same as the one on the previous Friday, except that it would not count towards the students' grades. No student ever scored as well on Monday as he or she had scored just three days before. The point, of course, is that if we're interested in real education, we have to utilize methods that promote *learning*, not just test performance.

Eventually the death of morning lessons came from my own fatigue. It was simply too much for me to keep up with them amidst the rest of life and the new baby.

During this lull in my "teaching," I rediscovered my children intellectually. When Whitney and Brandon had been three and two, it was appropriate for me to initiate a steady stream of activities and to guide most of their games or outings. They had *wanted* my initiative and active participation. In fact, they had followed me around and wanted to participate in everything I did. But now, at six and five, they had their own ideas and games and pretend world. These didn't have anything to do with me or what I might be interested in "teaching" or planning for them. And they needed time to pursue these things. It was very good for me to rediscover the reality that children learn all the time, that they learn a great deal through play and learn best what they're interested in.

So, lots of interesting subjects that I would not have thought to "teach," and even "academic" subjects that I *was* interested in presenting, emerged spontaneously through Whitney's and Brandon's pursuits. When I did step in to help structure their learning, I could now draw upon their interests for much more effective lessons.

One of the children's pursuits at the time was building. They used Legos and blocks and we also kept a lot of wood scraps that they found endless uses for. Well, I took their lead and it became quite easy and relevant for me to introduce mathematics topics like measurement and geometry. So even though our morning "lessons" subsided for a while, learning and education continued to thrive.

I have since resurrected morning lessons in different forms that change periodically. And I have grappled with the right balance of structure versus freedom in our home. Ideally, I've decided, the children should have some responsibilities and some good habits, and then plenty of time and assistance in pursuing their own interests. Responsibilities include things like care for their person, their home and environment, pets when they have them, meals, the yard and garden, etc. Good habits include things like reading, keeping a journal, writing letters, using the dictionary and other reference books, fixing and mending things, and saving money and keeping a budget.

The way we operate now, maintaining responsibilities and good habits, along with helping the kids pursue their own projects, plays a larger part in our homeschooling than do scheduled lessons. We have specific expectations for the children, like writing two letters per week, keeping a daily journal, or cleaning the bathroom, and we have a chart to record things. However, they do these things on their own, not at a scheduled time. While less structured than our previous lessons, these responsibilities and habits are perhaps more important because they are part of the daily rhythm of life we are trying to pass along to our children. Hopefully these will become second nature and contribute to their lifelong learning and living.

Right now, morning lessons are primarily reserved for math and Spanish. We do math work together daily and we have a tutor that comes to the house weekly to help with our Spanish. Periodically other topics come up that require structured attention and we might focus on, say, grammar or geography, for a while. But generally I find that most subjects are learned quite well less formally: in our regular writing activities, reading together or independently from a variety of sources, topics in the news, conversations at home or elsewhere, or special interests that the children take up on their own. I choose to make math and Spanish more structured because Keith and I value them, just as we value regular reading and writing, but we haven't found ways to make these as automatically a part of the regular rhythm of our lives.

It's important to Keith and me that the children pick up on what we value and how that fits into our adult lives; and it's important that they are given proper respect for what *they* value. This applies regardless of how much or little structure we are currently operating with. It is a deep part of our decision to homeschool and our overall approach to parenting. I think that children are about the business of growing up, and they seek to learn what their parents (or other role models) know and do and value. That's what makes learning real and relevant instead of abstract and artificial. Children want to cook or fix cars or work on a computer, if that's what the adults around them do.

Children are also about the business of defining themselves. They need time and the resources to develop their own interests. This, too, makes learning real and relevant.

Homeschooling is really just one facet of raising children. We feed them good food, we clean the house, we take them to church. We read to them and teach them to read. I read my own books and they read theirs. We play together and they play with each other or by themselves or with their friends. I'm sewing a quilt and someone may help me out for a while. Whitney may gather flowers and press them and I may join her to dissect a flower and learn about the parts. Then we may use them to decorate homemade papers. I write letters and they write letters. Then I am embarrassed by a dear friend into actually having a lesson or two in *how* to write letters. We all learn Spanish together. I practice the most but we all, including Haley our nineteen-month-old, can speak some. I teach math in the morning but Brandon teaches in the afternoon when he shows Kyle how to keep football scores or how to build taller towers; and Whitney teaches in the evening, calculating my grocery bill before I can get to the checkout line. Brandon studies architecture, U.S. History, and any sport known to man. Whitney studies wildflowers, dance and art. Kyle learns to read and add, swims in the deep end, and loves toy animals and cars. Haley studies fish and birds and likes to play football with her brothers. It's all about living and learning.

I've heard homeschooling called the "mothers' milk" of education. And I think it's a fitting analogy. For years, we as a society were convinced by "experts" that formula feeding was superior to nursing for both baby's nutrition and mother's convenience. Now we are coming full circle with the realization that nothing comes close to mothers' milk for overall nutrition, immunoproperties, brain development and emotional bonding from the experience of nursing. We've been similarly duped, only far moreso, educationally. What can compare within an artificial institution, to the natural education of living and learning within one's family and the world?

Homeschooling is empowering. It means taking control and making decisions for one's own family and one's children instead of abdicating these rights and responsibilities to others or simply complying with societal norms. Particularly for African Americans, schools are by and large failing our children even while they have convinced us that they know best. And societal norms are not effective in supporting our children to be happy, strong, and smart.

Keith and I have this ongoing discussion about the aftermath of integration. It seems that in many respects where there were no alternatives we fared *better* by taking care to teach our own in small (segregated) Southern schools where education was part of the larger communal care, hope, and commitment. That "it takes a village to raise a child" still holds true. We need communities and cooperation and support for each family. We've gone awry to take childrearing, and education as part of that, too far from the individual, family and community, out to these nebulous experts and institutions.

    My husband has expressed the opinion that every Black family should homeschool, and that schools are ruining our children and therefore our communities irreparably. Perhaps this is unrealistic. But certainly if we spread the word about this alternative then every Black family could at least consider it, which is the beginning of regaining control and making choices about our children's education. Some families will choose to remove their children from school. Some will stick with schools but be more informed. Some will perhaps create other alternatives, like cooperating between families. Of course our whole society now is dependent upon schools and having our children occupied away from home for most of the day. Many of us haven't learned to relate well to our children, or we need to work away from our children. But there *are* ways and possibilities, if only we will conceive of them. ❖

Pamela Sparks

Whitney, Brandon, Kyle, and Haley Sparks—on the trampoline

Left: Whitney and her ballet class

Whitney Sparks
Houston, Texas

COLORS, NUMBERS, MATH, AND GREEKS

My name is Whitney Sparks. I am ten years old. I quit school when I was five years old in preschool.

I have an interest in nature, books (reading), writing, art, swimming, ballet, drawing, music, math and Greek myths. I like almost everything. I'm interested in many things. I like dolls and names too.

I know a very good doll maker, Lawan, whom I asked to make a doll especially for me. Almost immediately I started thinking up hairstyles, clothing, and looks. Lawan asked me to think of a name so she could decide who the doll might be. Well, I was thrilled at the idea because I do like thinking up pretty names. One reason I like names is because I like pretty words and their meanings. When you're choosing a name, you can choose a pretty sound *and* a pretty word *and* a pretty meaning.

Another reason I got interested in names (although I was already very interested anyway) is because of the Greek myths and the names that came from Greek myths. For instance, take the name June. The Greek goddess Hera (the Greek god Zeus' wife) had a different name in Rome— Juno. Juno was the goddess of women and marriage, so June is now the bridal month.

I also like the Greeks because I take an interest in math and numbers and the Greeks were famous for their skill in this area. To go even further, I think colors have a lot to do with math. And I like colors too.

I like the colors of the rainbow. There are said to be seven, but you more often see just six—red, orange, yellow, green, blue and purple. Here's an easy way to put them together: take red, yellow and blue in this order and leave a space after each color. Then mix red and yellow and put the orange you get in the space between them. Mix yellow and blue and put the green you get in the space between them. Now, imagine that red, yellow and blue are in a circle or triangle. Mix red and blue and put purple in the space between them. That's one of the many very neat tricks I've learned with colors of the rainbow. You can do more tricks with colors and math by arranging colors in circles and triangles. And by the way, the seventh color is indigo. It goes between blue and purple.

One of the reasons I connect colors, numbers, math and Greeks is because the Greeks had a color and a shape for every number. For instance, with the number nine, the shape had nine corners. This shape, of course, is called a nonagon. I can't remember the color for nine.

When I get interested in a subject, I normally look it up in the encyclopedia or other books I have, although it depends on what kind of topic it is. For instance, I got interested in castles recently. My brother Kyle was looking at some picture cards of castles, and I came downstairs. I saw the castles scattered about the floor and I said, "Oh! wow! I didn't know we had these." I'd always been interested in castles, but never really studied them. So now I found a picture card of the castle Neuschwanstein. And I said, "Oh! This is a beautiful castle." I love Neuschwanstein. It is located in Bavaria. I was immediately attracted to it because it is so beautiful. The picture we have is taken from the snowy mountains surrounding it. You can see a frozen lake, more mountains and beautiful snow-covered evergreens. I have another picture, closer-up, in a book, of Neuschwanstein in summer or fall. The lake is blue. And there are green mountains with snowy peaks and green covered hills. The trees are greenish red and the picture is darker than the winter one. The winter picture brings out the white towers of the castle. The summer/fall picture brings out the red and green base around the main entrance. Me and my brother Kyle were talking about this castle because both of us were immediately attracted to its miraculous beauty!

So after I'd finished admiring the winter picture of Neuschwanstein, I looked castles up in our encyclopedia. At the end of the article they had some other suggested articles to read in the encyclopedia. I wrote them all on a piece of paper. And for some of that afternoon and the next day I looked them all up.

That is basically how I explore my interests. Sometimes, though, it has to do with nature. So I will go on a nature walk, or I will look it up in the encyclopedia but then also check it out for myself.

In other things like ballet, I find out through friends. I started when I was about six. My friend Kai was already dancing and she invited me to see one of her classes. I went and I loved it. I met her teacher, Kimiko-san Sugano. And I told my mom that I would like to dance ballet. Soon afterward I started. I think I did pretty good. Kimiko-san seemed to like me. In fact, one day after ballet class, me and my mom had to go to the grocery store and when we were just about to leave, who should we meet but Kimiko-san, with her daughter Arlene, who is a professional dancer. After we finished saying hello, she asked me to take off my shoe and show Arlene my foot. She seemed to think I had a foot for dancing—at least she was telling my mom and Arlene that. I was very pleased. In just a little while I was in the second level class. But later I decided the class was too much for me and I quit.

I tried a new ballet class after that called Fantasy Ballet—and it was! From what I can remember, that class was not someplace you would go if you wanted to be a ballet dancer when you grow up, like I do. We did a junior performance of *Copelia*, which is a dance about a doll. *All* of us played Copelia. I recall the teacher saying, "Well, we don't want to have any fights so we'll all be the doll." I felt completely embarrassed dancing that performance. Afterward, I quit ballet for the second time. Much later, I went back to Kimiko-san. I was eight. I enjoyed the classes thoroughly.

I was just about to move on to the third level when we moved to Houston. Now I'm taking ballet classes at Shelly Power's Academy of Dance. I auditioned for the Houston Ballet Academy but I found they went a little too slow and it was impersonal because it was such a big studio. Well, they suggested Shelly Power's Academy of dance because Shelly Power used to be the director of the Houston Ballet Academy, and also danced with the Houston Ballet. Shelly Power's Academy of Dance is bigger than the class I used to take, but still just as personal. I'm enjoying it very much. And that is my ballet story. Now I'm thinking about taking jazz.

I have some advice for parents who are just starting to homeschool and that is: you don't homeschool like a school. Homeschooling is not parents tutoring their kids. When you homeschool, parents are simply sharing their experiences with their kids, ways to learn about new things, ways to learn about everyday living. Whereas in school, what you're doing is learning the basics—reading, writing, math, etc.—from a teacher who has little time to spend with each child and no time to teach or do things in different ways. There's only one way to learn math in school because the teacher doesn't have time to show you many ways to add or multiply or whatever.

The main reason you would choose to homeschool is so you can free your mind to do anything you want to do. You start off with the basics, but then you *use* these skills. In school you may not learn to use them, and so they become useless. Then, as Black homeschoolers, you might learn about famous Black Americans who used their skills to do things, like George Washington Carver, who invented peanut butter. You can tell that there was a lot more than his knowing how to read and write and multiply. He knew how to grow things. He knew how to combine ingredients to create things.

Homeschooling should allow you to see your child the way he or she is; and then to supply your child with things he or she wants or needs—even if what your child is interested in doesn't seem worthwhile or useful to you—because a child is *always* learning.

I much prefer homeschooling over schooling. I think homeschooling helps you see life, especially if you do it without lesson times or hours. But I don't think you should hate, hate, hate school. I think that if you want to find out about school then you should simply ask to try it out. After all, some people like it. And a lot of homeschooling parents encourage their children to go to college. Like me, I want to go to college. And my little brother Kyle asked to go to preschool. Now he's going to preschool on Tuesdays and Thursdays and still getting his home education too. And I predict that he will homeschool after this.

Homeschooling is not all freedom. I still have a lot of work to do even though I'm homeschooling. Each morning I have to brush my teeth, make my bed and get dressed. Then I have to do my devotional reading and if I haven't done my journal the night before, I have to do that. And then, even if I'm hungry, I have to eat fruit first. I hate that. And then most times we do morning lessons which includes math and learning about writing. On Thursdays I have even more to do. I have to write two letters and I have to write out Spanish sentences because I take Spanish on Friday mornings.

This morning I have to write this essay. This morning I would *like* to work on a 1000-piece puzzle. I also might like to watch cable. And another thing I'd like to be doing is playing outside in the snow. And I really think I should because like I said, I would be learning something and I don't normally get snow where I live. But I guess this essay is more important right now.

Whenever I think I don't get enough free time, my mom says I get enough. Which is true I guess, because yesterday I did spend the morning playing in the snow.

I don't think I would have been able to get interested in names and Greek myths if I hadn't had time to follow my own interests. By studying names or Greek myths (I don't know which came first) one thing led me to the other. And once I got onto Greek myths I studied and am still studying all the gods and goddesses in the myths and their similarities and connections to Egyptian and Roman myths and gods and goddesses. And this helps me study the meanings of words. For example, the word arachnid, which names an animal group that contains spiders, comes from a myth about a girl named Arachne who was a weaver, and Athene the goddess of wisdom. All kinds of things have sprouted from studying Greeks and Romans and their myths!

The best thing about homeschooling for me is that I get to learn everything about everything, everywhere around me. And I get to make friends with people everywhere including friends who go to school.

I like peaceful thoughts. I do believe in God. And I believe there is Heaven. And I believe that there can be Heaven on earth. I like the thought that there can be a perfect world. I believe our world is like a pretty picture with a clear screen of shadows on top of it. And I believe to go behind that screen is to see everything as a perfect world. It doesn't mean that people won't die, it just means that we don't think of dying as so sad, and we don't think of them as apart from us. So we would be thinking more of people's souls than their bodies. And a perfect world doesn't mean that there won't be a dead leaf on a tree. It just means that the dead leaf will still be beautiful. You don't have to worry about other people if you see the perfect world. If you see the perfect world, you won't worry about somebody who can't see behind the screen because you realize that everything is O.K. really. It's hard to keep this perfect world going in your mind. But don't worry, it is O.K.! I think that if we do see the perfect world at least sometime in our life, we can see a little bit of what Heaven will be like.

I hope I have brought nice thoughts and perspectives to you by writing this essay. ❖

Brandon Sparks
Houston, Texas

A LOT MORE TIME
TO DO WHAT YOU LIKE

I am Brandon Sparks. I am nine years old now, and I have been out of school since I was four. I like sports, movies, cars, and history the most. My hobbies are collecting and trading sports cards, reading books about presidents, and looking at new movies. I have two sisters, a brother, and a lot of friends. I like homeschooling since it gives you a lot more time to do what you like to do.

When I wake up in the morning I usually make my bed, write in my journal, and do my devotional reading (which is like reading of prayers). Then I usually turn on some music, get dressed, and go downstairs. I usually have some math to do. On Thursdays I write letters or work on Spanish. After my morning work, I usually go outside, play football, maybe go check the mail, ride my bike.

I think kids can learn a lot better when they're not forced to learn. And homeschooling gives them the opportunity to learn on their own. I think kids don't like to be pressured. A lot of them like to learn, but they don't like the way they are taught in school. If you become a homeschooler, you may be taught by your mom or dad but probably in a freer manner than school. And when you're being taught at home, you're your mom's or dad's main focus—you're the only person, the entire class. And I think parents have a certain bonding with their kids. Your parents might choose to make you do math, but when you're homeschooling there's not the same kind of pressure on you that you get in school, pressure to get good grades. I believe homeschooling has made me enjoy things—like math—that school kids might not.

We've been doing a lot of math and I've been working on symmetry. When I see symmetry coming up now I take notice, because my mom made me aware of it. So now I *like* doing symmetry.

Brandon (right) and his friend Jonathon Carroll

My mom also tells us to read a chapter everyday in a book. Lately I have been enjoying reading more on my own. Today I read three chapters in my book, and my mom didn't have to tell me. Right now I am reading three books: *The Boxcar Children, Encyclopedia Brown,* and *The Shadow.* All are really good books. My favorite things to read about are history and the presidents. I know a lot about the presidents but I would always like to know more.

I also like geographical stuff. I am planning a trip for my family across the country. I am learning a lot about the states and I'm learning about historical spots in the country. I also like mysteries and piecing together clues. Most days I like to look in the newspapers at the baseball standings.

These are some other things I like to do: I like playing with sports cards. I like going outside to play football. I like writing stories. I like working at my desk, being creative. I can make up my own teams with football cards, make up my own stories. I like playing with cars. I like playing on the computer. I think kids learn a lot from these types of things. I have learned a lot about maps by making towns for my cars and by building with blocks.

I am playing football. My team is called the Bellaire Bears. I play defensive tackle, kicker and left guard. My best friend, Jonathan, plays quarterback. You have to have a lot of padding. It is fun and challenging. All of the people on my team are schoolers except for me. Most of my friends are homeschoolers except for Jonathan. I do not think it's hard to be friends with school kids. I've made a lot of friends on my team.

I think everything could be a learning experience. You just have to know *how* to make it a learning experience. One time I was playing basketball and I noticed a math pattern. One team kept scoring two pointers (two, four, six, eight, you know). And the other team kept scoring three pointers. And I noticed that the scores kept meeting up: two, four, *six,* and three, *six,* and then they met up again at twelve, and so on. All the times the scores met up were in the six times tables. This is because three times two and two times three are six. With math patterns like this, sports is a learning experience as well as fun.

If kids had the option to do anything with their time, they would probably do something they *like* to do, which might mean watching cartoons sometimes. But they would be learning on their own even though they weren't aware of it. I do not just like to watch TV. There *are* shows I like to watch, but that's not all I do. And I do not believe that if school kids had more free time they would only watch TV, either.   There are other things kids like to do, like play games. Some kids play instruments, and some kids collect things.

Once I was talking to my mom about how parents treat kids. When adults hit adults it's always recognizable that it's bad. But when adults hit kids, nobody says a thing. Whenever something big happens in a family, like moving, a lot of parents never tell a child until it's happening. But it affects the child's life too. So why not, I wonder? When we were moving, my dad told me straight away.

I think homeschooling is a lot of fun and I hope more families decide to do it. ❖

Indira Curry, Cleveland, Ohio
interviewed by Janet Taylor

CHALLENGING MYSELF

At the time of this interview, April 1994, Indira was eighteen years old. She had been out of school since she was fifteen and a high school sophomore. (When she started homeschooling, she immediately promoted herself to junior level, since in school she'd been taking Advanced Placement classes and working at junior level.) She lived in her parents' home, but in a separate apartment above the family living area where she supported herself financially. Her father worked in lead abatement, removing lead-contaminated paint from houses and then repainting. Her mother took care of foster children. Indira herself had worked at a number of jobs since she was sixteen, and among her list of homeschooling experiences was an internship, which lasted over a year, at NASA's purchasing logistics department, through which she earned a full college scholarship. She completed her independent version of high school at the age of sixteen, and officially graduated at seventeen. (She received a diploma from Clonlara's flexible and widely praised Home Based Education Program, which operates out of Ann Arbor, Michigan.) Indira then enrolled part time in a community college, and began studying to become an architectural engineer. Her other interests and activities include creative writing, art, and dance.

Janet Taylor was a twenty-one-year-old college "rise out" at the time of this interview, and she was traveling across the country interviewing unschooled teenagers in connection with a book and a video project.

Janet: Why did you move into your own apartment?

Indira: I wanted to see if I could make it on my own, but yet still be close enough to home to have that parental guidance. So that I could say, "This is my money that I'm managing." I didn't feel, when I was at home, that I could do that. Because even though I'd give my parents money—like half of my checks every time that I got one—I could never really see where it was going. I wanted to be able to say, "This is what's going for that." I wanted to know what direction I was heading into, and where I needed to improve. Not only that, but I wanted to see how neat I am, to see if I could make it by myself.

Janet: Starting from the very beginning, like kindergarten and pre-school, what was your schooling?

Indira: For kindergarten and first grade I was in a public school, and then I went to a bilingual school in Cincinnati for second through part of fourth grade. I was learning German there. They actually taught the children and cared about the children. It was really neat. And then I came up here to Cleveland and couldn't find a school that was as extensive as that one down in Cincinnati. So I went to a private school for the rest of fourth and fifth grade. And then after that I went to public school for sixth grade through ninth grade, and then I came out for two years and did homeschooling, and graduated that way.

Janet: What were the guiding principles underlying your homeschooling? Did you follow a curriculum or did you have complete freedom?

Indira: I had complete freedom, as long as I tried to stick to some type of curriculum myself. And I had the freedom to choose how that curriculum would go. I had been in school for so long that I pretty much knew how everything operated. But it wasn't like, "For fifty minutes here I'm going to do this, and then I'm going to do that." I didn't do that at all. I had books I read, that I researched. I went to the library, I made my own subjects up.

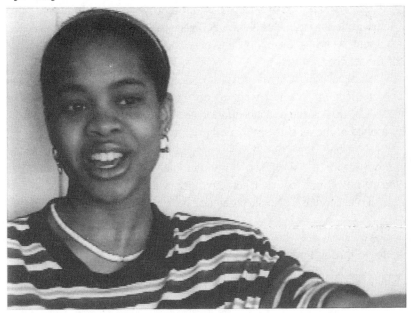

Janet Taylor

I said, okay, this is what I'm going to go into. I did extensive research, and then to make sure that I was keeping up with everyone else, I would go over to my friends' houses who were in the same grade that I was in so that we could compare notes. And I wound up finding that I was actually higher. I also went to a community college and took some courses there as well, to make sure that I was up where I thought I should be.

Janet: Why did you start homeschooling?

Indira: Well, for a couple of reasons. One, because school wasn't challenging enough for me academically.

Janet: Can you give an example?

Indira: For English, here I was in ninth grade and I was in the highest class that you could be in, and yet we were reviewing things that I had done in sixth and fifth grades. I'm like, why are we going over sentence structures? I mean, we should be beyond that now. Help me out with my essays, help me make them more college-like, or whatever. They were dealing with menial things and it was unnerving me.

Or like with biology. I didn't want a review anymore. I was sick of doing microscopes. I'd been dealing with microscopes since fourth grade. I'm like, this is *wonderful*. If you're going to have me looking under a microscope, however, just give me something more, not the same thing that I've been doing. Give me something else to look for, whatever. But it was pretty much review.

So I was kind of waiting, sitting there waiting, thoroughly bored. And I'd gotten to the point where I was tired of trying to make every assignment a challenge for myself, only to find out that it wasn't *exactly* what the teacher wanted.

I never showed my absolute potential in school, because it was never challenged. When I went to my counselors and told them, "I am bored stiff, this is the second quarter, we're almost in the third quarter," they looked at me as if to say, "You are crazy."

Not only that, but things were getting kind of rough in the school. My mom was like, "Well hey, if my daughter can't get any protection and if you're not going to teach her anything, why is she here? What's the point? To eat lunch?" So she snatched me out of school.

Janet: And how did you quit? Did you just walk out one day, did you have to go through paperwork? What happened?

Indira: Walked out one day. I don't even remember there being much paperwork. My mother got in contact with Clonlara. And when she did they were like, "We'll do all the paperwork and everything, you don't have to worry about it. We'll contact the school." They just sent us some papers and we sent them on to the Board of Education.

The school was really mad. I was still a high B and A student, so they weren't too happy with me quitting. The school *and* the Board of Education.

Janet: When you did make the decision to leave, did anybody try to convince you not to?

Indira: Everybody [laughs].

Janet: Like who?

Indira: Everyone. The last few days that I was in school, I remember just sitting there crying because everybody in my classes were just like, "No, you cannot leave." If nothing more, they'd argue, "Because we're not going to see you anymore." Everything that my mother had said, and the things the few homeschoolers I'd met had said, it all went out the window when these persons in school starting saying all these rumors about what homeschooling was like—these persons who were in school and had never even so much as *thought* about homeschooling. At the time I thought that homeschooling was kind of a small thing, like one out of every thousand kids were doing it. But once I got out it was wonderful. I got to see that there were so many more homeschoolers than I thought, and that they were also meeting *their* challenges. Coming out of school really became like the perfect challenge. Suddenly it was like, "Oh, I have a broad scope here. Here are my horizons." I felt like Columbus exploring the new world, as it were. I was exploring a whole new education.

Janet: Everyone always wants to know about homeschoolers' social lives or their lack of social lives, and gee, so do I. Tell me about your social life, before and after.

Indira: Well, my social life before. . . it actually wound up being the same before and after. Because before, while I was in school, even though the homework wasn't necessarily hard it was very laborious, because you had to continue to do it and there was so much of it. So spending time on the phone, or going to the mall or whatever, I hardly was able to do because I had some school project that I had to work on.

Coming out of school was an adjustment for me socially in the sense that I wasn't able to see my friends as much because they were in school and here I was out of school, roaming the world. That was a very interesting adjustment because I was like, "Well hey, let's go do this."

Janet Taylor

And they couldn't, because they were doing schoolwork. However, it's adjusted quite well. Especially the older that I got, you know, when I got my license it was like, "Hey—beep beep—let's go somewhere!" I had more free time to be able to go to weddings or anniversaries or have parties of my own, so in that way it was fine. Actually, it got better.

Mostly, all my life I've socialized with those that were older than I was, so that never changed at all. I just continued with that. So that was fine.

Janet: How did you go about learning the more difficult subjects, such as math? Or perhaps I should say the subjects commonly *assumed* to be harder than the others. Did you have a textbook?

Indira: Yes, I did have a math textbook. And then I continued by taking classes in the college, in community colleges. I focused on math and other difficult subjects there, because my mom wasn't necessarily completely adept to teach them to me, and my father was at work and when he came home his brain was completely tired. He didn't want to sit down and say, "Okay Indi, let's go and do this math, or whatever," even though they would review me on it. So I said, I want to make sure I have this down pat. Then, whatever else I needed to work on, I went to the libraries. And then I made sure that I never lost those basic things by studying with my brother and constantly teaching him more things. Even if he didn't understand it at all to begin with, I made sure that he understood it and was able to see something new, something that I knew and was able to teach him.

Janet: What role did—or do—your parents play in your education?

Indira: They were there more like the way guidance counselors would be. They gave me freedom, but whenever I was having a problem, or whenever I was about to make a major decision about education, they were always there to say, "Okay, Indi, let's think about this a little bit, let's sit down, let's talk about it some more. Hey, that's a good idea, go for it." So they were more like my guidance counselors, as well as my little light bulbs, because they would give me different ideas for different projects.

There was always some type of creative project that we were doing as a family, or if we went traveling somewhere there was always something to learn together. It was like, "Oh, this is an idea, why don't you explore this?" And I'd be like, "Oh cool, yeah, let's do that."

They were also rooting for me. They helped me out because they would say, "Indi, this is what you really like to do, so go on and do it." And if I was scared to, then they gave me that extra push that I needed in order to continue and to have courage to say, okay, I'm going to explore this anyway.   Whereas I know if it had been a teacher in school—depending on their love for teaching and for actually letting an individual explore their own freedom and their own parameters—I might not have pursued some things.

Janet: How is directing your own education different from someone else directing your education?

Indira: With someone else directing my education, it's different in the sense that they're giving me goals that they feel that I have not reached. They may not necessarily know that I have reached a goal already. So, school wound up not being a challenge for me. With me directing my own education, however, it was better because I'm thinking, "Have I reached this point, can I go even further?" It was more challenging to me, because it made me raise my own levels even higher. It made me say, okay, I think you're at this level, but I want to be at *that* level. It forced me to push myself even more. I was my own challenge. Like in a race, if you're the only one then you race against yourself, or against time, or against your own strength. And that's kind of the way my homeschooling wound up being. I raced against my own knowledge. I think that that was really neat for me. And then, if I didn't quite succeed according to my own goals, I didn't feel so bad because I knew at least I was at a standard level, even though I always wanted to be above that standard.

Janet: How do other people react to you when they find out you're not in school?

Indira: [laughs] Well, when I tell people that I was in homeschooling, at first they look at me as if I was crazy, like I'm some alien from Mars. The first thing that pops up in their mind is, well, two things. One is, "How are you getting an education?" And then two: "You have no social life." Yet, they see me and they're hearing me talk. They're seeing that I'm very social and open with communication. They see that I'm not vocally illiterate. And so then they're like, "Well, maybe this does have something to it." And then you wind up spending half an hour trying to explain to them what homeschooling is all about. Or they'll act like they know what you're talking about, when in actuality you know they don't know. After awhile you're like, "You really don't know what homeschooling is, do you?" And then you try and teach them, but it's so radical for them. They're just like, "No, you couldn't be learning anything on your own." But I really am learning something here.

Like with my job experience that I had out at NASA, I dealt with it everyday as if it was a learning experience, as if it was a classroom. I tried to come home everyday and identify something that I'd learned, and to put that in my own little notebook of life. If I felt that I was weak in a certain area, the next day I tried to focus on it. Every day had its own new challenges, so I always had something to try to accomplish or overcome.

But after a while people begin to accept you. They begin to see that you're normal.

Janet: When you first quit school, how did people react?

Indira: My mother's friends gave her a hard time, and they would constantly try to quiz me when I first came out, as if I wasn't learning a thing, as if I was just sitting there. They'd come over to the house and say, "Show me your curriculum." Show you my curriculum? Why do I have to show you? But I did it anyway, because I wanted them to see that being a homeschooler was valid.

Public school is not for everyone. Private school is not for everyone. They have a certain way of teaching and it's not necessarily the best way for everybody. Some people just never adjust to learning in school, but that doesn't mean they are learning disabled or that they are slow. It's just that the way of teaching that's considered standard in schools, it's very rigid and it doesn't adjust to personalities. I would not recommend public school to anyone.

Janet: When you did quit school, did you go through a period of time when you didn't have much motivation, where you took sort of a vacation where you had to switch gears?

Indira: When I first quit school, I hated homeschooling. I wanted to be in class just for the simple reason that that's what I'd done all my life. But change is good. So yes, I took a vacation. I had to. My vacation really wasn't an enjoyable one, because I sat there and cried, for like a good month and a half. I was also taking a couple classes, some math classes, with some other homeschoolers who had a private tutor. That was about the only time I didn't cry. But when I'd go home, I'd cry again, because it was such an adjustment for me to have to think, "Oh my goodness, now *I* have to come up with *my own* assignments." And I was thinking to myself, what if I end up digressing instead of progressing? For a little while I was in this negative outlook. It was like, oh Lord, woe is me, I'm not going to do well. I'll wind up being lower than anyone in my class.

Janet: Do you feel like you're proficient in all your academic subjects?

Indira: Yes I do, especially proficient enough to fit in with my peers.

Janet: Is there any academic subject you feel you don't know enough about? Speaking according to what public schools would have you learn. Any of those subjects?

Indira: Chemistry.

Janet: Who *does* know enough about chemistry?

Indira: I would say I don't know enough about chemistry. Maybe physics even. The sciences, some of the sciences.

Janet: Do you have an interest in those kind of things?

Indira: Yeah. I do have an interest and one day I definitely would like to go on and find out about those in more depth.

Janet: How did you get picked to work at NASA? Was it real competitive or anything?

Indira: Actually it was, I guess. They sent fliers out to different schools, and I was taking a computer repair class at a business school in Cleveland. My teacher said, "This will be a great opportunity for you," and I said, "They won't hire me—this is NASA!" He said, "You never know. Just do it for me. Go interview just for me."

So I called and made an appointment. I went through the interview, and I was chosen! Afterwards the interviewer told me she had interviewed, just in that one day, thirty-five kids, and she had only picked four.

Janet: Why do you think you got the job over the other kids?

Indira: I think for a couple reasons. One, I didn't have that school mentality. Because I was a homeschooler, I'd had to assume more responsibility. Homeschooling made me aware of the adult world, how to function within the adult world, and put immaturities behind me. And so I was able to present myself in a more mature fashion. The person who hired me, she really doesn't like teenagers, because of the immaturity. She picked mature kids. I could use my communication skills; I could talk with her and relate to her in an adult fashion. And that was very necessary when I got out to NASA, because that's all I was dealing with, was adults.

Janet: How did your work at NASA fit into your overall life and education?

Indira: Well, it gave me exposure as to what the working world was like. How to deal with adults, where I needed improvement, where I was doing fine. I didn't really have too many adjustments—I don't know if that was because of adrenaline, or what. I was ready every day. It wasn't one of those things like, "Oh, I don't want to get out of bed today." I was *up*. Which was, in a way, surprising. Because when I was in school, it was like oh, I have to get up again. I didn't want to get up. But going to work at NASA, I willingly got up. I knew that this was something that was going to be very beneficial for me in my adult training.

Janet: Have your schooled peers ever influenced your outlook on work?

Indira: No.

Janet: It seems that they're working their minimum wage jobs, and so many of them don't like their work. And here you are, you *like* the work you've done.

Indira: OK, from that standpoint, yes, they did influence me. Because I knew that I did not want to be flipping burgers at McDonald's, saying hello, may I help you, what's your order? I wanted more of an office-type experience. And to actually be able to fulfill that at my internship, that was great.

Janet: You are now going to college, right? [Indira nods.] Tell me about college.

Indira: College for me is a big adjustment. Because I feel like I'm going back into school.

Janet: Is it a negative experience?

Indira: *Yes* [makes disgusted face]. It's very negative.

Janet: Why are you making yourself go through this?

Indira: I'm making myself go through it for one reason and that's it. And that's to be able to have enough knowledge to be able to go to the Jehovah's Witness World Headquarters in New York and work there as an architectural engineer. Even though I know they'll train me, I would like to go in with at least some skills. Hopefully the class that I'm going to be taking next—engineering drawing—hopefully it won't make me feel like I'm in high school anymore.

Even when I was in high school, I couldn't stand it. I mean I saw the way kids acted and it was like, "Don't you understand? We're here to learn, we're not here to gossip about he said/she said things or act the fool." I mean yes, I love to have fun, but when it's time to study, let's study. And I don't feel that, even in college. In fact I actually feel like the students are despicable, they make me sick, and I'm one of the youngest ones there. Like in every class that I go to, persons are between the ages of mid-twenties on up to like forty-five, fifty years old. And they act like children. When I left school, I'd completely gotten away from that, and it was hard to have to adjust back into it. Really, if I could take the courses that I need at home, I would. I *would not* go to college.

Janet: Do you go full-time or part-time?

Indira's bedroom artwork (by Indira)

Indira: Part-time.

Janet: Have you ever encountered any prejudices due to your educational background?

Indira: Yes. I have actually been turned down for some jobs because they didn't understand the concept of being unschooled. And even when I do get a job, they sit there and they just constantly ask questions. It winds up not being an interview about me, but about my schooling. That prejudice is no problem because I can overcome those hurdles.

But I do find that sometimes when I'm talking to someone, just in normal conversation, and I let them know that I was a homeschooler, they're like [in a snooty voice], "Oh, you were a homeschooler." And then I play it up. "Oh yes, I had my own private tutors. And I was able to go on trips and I was able to do this and that." And then they actually begin to see the tip of the iceberg. But the first gut feeling that those people get is horrible. But I did too. I can kind of understand their reactions because when I was in public school, I felt the same way. It was like, "You're homeschooling? *Why?*" But now that I'm at the other end of the stick I'm able to be a little more lax with skeptical persons and try to describe it to them a little bit better so they can see the benefit of being a homeschooler. And then after a while they begin to understand and they respect you for it.

Sometimes I'll get a really positive reaction. You know, like, "You chose to be a rebel." I've been called that. To defy public schooling or private schooling, to set out on your own.

Janet: If you had to do it all over again, how would you change your educational path?

Indira: After fourth grade I would have come out of school. And I say fourth grade because I loved that bilingual school. I loved taking German and I loved those teachers. In every grade, those teachers cared about you. They were interested in challenging every student, and they did. But after that, there were very few teachers who decided to help me explore education in my own way, or even to make it interesting and challenging to me. So I probably would have come out after fourth grade. I might take a couple college courses like I did when I was a homeschooling junior and senior.

Janet: In what ways have your parents been role models for you, if they have?

Indira: In a lot of ways. One, religiously, definitely. Training me. Morally. They've also been role models for me education-wise. Studying was always something we did as a family so it wasn't like, oh you have to sit over there in the corner. It was never treated as punishment. It was like, "This can be exciting!" Like when we'd study for Jehovah's Witness meetings, we made it interesting, we'd get all the books out. And if I didn't understand, they didn't say, "Oh well, you'll understand one day." It was never that. We sat down and we had a little children's book called *My Book of Bible Stories* and they'd open it up and they'd read it to me, allowing me to see visual aides and to understand it on my own level. And it's always been that way. It's always been continual progression that way. Even when I was in public school, my school projects were family projects. If I had to get something done, my parents got excited. You know, like this is a big time now. Drop everything. My father would come home from work, my mother would hurry up and finish cooking and then we all went to the store, and we all had different ideas about how the project could be. Ideas were flying! Their attitude made education fun for me. So by the time I got into homeschool, I pretty much knew how to make it exciting. I knew what direction I wanted to go into, how to make everything *work*.

It was wonderful. It was like, oh wow, now I can finally *do* these things, that all this time my parents have been guiding me and directing me and helping me to see that I *can* do.

Janet: Homeschoolers don't automatically have a rite of passage into adulthood, compared to graduation and senior prom. Was there a time when you knew you had passed into the adult world?

Indira: Well, I did earn high school credits through Clonlara, just by keeping track of my projects and learning in different areas, so I could have graduated in January, a year and a half ago. I think I had seven credits over than what I was supposed to.

Janet: How old were you, sixteen?

Indira: Yeah, I was sixteen in January. Why I waited until June, when I was seventeen, I don't know. Well, actually I do know. I waited until June because Clonlara has annual conferences. In this three-day conference they also have a graduation ceremony. The graduates go on stage and receive a diploma from our principal. It's wonderful to actually be able to meet her and meet our director and everything. And the principal gives the diploma to your parent or whoever it was that was your main tutor and helped you along in your homeschooling. And then that person gives the diploma to you. And when that happened, right then I knew that it was like, okay, I'm ready to face anything now. I think I have learned enough to be able to face new challenges, new learning experiences, and have a positive outlook on them. Or if they are something negative, to find a way to make it work out. It was the most wonderful feeling. I dressed up really nice—my mom made a dress for me. It was the best feeling to stand up there and see people sitting down watching you and it was like, hey, you did it.

Janet Taylor

And then you were allowed to talk and say how you liked homeschooling, how you adjusted to homeschooling, why you *stayed* in homeschooling. It brought back all the memories. Just a couple years before I'd been like, "Grrr. . .I don't like this," and now I was like, "Thank you so much!" It was just so encouraging, it really was. It showed me that all the trials I'd gone through, all the bad looks, all the mean talk I'd received from persons for coming out of school—just everything, it was worth it. Everything passed over my mind and I was able to see it all at once. So that was my rite of passage.

Janet: How did your relationship with your family change once you started homeschooling?

Indira: I found that when I started homeschooling, the best thing was that my parents and I had already kept a close relationship. Because I needed their support then more than ever and they were there to give me that support without me bucking. That was the best thing, because if I had not been close to them I probably would have dropped out of homeschooling—like you can really drop out of homeschooling [laughs].

They were allowing me to see a new aspect of freedom. I know I would not have had that if I had been in public school; it would not have been there. It was more like, "Indi, we're giving you these suggestions, now it's up to you to decide how you're going to do it, but make sure it sticks within these general guidelines." Whereas if I was in school it would have been like, "Indi look, your teacher said do it, do it." There would have been no questions about it. However, because I was in homeschooling it allowed me freedom to decide well yes, I want to do this, and no, I would not like to do that. That was so much better. That freedom allowed my transition on into the later teenage years to go so much smoother. My freedom was given gradually, whereas had I stayed in public school it wouldn't have, and then even at eighteen it would have been, "Well, you're still just a child."

But because I came out of school, my parents could see maturity. "Yes, we see room for improvement, but we do see maturity also." And because of that they could say, "Well yes, we'll allow you some more freedom. Do you think that that's wise?" And then leave it up to me to decide.

Janet: What advantages, if any, do you think your schooled peers have over you?

Indira: I think my schooled peers have the advantage of being able to take school pictures [laughs]. That's about it. Nothing else.

Janet: What kinds of challenges and difficulties have you faced as a homeschooler?

Indira: Two things. One, getting adjusted, the period of saying, "Okay, you are no longer in school." And then, myself. *I was my challenge.* It was up to me to make that transitional period go smoothly, and to find where my educational nook was, where I thought I could succeed. You know, how far did I want to go, and what were my goals going to be? Another challenge was trying to everyday write down my hours, to document my activities for Clonlara so they could give me credits. Because I wouldn't write them down every day. I should have had this big chart just plastered on my wall. That was a challenge, trying to keep up with my documentation.

Janet: What sort of advice would you give to new homeschoolers?

Indira: I would tell them to focus on their interests. Even though they might start off like I started off, you know, doing it the way the school does, going through a curriculum. However, the more that I learned, the less I followed that curriculum. New homeschoolers should turn to their own interests and focus on those and explore those to the fullest.

For me, having experienced both worlds, I could compare a school to a jail. Coming out and going into homeschooling, it was like that jail door opened and I had freedom to walk out when I wanted to. I think new homeschoolers would benefit from thinking of it that way: they are now out of jail. They can now go and explore things that they may not have had the privilege of knowing about while in school because the teachers had a set curriculum. Explore everything. Follow your interests. Yes, follow some other things too. You know, like if you're really strong in math and science but you can't stand English, continue doing your English. Don't abandon it, because you'll need it later on. But if you focus on what makes you happy, or what your hobby is, what your interests are, then it seems like all the rest kind of falls into place. ❖

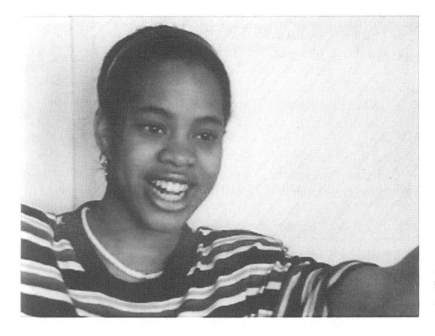

Janet Taylor

Donna E. Nichols-White[*]
Redmond, Washington

FREE AT LAST

THE CURRICULUM OF INDEPENDENCE

When asked, "What type of curriculum do you use?" I'm usually stymied. To say that I don't use a curriculum would be misleading—I do use one. It's not wrapped in a package, ready to use and foolproof. Rather, our family has discovered it through trial and error. Ours is the curriculum of independence.

This curriculum is flexible and can be changed easily if the need arises. It is tailored to the user and not to the teacher. Our time schedule is open and demands no starting or stopping of learning. With this curriculum the child is free to explore and the adult is free to back off and encourage. This curriculum promotes respect for a child's play. While other children were being enriched in preschools, mine were playing at home. Their imaginations soared to heights that I couldn't remember having reached. By keeping them home I did not become dependent on the parental relief preschool would afford me, and they did not become dependent upon someone telling them what to learn.

When I began to homeschool I depended on a structured curriculum for security, but only for three months. I quickly discovered just how much the kids could learn without it. I may use one again in the future but it will be as a supplement—not a life.

I take my children to parks where they can feed squirrels and birds, fish in creeks, climb trees, and hike through woods. I let nature do

---

[*] Editor's note: Most of the material in this section was culled from Donna's unique multicultural magazine for homeschoolers, *The Drinking Gourd*. Subscriptions are $15 per year (six issues); a single issue is $4--The Drinking Gourd, P.O. Box 2557, Redmond, WA 98073, (800) TDG-5487. As this book goes to press, Donna's oldest son, Khahil, is ten years old. Latif is eight, and Rukiya is three. Because Donna wrote these pieces over a period of years, they refer to her children at several different ages.

the teaching and I give information when asked. My nine-year-old occasionally uses a math text but most of his math has been learned from counting money. We read books, laugh, and work together.

When I say that my children know how to cook, clean, garden, and care for babies, I am considered academically negligent. When I downplay academics for a child who is under the age of ten, I am considered old-fashioned or primitive—and not mindful of what my children will need to know in order to survive in our technologically oriented job market. People want to hear that I spend three to six hours a day passing on academics to my children. They want to know that I have formed or molded them. To make matters worse, they believe that I work hard at homeschooling. This is a dilemma for many homeschool parents. How do we explain that, for the most part, we do not mirror schools, and that we do not want to? How can we give people truthful answers to their questions, yet without confusing or alienating them?

I am in contact with many people who are interested in homeschooling and I fear disappointing them by destroying their mythical version of our lives. Our family, like countless others, defies the conventional approach to education. We have proven that schooling is not necessary, and this we have discovered through trial and error. Our experiences have enabled us to become independent of dogmatic education. Ours is the curriculum of independence.

DOING WHAT WORKS: THE ROAD TO UNSCHOOLING

When I started homeschooling my children, I wanted to out-school the schools. Whatever was taught in school, I planned to teach more of it. Whatever grade my sons were supposed to be in, I'd teach one grade higher. Whatever the national average was for their schooled peers, I'd try for better. I envisioned three- to six-hour school days in my home, with the children obediently studying from tomes that each weighed a minimum of two pounds.

Over the years I have discovered that this is how children are *taught*—not necessarily how they *learn*. I have concluded that it's schooling, rather than "learning disabilities," that impinges on a child's learning. I have also decided I will not waste precious time competing with the schools. Schooling damages Black students the most; no other group of students fail in school at the rate they do. Why copy failure?

So, I decided that I would not harm my children by "schooling" them. I watched and noticed that they learned a lot on their own. At the ages of five and three, they spent their days exploring, using our encyclopedias to research the animals they encountered, building simple electronic circuits, and listening to lots of excellent literature.

Well, I thought, this is the road to unschooling. Now, what do I do with all the academic supplies I've already purchased? Are they completely useless to a self-directed learner? I had amassed an excellent collection of reading, writing, spelling and math textbooks—the best there was to offer—but I wasn't using them. I felt like throwing them out or selling them, but fortunately, I didn't. I eventually found out that the books weren't useless; they just needed a new use! Let me explain:

When Khahil wanted to read, I taught him phonics, because I knew that *I* couldn't tolerate reading lessons unless phonics were included. Six months of occasional fifteen-minute phonics lessons did the trick. He enjoyed phonics drill, but eschewed the Sullivan Readers I had purchased.

When Latif decided to learn to read, Khahil pulled out an unused Sullivan reader (a phonics program) and sat with him for three days until Latif completed the book. When Latif did cartwheels, Khahil did cartwheels; when Latif sat, Khahil sat; When Latif jumped, Khahil jumped. By the end of three days, the 64-page book had been read—while the boys cartwheeled, sat, and jumped. (Rukiya, too, is now becoming an early reader; any phonics instruction that Latif receives, she participates in also.) And so, the curriculum has a use after all.

We keep math books that span kindergarten through college level in our home, and the boys use them as resources. We've never completed a math book in the conventional sense; instead, we skip a lot of the drill work and do what *they* think is the interesting stuff.

We have many do-it-yourself type science books which promote independent learning. Do I feel a need to direct all of the science experiments? No, and I don't feel left out when they prefer to do things their way.

There is one type of textbook that I have not collected so far: the history textbook. Instead, I collect biographies and historical references. These I pre-read, because I do not want to hurt my children by presenting the popularized, incorrect view of world history.

My sons also research everything they're interested in by reading the encyclopedia or other reference books that we have in our home.

And throughout the years I have supplied the boys with books that supported their other interests, whether they were "old enough" for the books or not. For Khahil that has meant high fantasy, chess and electronics. For Latif, airplanes, earth movers, and cooking.

Do my children use our curricular materials and other books enough to disqualify us as "unschoolers?" I think not. *Schooling*, certainly, is not what we do. You see, we've turned the curriculum into resources. The books no longer hold sway over my home. The power of the almighty textbook has been reduced to the minor role of a less-than-perfect resource material. And that's exactly how it should be.

I've come to see schooling and its accompanying curriculums as a crutch. My children are not crippled now, and they will not have crutches to support them when they become adults, so why start out with them?

No curriculum should be allowed to hinder a child's education. The child is the learner, the curriculum a resource, and the parent a facilitator—not a *teacher*. I find things that satisfy my children's curiosity, and they do the rest of the work. I supply the tools and materials, and they do the building. I'm in the business of putting myself out of a job (as a parent), and therefore I promote self-teaching. Is it easy? Not really. I have had to learn to get out of their way; I have had to redefine my role: support, not leadership.

Are the boys performing at grade level? At least. Are they ahead or behind their school-age peers? I'm not sure. Do I worry about these things? Sometimes. But I no longer spend my days worrying about their standing according to standardized school-type measurements. Measuring up to an arbitrary standard of academic excellence, which has no bearing on how children actually learn, is what schooling is all about. Competitiveness is a mainstay in American education, but I am no longer interested in competing with the schools. Homeschooling is all about doing what works, and self-directed learning—unschooling—is what works for us.

HOW SHOULD I TEACH MY CHILDREN ABOUT US?

I shall read them the book *The Autobiography of Miss Jane Pittman*, by Ernest Gaines, which chronicles a girl's life from slavery to the civil rights movement, and contains beautifully written African American dialect. I shall also read *Now Is Your Time: The African American Struggle for Freedom*, by Walter Dean Myers.

Using these two books, I will devise an American time line. It will begin in West Africa and move on to the New World and its native inhabitants. We will add our own relatives, starting in the 1800's. We will augment our time line yearly, including all of the dramatic migrations of people to America.

With these two books as our guides, we will cover

- history (why and how did the early settlers reduce the population of the native people of the New World?)
- astronomy (the location of the North Star in the early 1800's. When I was a child, my grandfather would take my mother and me out at night and point to the North Star. He revered that star. It was a part of the Big Dipper, The Drinking Gourd. It was the map of my forefathers, and I named my magazine after it.)
- cartography (a map made it more possible to escape the horrors of slavery)
- sociology (what social conditions enforced slavery?)
- math (the economics of slavery, desegregation, and forced bussing).

The time line forms the basis of our history program, because I have never read a good history textbook. I was taught (in school) that slavery was good for the African people because the Africans fought tribal wars all the time and slavery civilized them. I was also taught (in school) that my forefathers were rather docile and content as slaves—and I was *not* taught about the oppressiveness of the slave system.

I shall share with my children an accurate account of the history of America—one which includes *our* history. That's how I'll teach my children about us.

COOPERATION: A REAL WORLD HABIT

I encourage my children to work together. I show them how to cooperate with each other. I play games, read books, and do puzzles with them, and so they have a firm foundation working together as a family.

Contrary to the teachings of popular child psychology, I do not encourage my children to make separate friends from each other. Nor do I encourage them to exclude each other from their lives. I let them know that I do not have child-free days—and that they cannot have sibling-free days. I think cooperation is a real world experience and habit that takes a long time to develop, and I think it should be developed in the home.

This doesn't mean my children have to be together all the time. Natural separations because of differing interests, games and hobbies is fine. I just do not allow *unnatural* separations based on age. At our house, you would never find a room where only ten-year-old boys were allowed.

I tell my children that when they become adults and run their own companies, they may be business partners. They might as well get accustomed to working together now.

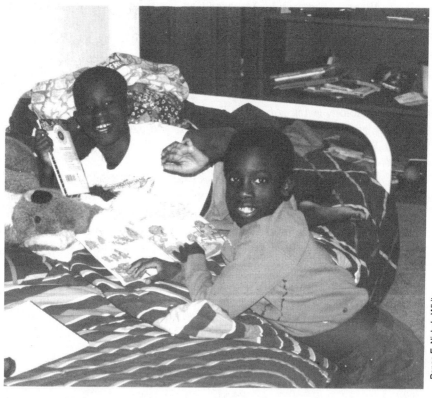

Donna E. Nichols-White

BEYOND MY REACH

Last week while talking with my mother-in-law, I learned something new about my husband's childhood. We were discussing how children should surpass their parents, and how the goal of parents should be to ensure this. We commented on how many of our friends' children seemed stuck and were not doing as well as their hard-working parents had done. My mother-in-law told me that even though she had not considered herself well read, she had purchased a set of encyclopedias for Cliff when he was in the fourth grade. Her own childhood had been devoid of books, and she was determined to give her son more.

Educators cite that the home is the best predictor of academic success. Good readers supposedly have parents who are avid readers. In the case of my husband, this is not true. Neither of his parents are avid readers—but he is, because his mother reached beyond her experience and supplied him with the tools he needed.

Her actions made me ponder, "Am I supplying the tools that will make my children better than I am? Am I improving the next generation of my family? Or am I encouraging my children to stay stuck at my level? What is my equivalent of my mother-in-law's encyclopedias?"

Our home is filled with thousands of books, which have been collected since my childhood. There are books that were passed down from my grandfather, books that friends and family found for me in used book stores, books we've purchased at library sales and book stores. These books include the works of Langston Hughes, Zora Neale Hurston, Shakespeare, Lewis Carroll, James Baldwin, Chaim Potok, Gabriel Garcia Marquez, and countless others. Until last week's conversation, I had always assumed these books were sufficient for my children—after all, I knew that school libraries are not as extensive as mine. Now I realize that these books are merely a reflection of my own comfort level. Even though most people would consider this level highly literate, I need to find resources that expand *beyond* my comfort level. I need to extend my reach for the sake of my children's future.

One criticism of homeschooling is that the world of the family is too limited for children to learn the skills they will need in the future. Ironically, *classrooms* are small in scope and limited in area, resources, and adult interaction. Many teachers claim that they bring the world into their classroom, but this is not possible. I, on the other hand, am able to expose my children directly to the real world, not just a classroom imitation of it. The schools are trying to prepare children for a way of life that is already extinct. The skills they say children need are not preparing children for *today's* jobs, much less tomorrow's.

Educators stress the need to teach teamwork, and they insist they are achieving this goal. Interesting, then, that so much money is spent teaching grown up businessmen (who have presumably already been schooled) to respect women and people of different races, religions and ethnic groups. If your education is received from homeschooling, you cannot help but learn teamwork, because a homeschool family truly is a team.

Educators claim that they teach socialization—and that this is necessary. Instead, they should concern themselves with their students' lack of higher order reasoning and thinking skills. These thinking skills are more important than any adult-imposed pseudo-socialization.

I have thought this issue over seriously. I know that homeschooling my children, as opposed to schooling them, is already a world beyond that of my childhood. Still, it is only the beginning. I feel a tremendous responsibility to stretch beyond my world in order to prepare my children for the future. I must explore new ideas and resources that will enable my children to soar beyond my reach.

TOOLS, NOT TOYS

I believe we are the sum of our experiences. I offer my children exposure to technology, along with the philosophy of using technology as a tool—as opposed to being ruled by it.   From the time they were able to pull up chairs to the stove and cutting board, they were allowed to cook. They chop vegetables with the same knives that my husband Cliff and I use. They sauté, stir, boil, and bake just like adults. At two, they've known how to use every appliance in our kitchen. Of course they're messy, but the reward is children who can cook.

Donna E. Nichols-White

Cliff repairs our cars and appliances. I remember him waiting until eleven p.m., hoping Latif (at eighteen months) would be asleep when he worked. But Latif always knew when it was a repair night, and he was out there under the hood alongside his dad until past midnight. Whenever we work, our children are by our side. Yes, working with them underfoot is difficult—but the reward is self-motivated children, who think learning is fun.

My children install, test, and use most of the educational computer software that I sell. One of their favorites is Interactive Physics 2.5, designed for high school and college students. In addition to the program, Khahil is reading *The Cartoon Guide to Physics* by Larry Gonick and *Thinking Physics* by Lewis Carroll Epstein. Their computer physics activities and Khahil's reading are self-directed, not parent enforced. I never limit them to "age appropriate" resources, so they utilize, enjoy, and appreciate high level materials. Science, math, problem solving, reference and brain-teasing books abound in our home. These books are *used*, and the children enjoy them. I supply my children with tools, not toys. In this way they can build, create, think, and utilize today's technology.

GENIUS HOMESCHOOLERS

No wonder that homeschool mothers cringe when they read about genius homeschoolers in the news. The reports contains stories that go like this:

Homeschooled Physicist Discovers the Sixth Dimension. Nine-year-old Jeremy Stephens has never attended school but, without expensive labs and materials, he discovered the sixth dimension. "I discovered the sixth dimension while milking the cows," young Jeremy told reporters...

Of course, after this story is carried by UPI and Associated Press, your neighbors begin to look at you in awe. Then you, knowing that all your kids have discovered is how to catch grasshoppers, are left with the feeling that you have done something wrong.

Genius homeschoolers? Like the students in college who break the grade curve, these amazing children and their parents, through no fault of their own, have caused undue pressure for you. People hear about them, and then ask you questions like, "What type of curriculum do *you* use?"

If you are structured in your approach to homeschooling, you'll have an answer. If you are like me, you will have to think of a way to change the subject. After all, Jeremy Stephens is a hard act to follow.

Last summer I asked a neighbor when her children would start school (okay, I had an ulterior motive). When she asked me the same question I replied, "My children don't go to school." She responded, "I meant, when does your homeschool start?" I frantically searched my mind for an answer and replied, "Uh, we homeschool year round."

Of course, most people assume that in order to produce an outstanding homeschooled student, a parent must log at least thirty hours a week of teaching. Nothing could be further from the truth. If I taught my children school-type lessons for thirty hours per week, they would beg to be sent to military school, where they would be a lot happier.

The question is, how do I explain my typical day? I have to leave out the fact that if I don't have coffee by nine a.m., I will suffer serious withdrawal symptoms—either leave out that fact or lose my organic den mother status, anyway. Next I have to admit that I make business calls before I shower and dress, and before my children forage for their breakfast. (I nursed them for three years, so they are big enough to feed themselves!) Maybe I could explain that showering and dressing covers the subject of hygiene.

Perhaps I could say that our daily trek to the post office is a field trip, whereby we study occupational education. Our math lesson could be the number of spiders the children snagged or the number of guppies the turtles ate. Let's see, it would be about noon now, what's next in our home "school" day? Oh, I know. Khahil and Latif play with each other for about five hours straight, stopping only to graze in the kitchen. Rukiya, age two, will now put on her only-child act and demand my attention until dinnertime. While I prepare a nutritious meal (often with my sons' help), she booby traps the kitchen.

After we eat we read, draw or play games. The magic hours in my day come after Rukiya, two years old, falls asleep. Then I get to work until the wee hours of the morning, which is why the next day starts with coffee. Did I forget to mention house cleaning? Oops! I missed it again.

Of course, throughout the day books are read, piano lessons are practiced, and issues are discussed. My sons do have one "unit study"—trapping squirrels with pistachio nuts and home-made net traps. I've been informed that my job is to pick the squirrels up and place them into a container.

Oh, I mustn't forget, three of the approximately twenty thousand homeschoolers in Washington State came over to play for three hours. That should cover what educators consider the most important subject area, socialization.

Donna E. Nichols-White

Latif on a night-time bug hunt

I know all this is not what people think of as a homeschool. I *have* read stories of highly structured homeschools. I just haven't known anyone who *runs* one, at least not for more than one year. I know hundreds of homeschoolers, so you'd think I should know at least one mom who takes a highly structured approach—but I don't.

As for the super homeschoolers we read about, many facts are omitted from the reports. Some didn't read until they were over the age of ten. Some can't tie their shoes (and neither could Einstein). Their parents allowed them to follow their interests instead of making them learn from a prescribed curriculum. Their parents were not usually affluent (most were barely middle class). Many come from one-parent families. And some have never even cracked a textbook. So, if your children share any of these attributes, relax. You are the parents of geniuses!

LOOKING FOR FAMILIES LIKE MINE

I joined a homeschool support group when my sons were only the ages of two and four. The members welcomed me. They were all white, and a couple of them went out of their way to form friendships with my family.

In spite of what people believe, homeschooled children are very socialized. Since they do not attend school, the younger children's days are filled with play. Our support group planned weekly field trips. The Boys and Girls Clubs opened their doors during school hours for homeschoolers' activities. If I desired, my children could participate in an activity every day. But I still felt strange in our group, for even though they homeschooled their children, they were not Black.

In the homeschooling world, I have noticed that white families have supports that are non-existent for Black families. Our history, needs, and desires are different. No matter how much equality society thinks we enjoy, we are still far from equal in opportunity. In order to improve our lives as homeschoolers, we must again pave our own path. Professional educators fail us because they don't know our needs, and even if they did, they wouldn't help us to satisfy them.

I needed to know if there were other families like mine who did what we did, so I decided to start a magazine. I wanted to find out about the homeschoolers who were rarely mentioned: African Americans, Latinos, Asians, and Native Americans. I wanted to publish a multicultural home education magazine that would explore home education from diverse perspectives. I couldn't type, had never written anything larger than a shopping list, and didn't own an operable computer. But my husband purchased a computer for me, a friend showed me how to operate the software, and I took off.

My magazine is called *The Drinking Gourd*. It was named in honor of those brave and determined Africans who refused to accept slavery and escaped to freedom, in honor of the strength of my ancestors.

Since I began *The Drinking Gourd* I have been contacted by people of different races, ethnic groups, and religions throughout the world. The most constant message I receive from these people is that they want to be able to maintain their culture, history and identity. It seems that schools are designed to destroy what is most important to the people they supposedly serve.

Through this project, I *have* found other families like mine, and I've found out that homeschoolers are a diverse amalgamation of people.

M.Y.O.B. WHILE H.Y.O.C.
(Minding Your Own Business
While Homeschooling Your Own Children)

Contrary to the stereotype of the perpetually *schooling* homeschool parent, a mother may soon find she has spare time for creating and developing her own interests. With the children working on their own projects, reading books, socializing with other homeschooled children, etc., she may even decide to devote this time to a family business. Since having a full time parent at home usually limits the family to one income, starting and running an at home business is a tempting idea.

"Starting a business while homeschooling? Surely you jest!" I hear some of you screaming. "What do I do with the kids, the baby, academics, dinner? Impossible. It might work for other people, but not me. I don't have any skills, talents, time, or startup capital."

I know what you're thinking, because I've said these things myself. When my first son was born I felt like I was the hardest working woman on the planet. Of course, many others thought I was on easy street, being able to stay home and just care for a baby. Since then, another son and a daughter have added to my list of "easy" jobs.

I have found starting and running a business almost as challenging as caring for a first child. With a baby, you stay up all hours of the night wondering when he will wake up for his next feeding because you know the minute you fall asleep, he'll awaken.

With self-employment, too, you stay alert for the moments when business will pick up, because you are too scared to sleep through an opportunity. After all, a home business that lacks investment capital requires an alert mind.

Motherhood doesn't turn your brain to mush, and neither does staying home with your children. Instead, it is ideal preparation for self-employment. Encouraging your children to be self-motivated and independent will help *you* become more independent.

I've noticed that when many homeschool dads (and working moms) see their children enjoying freedom from school, they begin to yearn for their own freedom through self-employment. Their jobs no longer seem like "great careers," but rather like heavy shackles.

"Okay, Donna, what do you do with the children? How can I work at home with four children? And what about the baby?" All these are valid questions—the answers to which only you can find out. A home business, like a home school, is unique. No two are alike.

A business, like the raising of your children, has to develop from your own talents. It reflects *you*. You stay committed because it is a labor of love. I am the product of a single parent household, and I grew up in the projects in New York City. By today's standards I was a deprived child. But in no way was I truly deprived. My mother equipped my family with a library that was the envy of the neighborhood, and stressed that we should have lots of alone time. Thanks to her, I've become a compulsive reader. My love of books, mathematics, science, and foreign languages wouldn't be considered viable *job* qualifications, but they have surely helped qualify me for my business. Learning from my children and reading the books I love have taught me much of what I need to know to become self-employed. In all honesty, I've accomplished more than I have ever imagined. I still have a long way to go, and I still struggle, but I love what I do.

During my years of working with *The Drinking Gourd*, I have taken my children with me every step of the way. They've been to printers, computer stores, stationery stores, and shipping companies. They've played while I interviewed homeschooled families. They've listened while I've received helpful advice from friends and acquaintances. They've seen me cringe at my major mistakes. They have gotten to know our staff and they're even learning how to edit (they love to point out my errors!). They have assisted in developing my product line by testing software, reviewing and critiquing books, and trying out new products. They know how to set up, run, and pack up a convention booth, and they answer the phones willingly. (I've told them they can't take orders until they can write quickly and legibly.)

So, when we don't get to do the math pages some week, or the handwriting hasn't improved, and the reading lessons aren't all covered, I at least know that my kids have learned something about how to own and operate a business. Occasionally someone rants and raves that my children will grow up and have to go to work, and punch a time clock, and be part of a team—and that they'll be unprepared for employment because they lacked a disciplined curriculum in my homeschool. I candidly reply, "When my children grow up, and run their own businesses, they will have to be able to perform every single job necessary to keep the business growing. They will have to be able to sweep floors and sign contracts. In other words, they will have to be independent self-motivated leaders. And by the way," I conclude, "My business *is* our curriculum."

PREPARING MY CHILDREN FOR THE "REAL WORLD" EXPERIENCE

Whenever I am accused of depriving my children of "Real World" experiences, I get upset. I used to imagine this accusation implied that I was either neglecting my children in some way or depriving them of growth. Some people, too, accused me of not being able to let go of my children. To many, it seemed, I was a selfish, insecure mother whose children needed to get away. One person stated bluntly that I had a deep-seated psychological problem. I began to avoid people who criticized my choice for our family. I thought it was wrong for me to have to defend my mothering, constantly, in my children's presence.

But it was not long before I realized that people were probably challenging me from a position of guilt. They had not gone the extra mile for their children. They were sending their children to school to face a world that they didn't have the courage to face themselves.

The real world experience for Black children is a cruel one, and parents know it. I have yet to meet an African American parent who is completely comfortable with the school their child attends. There is always either a real problem or the threat of one. And there is no income level exempt from these problems. In the inner city, teachers' expectations can be low. In the affluent suburb, teachers are often insensitive. At any economic level, racism exists in the schools.

Instead of challenging me, parents should challenge the schools. When they place their children in school they should ask questions: "Do you have close relationships with people who look like my child and share his culture and history? Do you like my child? Have you ever taught a child like mine? What is your aim in educating my child? What are your favorite ideas? What activities do you enjoy? What type of child would you consider a genius, and can an African American child be one? How often do you read, and what kind of books do you like? Do you value a child only if he measures up to your standards, or do you value him for himself? Is a child bad if he fails in school? What happens to the child when your teaching methods fail? What do you do when (not *if*) a child in your class is the victim of a racial slur or insult?"

Each parent should ask these questions before his child attends school. It is a responsibility—and most parents are not willing to accept it. Instead they trot their small children, who are too young to defend themselves, off to school, in order to experience the real world.

Many homeschoolers agree that this country's educational system maintains and perpetuates a class-based society. Most African American parents, too, are aware of this, but they do not work hard enough to change it. Instead, their children are sent to school, unarmed, to deal with the problems.

Many of my friends spend hours at school trying to repair some damage that school has done to their children. What I can't understand is: after they work this hard, they can't see any significant changes in the way their children are treated, or in the way the schools are run. They are also deeply concerned about their children's safety. Yet they continue to send their children to school.

In schools, only the people who are constantly affected by racism seem able to recognize it. If most of the Black boys in a particular city are placed in special education, people say this results from economic problems, the marital status of the parents, etc. Others will point out that they have or know of a child who benefited from special education who was *not* Black. They will not see the disproportionate labeling as indicative of a race and class problem—although in some places 50% of Black males have been labeled EMR (educable mentally retarded) or emotionally disabled. When the experts say, "Black boys are physical learners," it is not considered a racist statement. When people determine your educational success based upon your income, color, marital status, and religion, they are supposedly not biased.

Many parents perpetuate racism because they excuse their children's behavior as just being "the way children are." My sons were supposedly acting like Native Americans and doing war whoops with a neighborhood kid—things they had learned from the movie *Peter Pan*. They have also given each other "Indian burns." Cliff and I set them straight, and they know they are not allowed to play like that. We let them know those acts are insults to Native Americans, and that many Native Americans, like the Seminoles, helped our people during slavery. We point out the fact that many African Americans are registered with the different tribes today. As far as we are concerned, if our children insult Native Americans, they perpetuate racism.

When Black parents demand Afrocentric curriculums, many people call them racist, unamerican, and historically incorrect. They ignore the fact that history has been altered to portray the African American people as inferior. Maybe they fear having to admit slavery was a mistake that America *has yet* to learn from or repair. During slavery, literacy was punishable by death. Today, our literacy rate remains low. The situation does not seem to have changed much.

We who homeschool must begin to ask other parents, at what age should you subject a child to a system that is designed to make him inferior? If you put him in such a system, how much should you plan to work in it to assure his protection? And for how long?

Who is better able—me or the schools—to take my child aside and (in addition to the academic basics) teach him Nguzo Saba, the seven principles of Kwanzaa:

> Umoja—Unity
> Kujichagulia—Self determination
> Ujima—Collective work and responsibility
> Ujamaa—Cooperative economics
> Nia—Purpose
> Kuumba—Creativity
> Imani—Faith?

Am I really wrong to want to spend more years strengthening and preparing my children for the real world—at home? What qualification does the American educational system have that makes it more capable of preparing him for the real world than I? Do they know him well? Do they know his history? Do they even care?

WHY I CHOOSE TO HOMESCHOOL

The actors performed song and dance routines amidst squeals of delight emanating from their preschool audience. Khahil and Latif were having a good time. The room was filled with brightly colored high quality preschool toys. Phillipa and I had brought our children to a school on a Saturday, so they could enjoy this show. Khahil was four and Latif two years of age. They had never been inside a preschool before, and seemed thrilled.

I felt immense guilt throughout the entire show. Had I, by choosing to care for my children at home, robbed them of some important part of life? The preschool had more things—toys, books, and other resources—than I could afford to provide. There were certainly more children there than had ever been in my home, and the place looked stimulating. I leaned over and admitted to Phillipa that I thought I must be cheating my children. Phillipa, who is a teacher, asked, "What is it in here that makes you think this is better than what you are providing? Is it the toys? The books?" She couldn't believe that I felt I was wrong to keep my sons home with me.

When Khahil was born, I was overwhelmed with the love I felt for him. I thought, *nothing* will keep me from taking care of my baby. Most of my friends wanted to return to a job after giving birth, but I felt it was more fun to take care of Khahil. I enjoyed the experience of being a new mother.

Latif was born two years later, and though I was exhausted, I still preferred to be home with the boys. Having two babies to care for can be hectic, isolating, and tiring—but I loved it.

When they reached the ages of four and two, I found that loneliness was my greatest problem. I lived in a neighborhood with some moms who didn't work at jobs, but their children between ages two and five were in preschool. Adult company was nonexistent, because the moms were never around. We were also the only African American family and were excluded from most of the neighborhood friendships. I still enjoyed being with my sons, and felt there was no need to place Khahil and Latif in a preschool. They would probably have been the only African American students, and I felt they were too young to have to experience racial issues alone. At this time I began feeling the pressure of family and friends to "Let them go." I wondered, "What is wrong with keeping a young child home? What is so bad about being a full time mother?"

When Khahil turned five, it was time to break the news to family, friends, and neighbors that I was going to teach him at home. My reasons: Clifford's and my happiness with our life as a family, the low academic expectations of the public schools, my distaste for the "group think" encouraged by the schools, the appalling statistics reported weekly on the failure of Black children in school—regardless of their varying economic circumstances. We enjoyed having wonderful, loving and secure children. We were beginning to enjoy the rewards of our intensive parental involvement in Khahil's life. We did not want our joy to be disrupted by schooling. And most of all, Khahil was a Black boy—otherwise known as an endangered species.

Donna E. Nichols-White

Khahil was an early reader and he enjoyed learning, exploring and playing with his brother. Sibling rivalry, surprisingly, was not a problem in our home. Our sons played together all day long with a minimum of squabbling. We couldn't find anything valuable that school could add to our lives.

Every year reports tell of the problems in American education. Every year tests, books, and curriculums are "dumbed down." Yet, every year we are also told that schools are improving. We are asked to support (financially and otherwise) a system that fails the majority of its students, but most of all the Black child.

I listened to the stories of friends and family members who were having difficulty with the schools. Most of these people were good parents, yet their children performed poorly. Most of the blame was placed on the children, which I felt was wrong. I began to notice that school was an institution which always blames its failures on outside factors. Declining academic performance is said to be caused by single parent homes, economic factors, parental neglect, and a low level of parent education. My gut feeling was that instead, something was inherently wrong with institutionalized education, and my children were not going to partake in it at a young age. Spending large amounts of time with age-related peers encourages a child to think only like his or her age group. I thought children needed to be with a variety of ages, and that a young child needed a close relationship with an adult. I did not want my son to learn that thinking like everyone else was a good thing. At home he was able to make decisions, act upon them, and experience the consequences.

In the past seven years I have not read a single positive report in regards to the education of African American children. I do not like reading that African American boys are an "endangered species." When I read these reports I ask myself, "Why bother with school at all?" I couldn't possibly fail my children as acutely as the schools do. Obviously education in America is not designed to make us success stories, or else we would be doing better. African American people could not possibly be the least intelligent people on the planet. I think the institution of education in America is designed to turn us into failure.

African American people are educated away from their communities. Those of us who "make it" are not of value to those of us who don't. Few successful African American adults return to their communities to actively improve them. Instead, we should educate ourselves so as to improve the lives and communities of those who need assistance. This is one way for us to change the negative statistics, and rebuild our communities. Homeschooling is one way to reconnect us to our communities. I teach my sons the importance of family and community and our roles in each.

Clifford is an aerospace engineer. He works long hours and is an excellent provider for his family. I have been a full time mom for seven years. In addition to our boys we also have a daughter, Rukiya, age one. I publish and edit *The Drinking Gourd Home Education Magazine*, which was named in honor of the underground railroad. Between Cliff's job, my home business, and our children, our lives are filled. Through *The Drinking Gourd*, I try to bring together different racial, ethnic, and religious groups in order to support families and communities who homeschool.

Our home is filled with books and reading materials. We are a family of avid readers. Clifford reads for an average of two hours a day; I read between one and five hours per day. Khahil reads about three hours per day and Latif (who is learning to read) explores books about one hour per day. Rukiya, too, loves to "read" and be read to. We read together, alone and to each other. We attend library sales (all the books you can carry for two dollars!), borrow from the library, and also purchase lots of books. Books are in every room of the house. Our children are encouraged to read whatever they want to read. Khahil likes comic books and science fiction, and Latif likes books about airplanes, cars, and trucks. I believe in letting children pick books freely and I try not to discourage reading in any way.

Math is taught by counting money. Our children receive a small allowance which will increase as they mature. We plan to give the responsibility of household shopping and bill paying to our sons when they reach the age of fourteen. We do use math workbooks, but not as the main focus of our math work. We count, measure, and compare as we cook. Math is taught in real life situations.

Writing consists of picture drawing, birthday cards, and gift lists. Our sons write when their situations require it; otherwise their interest in writing is minimal. I have decided not to force handwriting skills at this time. History is taught through the use of biographies, family history stories, and museums. History textbooks are generally poorly written and inaccurate; therefore, we do not use them.

Science at home is fun. I supply science books and have the materials to support them. There is plenty of electronics equipment in our home: wires, batteries, lights, switches. I let the boys build robots and machines on their own. They make potions (with household products) by themselves. Science does not have to be *taught*, because our sons like it so much.

Our house is loaded with building toys. There are blocks, Legos (thousands) and Fischer Technics available and out at all times. The boys will build with these toys for hours and create stories and plays as they go along. Play is an important part of children's lives, and I respect and encourage it.

Since our children are young, we have decided to base their learning experiences on their talents and desires, and in this way to encourage them to love learning. We do not force feed them academics, we do not plan what they will do all day long and most of all, we do not entertain them. I think that when children are not supported in their talents they become frustrated and rebellious. I enjoy following a child's lead. As long as my child has special interests, I do not have to tell him what to think or how to think—he already knows.

I remember being force-fed information in school, in order to get me to perform well on tests. I completely forgot most of that information once the tests were over. I want education to be a lifelong process for my children, and not a temporary one.

I do not entertain my children, because I want them to develop their own abilities, and don't want them to be dependent on outside factors for stimulation. TV viewing is limited; I consider it a waste of our time. Playing takes precedence over TV. I am appalled by the negative images of Black people that television displays, and I try to limit my children's exposure to these images in particular.

Clifford and I share the responsibilities of family life. The only thing I have done for the children that he hasn't is to breast feed them. We work hard to care for each other and the children. If the children have questions or need to learn something, we are both available to respond.

I think we have the messiest house on the block, because it is always filled with kids. We entertain friends while most children are in school, and we enjoy the company of schooled friends on weekends. We attend to the daily business of *The Drinking Gourd*, which entails trips to the post office, UPS, the bank, and the printer. We visit friends, attend swimming lessons, soccer practices, science labs, and field trips. We lack the desire and the time needed to keep the house immaculate. When my children are home, they eat six meals a day in the same kitchen. I let them cook many of their own meals, and the mess doubles. Since I became a publisher, Cliff and the boys have taken over the laundry. I think I should develop a neatness curriculum!

Homeschooling is a satisfying experience for our family. We enjoy the closeness. We like, love, and have learned a lot from each other. My children have had positive early learning experiences which I hope will benefit them throughout their lives. If you are considering homeschooling, I would suggest that you do it based on your *intuition* rather than on your concern about the detrimental effects of institutionalized education. Ask yourself, "Does this *feel* right?" Schooling didn't feel right to me—not as an adult, and not when I was young. Throughout high school people told me I was living the best years of my life. I knew they were lying. I despised school and thought all of its trappings (proms, sports, debate teams) were con jobs meant to keep me there, and props designed to delay my maturity and independence. It would have been more productive to learn how to support myself and how to help others less fortunate than myself. Instead of suffering through high school, I desired real world experiences—apprenticeships, community volunteer work, hobbies. No, schooling has never felt right. Homeschooling does.

It has been five years since that day I felt guilty of cheating my children of the great school experience. My doubts are by no means completely erased, but I instinctively feel I am doing the right thing. Homeschooling is our family's way of life. We like it and we enjoy being a family. I love being a mother. We live a good life. At this moment, we have no need for institutionalized education; we're happy with things just the way they are.

FREE AT LAST

The back-to-school season seems like a national holiday. Department stores offer "back-to-school sales," clothing and school supplies are purchased in earnest, and after-school programs are implemented. Many parents breathe sighs of relief for since their children are returning to school, they will no longer have to find things for them to do. Schooling will eat up at least six hours of their child's day and what little time remains will be tightly scheduled: sports, homework, television, dinner, bathing and bedtime.

If you homeschool, these parents do not understand how you survive with your sanity intact. I am almost ready to stop answering the question, "How can you stand to have your children with you all day long?" But I do answer.

I tell people that in September our family is "free at last." We are free to awaken according to our natural rhythms, to be regimented only by the occasional early morning appointment. The children are free to prepare their own breakfast and decide what they are going to do that day.

We are free to practice our music lessons early so as to get them out of the way. We can read what we want to read, when we want to read it, and for whatever amount of time we want to read. We can explore nature for hours in a local stream. We usually have the stream all to ourselves because most children are in school. The undisturbed exploration enables the children to make new discoveries. My sons are free to be themselves, and not the stereotypical Black males that society expects them to be. My children are free from the preconceived performance expectations that schools publicly flaunt. They are free from the labels—educable mentally retarded, attention deficit hyperactivity disorder, etc.—that are given to an alarmingly disproportionate percentage of Black children. (I have read of no other ethnic group with such bad statistics.)

My children are free to work on projects for a few minutes, a few hours, a few months, or a few years. They are not limited to forty-five minute time periods. They are able to concentrate for long periods of time, while school ruins other children's concentration levels.

The back-to-school season is a wonderful time for us. Finally, we're free at last! ❖

Khahil White (center) with homeschooled friends Adam and Russell Powers

Latif and Khahil

Tanya M.N. Khemet
Renton, Washington

CELEBRATE THE CHILD

Parents get little time to sit and think. Sometimes all you can do is ride the roller coaster, enjoying the highs, waiting out the lows, never knowing what is around the corner. But once in a while you get a quiet moment to reflect back on your path and ponder the choices you've made. As you reflect, you see that some were not really choices at all; there was simply no other way that you *could* have gone. Homeschooling is one of the roads our family travels, and I realize now that for us, there could have been no other way.

On the bad—yes, there *are* bad days—I daydream about "going to work" and sending the children to school and day-care. Then the good days come along and I laugh at those crazy thoughts. I love my children and I love participating in their learning process. Just as it was a joy to see that first smile, it is still a joy to see the smile of accomplishment at a perfect paper, or the smile of wonder at first seeing the trick of the nine times-table.

Childhood is a precious and pure time, and homeschooling extends that time. I remember one day sitting on the bed with Miri (then nine years old), making paper planets and using them to talk about orbits, while Nefertiti (four) played in a bucket of water seeing what different patterns she could make on the ceiling with the sun coming through the window and bouncing off the water. Suddenly Miri jumped in, trying to see what patterns *she* could make. The paper planets lay discarded and forlorn on the floor, forgotten until another time. I picked up on a discussion about light, which we'd started a few weeks back. Light waves as energy, the refraction of light, the light spectrum. We had done some experiments we found in a library book, and this was a perfect review. Who would have thought you could have so much fun with sun coming through a window, a bucket of water, and your daughters?

Tanya Khemet

Nefertiti, Miri, and Kofi Khemet

This is the joy of homeschooling; learning does not have to be a scheduled and restricted activity. Instead, it happens unexpectedly as you move through life. Remember *your* school days. Think about the science classes when you studied light. All I remember of science is sitting through boring lectures, waiting for the experiments—though there was never enough equipment for everyone. And I think now, how did they manage to take the wonder out of something as miraculous as Light!? This is one reason we homeschool: to preserve our children's wide-eyed, open, honest hunger for learning.

Before I go any further, let me tell you about us, because homeschooling is just a natural extension of who we are and the life path we started when my husband and I joined our paths into one. We are Kofi Khemet, thirty-six, and Tanya Khemet, thirty. We have a growing incense business, Marimba Productions, that we run out of our home. Our students/teachers are Miri (ten), Nefertiti (five), Nehanda (two). From before our children were born we knew we were going to homeschool, and had begun to gradually prepare—we were reading and gathering resources. But life has a way of sending unexpected curve balls: Miri, my husband's daughter from an earlier relationship, had lived with her mother and been homeschooled there. Then, at the age of six, she came to stay with us. So here we were, with Miri suddenly at our doorstep challenging us to stand on our principles. It was time to jump in. Prefabricated curriculum materials were out of the question; we just could not afford them. So we started with a little reading book, part of a series produced in the Caribbean. It was simple, straightforward, and had beautiful pictures of West Indian children. We were also able to buy the books and accompanying workbooks one at a time as we needed them, instead of all at once. As for math, every morning I wrote out pages and pages of math problems. In this way we were able to pinpoint and reinforce problem areas.

Our business was still relatively new and still at the point where it required both of our attention all the time. School had to flow along with our topsy-turvy world. In the morning after breakfast, Miri and I would sit and plan the day. Our focus at first was reading, writing, and arithmetic. During the morning meeting, I introduced new words and concepts, and we worked on areas that had given her a hard time the day before. Sometimes Miri worked beside me, each of us doing our own work. Other times she would go off on her own and work in solitude. When reading time came, often I was not able to stop working, so Miri had to go with the flow, reading aloud to me at the computer or wherever I happened to be working. Of course if she detected that I had gotten engrossed in my work, she would try to skip over words she didn't know. Little did she know Mom could focus on two things at once! (From this experience I understand how children come all the way through the school system and remain illiterate. Learning to read often requires one-on-one interaction, teacher and student alone with a book. Most teachers don't have that luxury, and many children learn to fake it.)

Our school has no set times. It starts when we start and it ends when the work is complete. After school, there is arts and crafts time—we provide the crayons, paper, glue, and wall and refrigerator space for display, but otherwise stay out of it.

In our school the lesson plan is secondary to our children's ability and widening interests. For example, we did not start fractions until Miri had the necessary mathematical background *and* she expressed an interest by bringing home a fraction book from the library. A book given to us by a friend launched our formal study of science. The learning just flows from one thing to the next. The homeschooling parent-teacher is mainly a facilitator, a guide to the child's naturally driven curiosity. Children learn to walk not as the result of physical therapy exercises and scheduled lectures, but rather because of their determination, natural ability, and self-confidence. They keep trying, and then one day they do it. It's no different with math or reading. People think nothing of pushing a child to "know" the alphabet at the "appropriate" age, even when that child has no interest in it and may not even want to sit down. But we would think it ludicrous to say, "OK, you are twenty-four months old. Every day we're going to spend forty-five minutes studying the rudiments of tricycle riding." Or, "Now that you're six years old, it's time to learn to ride the bike without training wheels. Every Saturday morning at 8:45 we are going to study advanced bicycle riding, but first, these workbook pages."

People ask, "Why do you homeschool?" As I start to answer, so many reasons rush into my head all at once and demand to be heard, that I often sound incoherent. I appreciate this opportunity to put down my thoughts in an organized way, and I pray that I will assist someone in some way.

So, why *do* we homeschool? There are many interrelated issues that go deep into the fabric of American society. Let's start with the institution of public education itself. What we see is a megalithic institution, corrupt at its very core, that would take more energy than we will *ever* have to effect any change. We salute those parents and teachers will *ever* have to effect any change. We salute those parents and teachers who battle every day against that Goliath, but we have chosen to give our time directly to our children.

When schools were designed with the industrial age in mind, children were herded into the classroom because the country needed good factory workers. They needed to be trained and molded into workers who would arrive on time, sit quietly for eight hours, do the assigned work, and accept authority. In other words, schools were simply not *designed* to nurture the budding human potential. Similarly, the current debate about school reform does not come from a heartfelt desire to help our children really learn, but from a xenophobic need to be "on top." Those industrial age factories have grown into multinational corporations, and their plans for factories no longer include the American people. What they want from America now is workers who can think on their feet, work independently, and work as a team. So as the schools *seem* to improve, it is basically only to provide workers to keep the machinery going.

Consider, now, what black youth have to contend with in this institution. Remember that America never wanted to educate us in the first place; the school system has always given our children the shaft. Black children get the worst of everything: the dilapidated buildings, the incompetent teachers, the corrupt administrators. Furthermore, year after year they are subjected to a curriculum that denies their heritage, ridicules their culture, punishes them for who they are, and awards them when they adopt a foreign persona (i.e. assimilate totally). They are subjected to teachers who despise them and who may not even recognize their own racist attitudes. They are subjected to tracking that takes our best, brightest, and most creative and labels them "special ed," "learning disabled," "remedial," "ADD," "hyperactive."

Kofi, like many black males, can tell disturbing stories about his own school days:

In the mid sixties my family moved into a neighborhood that was dis-integrating as a mixed Afrikan and Jewish neighborhood and re-integrating as an all Afrikan neighborhood. I attended a neighborhood elementary school for the fourth and fifth grades and then was bussed to a warehouse known as the sixth grade center. Some interesting things I noticed during my tenure at these two institutions were that the more Afrikan the school population got, the less college-prep type work we did. For example, we had just started learning Spanish in the fourth grade, when all of a sudden it was oddly discontinued. We still had the same teacher; she just stopped teaching Spanish. I remember quite vividly, because we learned to count to ten, but we never learned all the colors. I didn't bother to mention the change to my parents, because as a child, I didn't realize its significance.

So, although both of my parents held college degrees, and my father was a Ph.D. in Medieval German and a former Spanish and German instructor, I didn't even learn enough to say, "¿Qué pasa?" so he could respond. I got better treatment in English class, where we used the S.R.A. system of reading education. All students worked at their own pace, experiencing independent learning and individual testing.

The story becomes interesting when we contrast my fifth grade year with my sixth grade year. The sixth grade center was a warehouse for children from all over the city, though it was still a predominantly Afrikan population. I was placed in both remedial math and remedial English classes. The year before I had been in advanced classes, both in math and English. In remedial math class I felt somewhat comfortable, because I had never wanted to follow the rules they laid down for math; I always wanted to discover a new, easier way to do the calculations. But in the English class I felt very uncomfortable. First, my teacher was a crewcut-wearing white male who kept a full size W.W.II bomb shell in his classroom. Second, we were reading the fifth grade *Dick and Jane* book as a group activity in class—not only a remedial text, but a *fifth grade* remedial text. I was at about seventh grade level at the time. I don't recall telling my parents about all this, possibly because I thought I was being punished for forging a note to my fifth grade English teacher when the whole class had done badly on a particular test and I didn't want my parents to know. So I kept it to myself, the fact that this reading material was way below my level. After reading the fifth grade *Dick and Jane* for the greater portion of a year, the teacher finally said we could read the sixth grade book, but we had to read it on our own and then take a test on it. The tests were given individually and orally, so he'd know if you hadn't read the material or didn't comprehend it. We finished the fifth grade book in early May, and school let out in early June. In that month I read the entire sixth grade, seventh grade, eighth grade and a good portion of the ninth grade book, just to prove to him and myself that my reading skills were as good as I thought they were. Why in the world had I been relegated to this class in the first place?

Before I went to the sixth grade center, I thought you had to *work* to move from one grade to the next, but before I left the center I checked something very carefully. There was one white male student who didn't come to class half the time. When he did, all he did was take up air space. At the end of the school year, I figured there was no way he would be going to the next grade. When I asked to see his end-of-the-year report card, he graciously showed it to me. It was blank. It didn't have anything on it at all, except his name-rank-and-serial-number, and the fact that he was to be promoted to the seventh grade. That was an absolute shock. I couldn't figure out how he could graduate to the next grade without doing anything, and here I was working my behind off for the same booby prize.

Well, let's call this an isolated incident. A mistake, even. That year my whole family packed up and moved to Ohio. The larger situation was different, but the scenario was uncomfortably similar. My new school was almost entirely white, in a college town which hadn't failed to pass a school levy in thirty years. The white children in the neighborhood (we were the only Afrikan children on that side of town) had all taken French in the fifth and sixth grades. So, when my mother and I went to the school to register for my seventh grade classes I specifically asked my counselor, Mr. Bateman, if they had any beginning French classes where none of the students had already had French. "No problem," he responded.

My first day in class? The teacher began speaking in French, and all the students could answer except me. I stuck with it for awhile, but it was too much; they moved too fast, reviewing material they'd already learned. Now, even though my father was fluent in French and could have helped me, I was just too embarrassed to admit that I couldn't keep up. So, I went back to Mr. Bateman and asked him for a reprieve. He told me I was stuck. Well, I had been going to French two days a week and English the other three days. I just stopped going to French and stayed in English. They eventually got the message and took me out of French. Later I signed up for German. No problem here, because everybody started off on the same footing, and besides, my dad had a doctorate. I knew I could pass German, and I took it all through high school on into college years.

Let's say that these are just isolated incidents. Let's say that the young Afrikan student who walked up to me the first week of seventh grade and asked if I was in the slow learners class in math and English was an anomaly. After all, he only asked me because all the other Afrikan students—all seventeen out of a student body of five hundred—all were in the same slow learner classes. Let's say that situation was the exception to the rule. The question *still* comes up in my mind: why is it that whenever I tried to take a class that would put me on track for college, I met opposition? Why is it that all through high school there were NO other Afrikan students in my Biology, Chemistry, Physics, German, or English classes? The only time I had any other Afrikan students in the classroom was in typing and shop classes in the vocational wing of the school, or in my remedial math or Algebra classes.

Yeah, I probably just imagined all of this. But the funny thing is that years later, right here in Seattle, a friend and I did a survey of math classes in one of the oldest Afrikan schools in the city, Garfield High. We found that although the school was primarily Afrikan, there seemed to be an odd pattern in the distribution of Afrikan and white students in the math classes. We attended math classes for a day and found that the remedial classes were packed to the gills with Afrikan students and one lone white female. The intermediary classes had some Afrikan students, but the more advanced the math classes, the fewer Afrikan students and white females. By the time we got to the calculus class there were no Afrikan or female students, period. It was an all white male affair with an Afrikan male teacher. Ironic, but true.

These experiences and others involving the public schools—*and* many of the so-called "independent" schools—have brought us to the point where we couldn't see turning over our children to others. We may call on others to assist in guiding them on their path, but we could never turn them over entirely for outsiders to "educate."

Now that Kofi has had his turn, let me share a vignette. I was in the library the summer after I graduated from high school, browsing. I came across a big coffee-table type book called *Faces of Ghana*, or something like that. I started looking at the photographs—primarily portraits—and I was stunned. The faces were absolutely beautiful. The book also had African poetry, traditional and contemporary. This floored me. Me, a high school graduate, honor student, college bound, and I had *absolutely no idea that Africans wrote poetry!!* Milton, Whitman and emily had been crammed down my throat, but *no one* had given me literature that I could hold on to. I was adrift in my life without a real cultural foundation! As I see it, the schools had failed me. That one book, which I found on my own, launched me on a *learning path* that is a *life path* that I am still on today. I give credit only to that teacher or teachers back down the line who taught me how to read. Or perhaps my mother did that. I should ask her.

Another thing that we must remember as we examine the school system in America: the school system was designed by Europeans for Europeans. We differ from them in many ways, including culture, customs, and even physical and mental development. Four hundred years of living in this melting pot has not changed our basic makeup. So turning an Afrikan child over to these authorities is like asking a bird to swim and then complaining that he has lost his gift of graceful flight. Journey with me to my childhood, or your own. I remember wonderful times with my parents and their friends. I remember all the loud and lively discussions, the dancing, the music. We are not a quiet people; we like to make a joyful noise. Take our children from our noisy homes and deposit them in a room with a bunch of others and say, "Now you must be quiet for hours." Some children will learn how to survive and excel. Others will not make the transition early enough to avoid acquiring a label in their permanent school record.

We start *our* school day with music and dance; that's our P.E class. We use drumming to learn the times tables. This is all a learning process for me as well as my students, because it's not the way I was educated, and it is very easy to fall into the trap of presenting the material the way it was presented to me.

The biggest lesson I have learned in my short experience with homeschooling is to respect my childrens' ability and willingness to direct their own learning. Once, Miri got involved in a project that started with a globe (bought for twenty-five cents at a swap meet). She wanted to work with it, and started by finding the names of all the countries in Africa. It took a few days before she had them all located and correctly spelled. Then she located the countries on a blank map and wrote the names in. Next, she wanted to see the flags, and she started drawing and coloring them. We started pointing out current news events in the paper about African countries, and she cut out the stories. Then Miri found pictures and stories about African people in an old *National Geographic* (again, purchased at the library for twenty-five cents). These, too, she cut out. She found pictures in other books, and we made color copies of them. By this time she had acquired a binder to hold everything and this became her "Africa Book." At the time this project started there were some subject areas that we were working on that I did not want to drop entirely; she needed to strengthen those skills so they wouldn't be forgotten. So we negotiated an agreement of a minimum amount of work she had to complete each day in addition to her evolving Africa Book. Miri decided she would get these out of the way; before anyone else woke up she was in bed doing her math workbook pages and had all the work done by breakfast, so she could spend as much time as she wanted on *her* project.

Suddenly, after about three months, it was over. The book was boring. She moved on. Neither wild horses nor I could get her to work on that book again. But she had a finished project she was proud of, and we had learned a valuable lesson about the power of self-directed learning.

Even more important than our academic schedule, or the assigned workbook pages, is the talking—the unhurried conversations in the grocery store, or in line at the post office. A cloud formation spotted in rush-hour traffic can spark an entire lesson in geography. Making lunch or dinner can turn into a discussion of the three states of matter: solid, liquid, gas. Children need time to ask questions without fear of ridicule, and explore their areas of interest without an agenda. We need the time to teach children how they should move through this world. Have we achieved anything if we educate people to recite the quadratic equation, but they don't know how to treat other humans? If they have the great classics of literature under their belt, but don't know how to be alone with themselves?

Different families handle the logistics of homeschooling in their own ways. For us, Kofi has taken on the majority of the responsibility for the business, while I have the majority of the responsibility for schooling. The home business makes life simpler, because I can put in work hours without the added problem of juggling with day-care; I commute just down the hallway. Also, I think it's wonderful for the children to see us working, to see that we *use* the skills they are learning. And the business itself provides a learning laboratory. Miri loves to go and sell with her father. She is an exceptional salesperson and adds up a purchase and makes change so fast she shocks many customers. If there is a math concept I can't get across, I just use an example that involves money, and suddenly mud becomes crystal clear. Sometimes when we've gotten a backlog of orders Miri and Nefertiti pitch in with the packaging, dropping incense into bags and bundling them in dozens. If you've got to work, it's so much nicer to have your family with you.

Now I know I have to touch on the socialization question, because it seems to come up almost every time the issue of homeschooling is raised. My answer is that we need to challenge some unproven assumptions. Let me start at the beginning. This country is actually conducting a large experiment in child raising and family life. The problem is that no one remembers that it is *an experiment.* Our unquestioned educational model is unprecedented in human history, and untested outside of the last 150 years. Yet it is pushed on millions of children and families. There is no stopping to assess the consequences of institutionalizing children so early. Women are encouraged, pushed, even *forced* back to work after childbirth. For those who are able to and choose to stay home, the subtle and not so subtle messages are unrelenting. Concern in their voices, people ask, "Don't you miss working? You must be bored, being at home all day."

But often what we view as normal may not really be the best choice; it's just what everybody happens to be doing right now. So to the people who ask the socialization question, *I* ask, "Do children really need to spend eight hours everyday surrounded by thirty children of exactly the same age?" For me the answer is *No*. The social circles we move in provide what our children need, as do the neighborhood children of all ages. And don't forget the family. Miri, Nefertiti and Nehanda—ten, five, and two—play together beautifully. Spring and summer come and they are outside with friends, visiting or being visited. When friends of their

Tanya Khemet

own ages are around they grow apart and argue more. I look forward to winter and quiet rainy afternoons, watching the sisters play and grow together. The family is stronger, more united, and there is also time and space for solitude.

Sometimes I feel inadequate to teach. I jump into panic, afraid I'll forget to cover some area. I imagine my child as a young adult in college, hampered because I neglected to teach some crucial basic chemistry, or how a bill becomes a law. Then I remind myself that there is little that *I* remember from high school. I managed to succeed because I learned how to access the information I need. The panic attack subsides, temporarily.

Another fear that assaults me at times is that I might not provide enough variety of experiences for an older child. I remember some wonderful experiences in high school—primarily after-school experiences, actually—like being on the track team. Along with this fear comes the realization that with creativity, any family can overcome this one. A strong homeschooling support group can definitely help; there is strength in numbers and you can get your group into activities just as if you were a school group. Also, in some states you have the option of using the public schools on a part-time basis, perhaps for a music class, advanced computer or TV/video production class your teen may be interested in. Search the community for classes/workshops, seminars, and volunteer opportunities.

There are three things we should remember if we feel we are unable to educate our children ourselves. One, in this society we have been conditioned to defer to the experts. From the minute you think you are pregnant you are supposed to run to an expert to tell you how to take care of yourself and your baby. We must remember that certified teachers spend very little time studying their subject matter; the bulk of their education is spent learning how to teach, how to be sensitive to the needs of several children, how to spot potential problems, and how to discipline. These are all areas that you get a crash course in from the moment your children are born. By the time they are ready for school, you've earned a Master's Degree in education.

I remember in my freshman year of college I spoke with my high school algebra teacher, Gary Phillips. (I remember his name because he was one of the exceptions, a true educator who loved young people and worked hard to make learning fun.) I told him I was taking calculus and he shocked me by telling me he had never taken it. In my freshman year of college, I had already gone further in mathematics than he had. Remember, when it comes to your children, *you* are the expert.

Two, *relax.* We will never be able to teach our children everything they need to learn for adulthood. What we can do is teach them how to learn on their own, teach them research techniques, teach them how to use the library. Instill in them the self-confidence to walk into situations where they might have to learn as they go along. Just think about your own work experiences.

Three, there is a wealth of materials available, even if you are on a limited budget. You may have to search a little harder and be more creative, but you will be surprised at what is out there. I had a hard time not jumping in and playing with the school supplies myself. Remember, the best resource of all is absolutely free: the library. Get to know your library system and I guarantee it will surprise you.

How do you start to homeschool? Start with trust. You must trust your children's innate ability to learn and to guide their own learning, whatever their ages. You must also trust yourself and your ability to know and do what is best for your children. That knowledge may come from the heart or the head, but you must trust it all the same.

If you are *removing* your children from the institution called school, rather than homeschooling from the beginning, pull out your extra reserves of patience. You have the additional task of deprogramming bad habits and attitudes about self and learning. Allow your newly liberated students *time* to adjust and find their own rhythm.

Sit down with your children and talk. Let them be the co-founders of your new school. Plan your days and lessons together. Define your focus and set goals. First, work with books and materials you have on hand, visit the library, read books and magazines by homeschoolers, and slowly build your library. There are some exceptional materials available, and there is a lot of rubbish. Many families start by satisfying the Board of Education requirements and purchasing curriculum materials, but they find they have replicated the school in their home. Instead, lay the foundation for your school in your relationship with your child. The state and the publishers can wait.

Miri is now at home with her "other" mother; the transition between her two families is made smoother because she is homeschooled. Nefertiti, my prolific artist and champion of fantasy play, has decided she is ready to learn how to read, so we are working on that. Nehanda? Well, she's in that special place of babyhood where every waking moment is a new discovery. So you can see that I am not an expert by any measure. You can find many people who have homeschooled longer than I have. Still, I hope to humbly yet loudly add my voice to a small but growing revolutionary front. Yes, make no mistake about it, there is a *battle* raging for the very hearts and souls of our children. The weapons I bring to this struggle are my love for my children, every talent and skill I possess, all the wisdom I have acquired, and the courage to take this leap of faith and do what I know is right.

As we shed the illusions and the self-hatred that is so much a part of our history as Afrikans in the Diaspora, as we learn to honor our ancestors and traditions, we must also renew our respect for our mother-wisdom. Not only must the bounds of white supremacy be removed from our minds, but so must the shackle of male domination. What I mean is this: if it tears at your heart to send your five- or six-year-old to school, don't do it. Mother knows best. If it feels right to delay teaching mathematics to your child, do it. If your student prefers poetry to prose, let them explore it to their heart's content. We all, mothers *and* fathers, must retune our inner ear to pick up the mother-love-wisdom channel.

We need to come full circle and return the process of teaching children back to the community and family. At the same time, we must look to the future. Our children need an education that enhances and challenges the uniquely human ability to think holistically. They need an education that nurtures the individual soul. And as we look to the past and the future, we must also remember the present. The experience of childhood and youth is a precious gift that we are each given only once. It should not be squandered in a hurried march to adulthood. We need an education that celebrates the child.

All praises due to the Creator. Ase. Amen. ❖

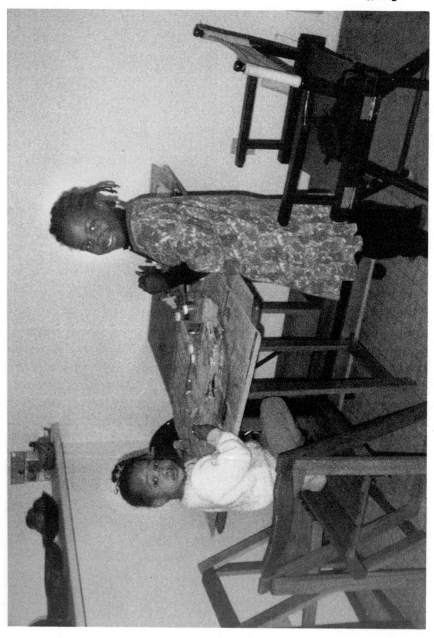

DC and Adam Clough
Port Orchard, Washington
interviewed by Donna E. Nichols-White

RESCUING A TEENAGE BOY

Cast of characters:

DC Clough, single mom working full time. At the time of this interview, she lived with her son Adam, and also with a nephew, Jimmy, and a niece, Stavon. Jimmy and Stavon attend school.

Adam Clough: fifteen years old, homeschooled for a year and a half. Homeschools in conjunction with a local public alternative school, which allows him to earn high school credits and to use textbooks and other resources. However, DC—not the school system—directs his education. Adam will be spending the next school year in Malaysia with his father, homeschooling half time and attending a private school half time.

Donna Nichols-White: interviewer, editor of *The Drinking Gourd* multicultural magazine for homeschoolers. See her essay in this book, "Free at Last."

Khahil White: Donna's nine-year-old son

Rukiya White: Donna's three-year-old daughter

Bruce: A counselor at the public alternative school who checks some of Adam's work and awards high school credits.

Donna (to Adam): What are your hobbies?

Adam: Basketball, women, and music.

Donna: Can you read music?

Adam: Uh-huh. Read the back of a CD cover [laughs].

Adam Clough--and his friend Sugar

DC Clough

Donna: Let's start from the top. If you didn't have to do the work that DC gives you to do, what would you do?

Adam: *Sleep!* You gotta be really specific here, because I'm being honest.

Donna: Do you like Legos and stuff like that? Do you like to build things? Do you like taking care of the horse? Planting the garden?

Adam: So you ask me if my mom didn't give me work to do, and I had to do something constructive, what would I do?

Donna: Yes. What is your interest?

Adam: I like writing stories.

Donna: What kind of stories do you like to write?

Adam: Detective.

Donna: And what do your detective stories consist of? Do you have a main. . .

Adam: Just a hero, a broad, a villain, and a bunch of club scenes and stuff.

Donna: We're gonna have to work on that. We have a hero and a broad, that does not sound. . .[trails off into laughter].

Adam: Okay, I'll put it more specifically. I have a hero, a woman that's mysterious that you're always suspecting as the murderer, a bunch of club scenes, and some kind of mafia or something.

Donna: And do you write for a certain amount of hours each day, just on the things that you like to write?

Adam: No, I write when I write. I don't really have like a set time. I just, if I'm bored or something and I feel like writing, then I just sit down and write.

Donna: So do you think you write everyday? Or whenever you get the opportunity?

Adam: Yeah, I do, I write a lot at nighttime.

***

Donna: How well did you read when you left school?

Adam: *Pathetically.*

Donna: Pathetically? And how old were you when you left school?

Adam: Thirteen? Oh no, fourteen.

Donna: Whose decision was it?

Adam: That was a dumb question. That would be Mom.

DC: Actually, you were thirteen, Adam.

Donna (to DC now): What was the catalyst that made you finally get your kid out of school?

DC: I was physically out of shape for the beatings! [Everyone laughs.] The beatings wore *me* out! No...it was the report cards, the lack of work, the lack of knowledge. It was a lot of things, it wasn't just one thing. It happened at the end of the semester, getting the report card and it's all F's. He can do the work, he just doesn't do it. And that was the comment all the teachers had—he could do the work, he just wasn't doing it.

Donna: They told me the same thing, and I turned out okay. Parents hate it when I say that! I'll tell parents in a minute I *hated* school. "Don't tell our kid that!" they say. That's how Cliff and I ended up getting to know each other in high school, because I hated school and he thought it's just what you have to go through. He's a straight and narrow type of person; I'm the one who says, "There's got to be a better way."

DC: But see, the problem was Adam was not learning. If you get an F in a class and you know the work—you *can* do it, you just *didn't* do it, there's a difference. Why that F, what kind of F is it? Is he not trying, or is he trying real hard and still not getting it? Adam was not getting an education, at all. He'll be the first to tell you that.

Adam: Yes.

DC: He knew it probably moreso once we started homeschooling and he could compare school to the things he was learning at home.

Donna: What was the hardest thing that occurred after you finally decided to homeschool?

DC: Where to start.

Donna: But you didn't start tough, you gave him a vacation, didn't you?

DC: Yes.

Donna: What was a reasonable vacation according to DC Clough?

DC: I remember we started like the middle of September, and we'd just go on the deck, sit in the sun, and read.

Adam: It was *nice*.

DC: He'd read the Bible to me.

Adam: Now she's starting to crack down this year.

DC: After this morning when we get home, you're gonna be working [laughter].

Donna: I can't argue with it, you only got a couple of years left that she might have you to torture....You only got a few more years to get it in, because society tells them when they're eighteen they're on their own.

DC: Please. The *law* says when they're eighteen they're on their own, society says usually it's twenty-three before they're ready to go out there.

Donna: How long did you want to homeschool before you did it, both of you? Adam, you didn't want to, or did you?

Adam: At first I didn't want to do it at all. Now that I've done it I want to do it for two years.

Donna: Do you think you want to go to college?

Adam: I'm definitely going to college.

Donna (to DC): Is that because he's been brainwashed like my children or because he wants to go to college?

DC: I think it's a little bit of both.

Donna (joking): Well, Khahil is going to college at about thirteen or fourteen, right Khahil?

Khahil: Uh-huh.

Donna: Now, DC, how long did it take for you to decide to homeschool, finally?

DC: I decided in the spring, and then we started that September. In spring of '93 the report cards came and I just knew there was a better way. I let him finish that year. And the way I approached it to him, I didn't say like, "This is what you're gonna do. It's gonna be this way and no other way."

> *"What really got me was, that June when he failed eighth grade, I sent him to a tutor two days a week for one month and she got him through pre-algebra, which they wanted him to spend a whole year on in the ninth grade."*

It was more like we talked about it. And once I went to the WHO [Washington Homeschool Organization] Convention and saw that there were a lot of people, that was it.

Donna: That was the first year I saw that many Black people. Over 3,000 people attended that WHO Convention.

DC: My decision wasn't because of the number of Black people there—that didn't influence me one way or the other. It was just something I needed to do. It didn't really matter what category you put the people in, be it for religious reasons or whatever. I just knew it was something I needed to do.... Adam had no choice in it, but I wasn't going to make it where it was going to be a fight and a struggle. And so I just approached it like we could spend time together. You know, I made it like it was going to be a positive thing. Even though he might have been afraid of it, he was like, "I'm gonna give it a try."

Donna: How did you first learn about homeschooling?

DC: I have no idea.

Donna: Do you know people who homeschool?

DC: Yes, I know people who homeschool. I can remember being young though, and still in school, and they'd do programs on homeschooling on talk shows. I knew it was out there.

Donna: And you hadn't read any books on homeschooling or anything? You went in cold.

DC: No, no, I hadn't read any books. There's a lady that lives a couple miles up the road who has horses, and her kids have always been homeschooled. And then there was a guy at work when I was at Boeing who homeschooled, he took his kids out because he was having problems too. They just weren't learning. And he's the one that told me of places to go for ideas, and told me about being certified to teach—whether you have to be or whether you should be, all that stuff. Then I did research into places where you could get certified and what it entailed. And there's so many different ways, everybody has their own opinion how it should be and how much time it should take, and what it should cover. And I didn't have the forty-five credits of college.

Donna: But Adam's officially under the school district anyway, though. He's considered a part time school student in a way.

DC: He is now, but when we started he wasn't going to be at all. It was like, "I'm taking him out and I don't want nothing to do with you again." You know, the deciding factor to homeschool was when he was in the eighth grade and he failed four out of six classes, and the other two were like D's. And I said, "Well, we'll just have him do the eighth grade over." And they said, "No, we'll just have him do the language arts in the ninth grade again, and we'll have him do pre-algebra over again in the ninth grade." And I was like, "But I don't want that. I want him to do the eighth grade over." And they kept trying to push him on. For *years* they'd been saying that, while I'd been talking to Adam about staying back for quite a few years. Probably from the sixth grade on, I'd say, "You need to stay back a year."

But every time I'd talk to the teachers and the counselors, they were against it. And finally their reasons weren't making any sense because nothing was getting done, nothing was happening with his education. And so I went to a certification class, and I'm glad I went because I did learn quite a bit, not just about the laws, but also about teaching styles.

Donna: Your class was a religious one?

DC: Yeah, but there was nothing religious talked about in it at all. *Nothing.* There was no religion in the classroom, in her speeches, in her books, nothing at all.

Donna: That's good.

DC: I was happy because it was not for a religious reason that I'm homeschooling. And it really wasn't an ethnic reason why I'm homeschooling, either.

Well, at the end of August the school called me up. Adam was spending the summer in Bangkok with his father. And they said, "Well, Ms. Clough, what do you want to do?"

"What do you mean what do I want to do?"

"Well, about Adam."

"What are you talking about, what do I want to do about Adam?"

"Do you want him to do the eighth grade over or do you want to put him in the ninth grade?"

I said, "Why is it when I talked to you about this in May and June you didn't want him to do the eighth grade over, it was all about going into the ninth grade. You didn't tell me I even had a choice." And I said, "So I've decided to definitely take matters into my own hands, and he will *not* be returning." CLICK.

What really got me was, that June when he failed eighth grade—to me it was definitely failing—I sent him to a tutor *two days a week for one month and she got him through pre-algebra*, which they wanted him to spend a *whole year* on in the ninth grade. But our tutor quit.

Donna: She quit? Elementary algebra is probably a cheap course. I'll look into one of my books for you. For the computer.

DC: The tutor that taught him pre-algebra, she worked with him on a lot of grammar and English. Algebra I is as far as she goes with math; English is her baby. She said any kind of English grammar, writing problems, anything, send them to me. But she can't take them any farther in the math.

Donna: If you lived nearby I could tutor you in Algebra.

DC: I'll bring him.
So, that was it. I feel like the school messed me over. I'm not saying it was all the school's fault, though. Because Adam has to take part of the blame too.

Donna: Yes, but keeping him home you can make him more responsible.

DC: He knows it. He knows it.

Donna: Now Adam, how do you study all your courses? How do you do your math? You used to have a math tutor, so now math is on hold for a while?

> *"I don't* connive *anymore. When I was in school I was criminal-minded. I'd think about teachers and I'd say, 'Ah, we'll fix 'em.' They just kept trying these little tricks and I'm so criminal -minded I got out of 'em. "*

Adam: Yeah, math is on hold.

Donna: You don't look too happy. You look like you liked math. So, you just have your core work in reading, mathematics, lots of writing? Do you do spelling?

Adam: Oh, I'm good at spelling.

Donna: That's right, he already spells. Did he get tested again?

DC: He gets quite a few tests in spelling.

Donna: No, I mean the standardized exams, or is the teacher just assessing him?

DC: All the teacher does is just look and see that he did the work and that's it.

Donna: But remember Washington's yearly requirement for testing or assessment?

DC: He takes the CAT [California Achievement Test]. He did that last year and he'll do it again this year.

Donna: What sort of conflicts, if any, come up between you and Adam about homeschooling?

DC: Have we ever had any?

Adam: No, no.

Donna: Well, there goes the other question—"How do you handle them, how do these conflicts compare to previous conflicts over school?" You have no conflicts.

DC: What happens is, you know, like with the imprinting animals do with their young. We do it too. You get it across that "I am the boss and you are my subject. . ." [laughter]

Adam: It's like she goes, "Do it." And I can't resist.

DC: Right. And it starts around Ru's age [around age three].

Adam: She is a dictator whose word is law.

Donna: She looks so sweet and innocent.

DC: Yeah, it started at such a young age that there's no problem. Like if I want a glass of water I don't say, "*Get* me a glass of water." I don't go that far.

Adam: She asks me, "Please get me a glass of water." I go, "No," and then I get up and go get it [laughter].

DC: This year is definitely different than last year. Because I was laid off last year so I was with him at home.

Donna: And you had time. But that was good though, being laid off that year. This year he's on his own during the day as he homeschools, and he still gets the work done.

DC: Adam, can you talk about your interests and what you learn and what are your days like and stuff?

Adam: Music, volume....

DC: I should ask, what do you do different now that you're not in school?

Adam: I don't *connive* anymore. When I was in school I was criminal-minded. I'd think about teachers and say, "Ah, we'll fix 'em." We'd do a progress report. Silly teachers. And then what I'd do is, whenever I got that progress report, the classes that I did good in I'd let them sign it and the ones that weren't good I'd just write a substitute. They just kept trying these little tricks and I'm so criminal-minded I got out of 'em till it was like a must thing. I'm very criminal minded. If you don't go directly to my mom to tell her what I'm doing, it won't get to her. I work my way out of it with ease. I've had times where I've lost tests, told them my dog died, acted depressed, and got to do it the next day.

DC: I think the question "what does he learn" also means, what are the subjects that you're learning?

Adam: History, math.

DC: What type of history?

Adam: Ancient history.

Donna: So what period is that? What's ancient to you?

Adam: Ancient history's like going back to the Homosapien, Homoerectus....

Donna: Oh, so you're learning archeology.

Adam: Yes, and paleontology.

DC: Last year we did the Bible. And this year we're doing this. We put Black history on hold.

Adam: Yeah. We're probably going to start that back up pretty soon.

Donna: But you can *integrate* it.

DC: Yes, we do, but you know, we're getting through this stuff now. What other things are you doing right now, Adam?

Donna: You study grammar together orally.

DC: Maya—

Adam: Maya Angelou.

Donna: Studying Maya Angelou. See, you do still have Black history.

Adam: She's good. I *love* her poems—"Why you pushing on me?"

Donna: "Phenomenal woman," I like that one.

DC: What are your days like, Adam? Explain your routine. Your school day.

Adam: My school day, okay. I wake up in the morning with Jimmy, we go into Mom's room and watch our daily cartoon schedule.

Donna: *Before school?*

Adam: Yeah. It's early, like six to eight. *What?!*

Donna: Go ahead, continue.

Adam: Okay. From six to eight, and when he leaves for school I go back to my room and sleep for one more hour till nine.

Donna: Do you feed him breakfast or anything?.

Adam: If there's no food, yes. But if there's cereal I say get up and get it yourself.

DC: He'll do the bacon and eggs thing.

Adam: I'll do the bacon and egg. I'll cook pancakes for him. I make sure he eats, but after that I go back to sleep, I wake up at nine. Sometimes I watch *Days*, depends on how much work I got. If I got like a serious work day then I just get right to work.

DC: *Days* is our soap opera.

Adam: From there I just crank up my stereo and get to work.

DC: What's "get to work" mean?

Adam: Get to work means jump on that computer and do whatever you're having me do, whether it be questions, or a program, or whether it just has me study—

DC: He has to read a book right now. What I do is I go through the chapter before he gets to it. Sometimes I have him read it. There's a junior high type level history book and there's a college prep. A lot of times I have him read the basics, called the Basic Approach. It's a lower level, first, just to get some ideas of what it's talking about. And then he reads the college prep one. And I go through and write down as many questions as I feel like writing.

Adam: See, Bruce has a test. Usually I take Bruce's test just fine, you know, a little fifteen questions.

Donna: That's the teacher's test?

Adam: That's not good enough for her. She has to pull out the big fifty-five test.

Donna: You make up your own test?

Adam: She makes up her own test.

DC: They're hard.

Adam: Fifty-five questions. We're talkin' *test*.

Donna: You should keep all the questions from her tests.

DC: They're in the computer. I read 'em off and he types them in the computer. And then after he's done typing them in the computer I go in my room and he has to work on them.

Donna: I could sell the book *and* your test.

Adam: That's harsh! Don't punish kids.

Donna: You know, I'm just getting tough. I'm tired of the half stepping. My kids have to know stuff when they go out in the world because there's nobody to take care of them. If you're going to do physics, do *real* physics. If you're going to do math, do *real* math. Don't Mickey Mouse.

DC: Oh yeah. No, I do a lot of questions. And he has to do them all. There's questions in the book, and reviews—a lot of times the questions I will put down on *my* tests are already in the book.

Adam: So she double whammies me.

DC: But he has to write 'em twice, he's more likely to remember 'em.

Donna: I thought my mother was bad.

DC: And I have them do reports on Cleopatra, Hannibal....

Donna: Well, you're doing Hannibal, that's Black history.

Adam: So is Cleopatra.

DC: The Parthenon. He didn't know about the Parthenon when we did Greece. In about another month we're going to be done with this history book and go back to something else. Not the whole book but half, and we'll take a break.

Let's see, what else? What are his days like? I come home in the evening and we take tests.

> *"You know, the biggest positive out of the whole thing is that he spends more time with family, like his grandparents. I had a cousin who died last year and we knew that she was going to, so we spent a lot of time going to visit her. I even had him sing the Black National Anthem to her one day. He spends a lot of time with my mother, and he's eating a lot of soul food."*

Adam: Or you just look over my work.

DC: I look over your work. And then you read. Forgot about the reading I make you do. And what kind of things you like to read.

Donna (looking at *The Math Kit* with Rukiya, Adam, and Khahil): This is the Greek Pyramid. And see, in there, they're explaining the history of mathematics which started in central Africa....Rukiya took the rubber band out. That has algebra in it—the Cartesian coordinates.

DC (reading from Donna's notes): "Did your relationship change after starting to homeschool?" You know, the biggest positive out of the whole thing is that he spends more time with family, like his grandparents.

Donna: Oh! Because he already spent plenty of time with you.

DC: Yeah. Especially the year I was laid off. I had a cousin who died last year and we knew that she was going to, so we spent a lot of time going to visit her. I even had him sing the Black National Anthem to her one day.

Donna: *You did?*

DC: Yeah, I made him write it down, write the words down. I figured if he wrote the words down that meant he listened to the tape enough times over and over that he knew it by heart.

Adam: I had it down cold.

DC: Came in handy today.

Adam: Yeah, it did. I was like, when am I going to use this?

Donna: It would have come in handy at Kwanzaa too because everybody said, well, let's sing the Black National Anthem—and who knew it?

DC: So that's one of the big positives. He spends a lot of time with my mother, and he's eating a lot of soul food.

Donna: But he gets both sets of grandparents. Grace wants to know, is your homeschooling experience tied to your experience as a Black person? We don't wake up in the morning, look in the mirror and say, "Let's enjoy this Black experience" [laughter]. But the fact that he's got two sets of grandparents and two different worlds to deal with, that's fun.

DC: And like one, like Grandma Eldean, is like. . .

Adam: Grandma Eldean is traditional. She's straight Walmart.

Donna: Traditional Black?

DC: No, she's White.

Donna: So how is she traditional?

DC: She flies kites. They go for trips in the winter.

Adam: And gardening and RV's.

DC: And she's like into Bonsais at Weyerhauser Gardens where she tends her plants. They have a house at the ocean and they fly the kites.

Donna: Oh, I'd like that. And you get to do stuff like that?

DC: And she takes them whale watching, you know, that kind of stuff.

Adam: It's fun.

DC: Where *my* mother is more like, "I'm gonna fry me up some cabbage," and, "Lets make some fried chicken." It's just different. Because my mother isn't wealthy or anything, she's downright poor. And then this other side—

Donna: It must be a nice place to be in. See, I don't have a wealthy set, a *well-off* even set of relatives. We're it.

Adam: Oh please!

Donna: We're it. They come to us.

Adam: Oh, okay. I thought you said *us*. Don't act like you're poor. I know you're living in the hood here.

DC: But that was one of the major changes—spending time with family. He can go spend a couple of days with a grandparent and do the gardening, or go clean horse stalls for Tina.

Adam: Shovel duty!

DC: He can do that. And he couldn't spend that time when he was in school, because the only time he had was just weekends.

Donna: What are the best resources or organizations your family has discovered for homeschooling?

DC and Adam (to Donna): You.

DC: The best resources? Adam's Grandma Eldean, she's a retired teacher. I gotta explain this. She was my fifth grade teacher and because I grew up with my father, she took care of me a lot. She's the one who got me into horses.

Donna: Adam's grandmother?

DC: No. She's *like* a grandma. She's like my parent.

Donna: An adopted grandmother.

DC: She's been in his life and my life forever.

Donna: That's right. She's the woman who saved *you*.

DC: Yeah, she saved me. She was my teacher, so I talked to her before I even made the decision to do this. She doesn't teach him or anything. But just to have the support of knowing she agreed and would be there if I needed it, was good. Then I found out about the Hall program, which is like a school for homeschoolers. All it is is a computer lab. It has all kinds of academic programs for anything you need to teach.

Donna: Is that in the Highline School District?

DC: No, it's Gig Harbor. But they also have books if you want them. The only thing is, the parent has to be there. They're not there to teach your child. They just have the resources. Last year I could be there with Adam, so I would take him. But I can't do that this year, and I wouldn't do it for all the classes anyway, because I still wanted the Bible, and I still wanted Black history—there were things I wanted. And then at the other end of the school, they have an alternative high school. That alternative high school's mostly for wayward children with clipped wings.

But still there was usage there because they had a counselor that could look over our schoolwork and give us credit. And it went into the school system as real school credits. If I put him back into school as a senior—no, it's not happening right now, because he'll probably go to college instead—but if I did, or even when he goes to college, I don't want to have him take a test to prove he knows this. You put a test in front of Adam and there is no telling what's going to happen, even if he knows the material. And so this way there's already paperwork proof that we've covered that, we don't have to cover it again. And that's what it does.

In going to them, Bruce can look over his writing, a story he wrote, and say, "Well, he needs to work on some grammar stuff. Here, here's a grammar book." And so there has been help and the support is there. They keep track of, like if we get through this history book halfway that's sixty hours of history, and he gets that credit. He has to get an eighty percent on the test that they give, but then he's gotta do my test too.

So there's been support through people like that, but I still like the fact that I have *control*. I can say, "This is what you're going to learn. You're reading Maya Angelou, you're going to read Walter Dean Myers." Next he's going to be into James Baldwin, he doesn't know it yet. But I don't want him to think that there's just a white world out there. I'm not saying I want him to deny it either, because he is bi-racial, but we know society is going to look at him as a Black teenager.

***

[DC and Donna have been discussing Adam's bi-racial heritage, and how he fits into the white world.]

Donna: It's a whole different way of life.

DC: It is. It's like you want that child to have that exposure because that's part of their heritage.

Donna: And it's part of their protection.

DC: Yeah, and it's like, how am I going to teach it?

Donna: Your friends were on your side, right? When you decided to homeschool?

DC: Yeah. It didn't matter.

Donna: Yeah, *your* family and friends don't mess with *you*.

DC: I had a lot of support. A lot of people think, "How can you do it?"

Donna: They think, how can you stand to have them with you?

DC: Oh no, not that. "How can you do it?" is like people think that they can't teach their child. You know, how can they be the *teacher*.

Donna: Do you see yourself as a teacher?

DC: *No.* I see myself as a parent that can do a better job than the school did....I guess all parents are teachers in that sense.

Donna: I don't think of myself as a teacher.
Oh......finances. You're a single parent. You raise horses.

DC: I do? I just *have* a horse.

Donna: You're getting another one.

DC: I'm going to try. I'm working on getting maybe something cheap.

Donna: So you're a single parent, self-supporting. . .what do you do?

DC: I'm an apprentice as a heavy equipment operator.

Donna: You're an apprentice who works all the time. You have a mobile home on five acres. What's the difference between raising Adam in Seattle, the city, and then homeschooling him and raising him out in the middle of nowhere?

DC: The difference? Well, we lived in Tacoma, in Hilltop, which is considered the heart of the ghetto.

Donna: It's always on TV.

DC: Yeah, Hilltop. And you know what? It ain't *nothing* like that. It really isn't. People think that it was nothing but Black people going by shooting each other. Our neighborhood we lived in was so diverse.

Adam: It was!

Donna: Seattle doesn't *have* an all-Black neighborhood.

DC: Everybody knew everybody. But it was getting bad. Matter of fact somebody had gotten killed, shot up, on the next block and that's when I knew it was time to go. Also I knew—even though it doesn't affect me because I'm an adult that can say no and I don't have the peer pressure—I knew that there were a lot of kids there that were like eleven and twelve, who could be led astray. Peer pressure's tough, it's tough.

Adam: When I was there, I wanted to be a gang member. Big guy, let's just go bump 'em off. Puh! I wanted to be a gang member. That's all I wanted to be.

Donna: Being *her* child?

DC: And then when I lived in Tacoma I was sometimes working swing shift. I had to be at work and not know what they were going to do. I lived with my father, so there was supervision there. But still, not knowing what drugs could have been offered them, and all that. And I'm not saying it's any different where I live now, because it's everywhere, you're going to have those temptations. But now, in the country, there are no hangout spots. It's like they can't walk down to the corner store, which before was a block and a half away and everybody hung out.

Donna: Where there were drugs, right?

DC: They can't do that anymore. My kids can't get a gang of people and just walk the streets or anything. They can't do those things that teenagers are doing. Not that they were doing them then—they weren't, because they were still too young.....The kids they grew up with in Tacoma, there's nothing to brag about in their lives now.

Donna: *Already.* You know, *we* lost a lot of friends. I now know that after I finished school, kids younger than me—even girls—were in jail. That was a big shock for me. How could they possibly have ended up in jail?

DC: Stavon has friends who are pregnant. Adam has friends who are in gangs, or dropped out of school already. And who's to say, he could have been there.

    Another thing—I don't know why people think this, that because I homeschool I'm not allowing my child to live in the real world. That I'm not allowing him those temptations that he's going to face sooner or later anyways. It's like these things people say to me, like, "I taught *my* child the difference between right and wrong, and I put them out there, and *they* knew not to do wrong," and all that stuff. And I can't—

Donna: Why fight it?

DC: I don't even argue with them, I don't even argue with it.

Adam: I know about the real world anyway. I already know about it.

Donna: You probably know plenty.

DC: Speak. It's your turn, you've got the floor.

Adam: See, people say you gotta be faced with the real world. I've been there. I've been tempted by every drug and all that. Drugs, sex, all that. Turned it down. So it's not like I'm missing the real world.

DC: But I also think that the drugs and the sex, that's not the real world. That's just temptations out there.

Donna: No. That's not even growing up. They say people go on drugs and they never mature. You know, it would be still twelve-year-old Adam when he was twenty-one, if he was high for eight years in a row. You don't get to grow up. I don't know, I think people are confused about what the real world is. And I think especially for Black kids, they think they should be exposed to the hood, or know how to walk down the block or do this, that, and any other thing....

***

DC: I think getting laid off and being home that first year and getting down to business was great. And I just lived poorly. I lived on the unemployment and I just didn't spend much money. I just stayed home, I didn't do anything out of the ordinary. I went to used bookstores and I used the books I have. And now, as a single parent since I'm gone all day, each night I leave a list and we go over things that need to be done.

Donna: You work hard.

DC: And some of the things I want done when I walk through that door. If not, prove to me you did *something* today. Show me proof of what you did today.

Donna: Everybody has to clean house and cook and do everything else.

DC: I kinda quit cooking for awhile there. I just said, "I'm the first to leave and the last to get home. I rest my case." And Adam did, he cooked me dinner too.

Sundays and Wednesdays is chore day. And then during the week they have to keep the kitchen up and that's about it. And my bedroom bathroom, they do that because they use it.

Donna: I've seen your bedroom bathroom.

DC: It's bad. Actually, Adam, you owe me a bathroom cleanup, supposed to be done yesterday.

Adam: Good job, Donna.

DC: From being laid off, I got a settlement. The first thing I did was buy a computer. I knew I needed help, and I knew that I'd be going back to work, and so that's what we did.

Donna (to Adam): How much of your time do you work on your computer? How much of your academics?

Adam: All. Pretty much all.

DC: Everything except for the book he reads.

Donna: And the math.

Adam: Yep.

DC: We do have an Alge-Blaster. Intermediate. We haven't worked on it. We will eventually. One thing we do, we might work on something and then something else will catch our fancy, so we'll drop the first thing for awhile and go to this, go to that. My goal is—he couldn't read and he couldn't write—I mean he was in the ninth grade and he was at sixth grade level. So that was my whole goal, and now I think he's pretty well caught up. Sometimes he still has problems reading, I think.

Donna (to Adam): Do you like to read now?

Adam: No, I don't.

Donna: Still doesn't like to read.

DC: I think he says that partly because it is expected for him to say it. He'll read a book and he'll enjoy that book. *Having* to sit down and read it is what he doesn't like to do, but once he's doing it. . .like with *Of Mice and Men*. . .

Adam: *That* was a good book.

Donna: That is a good book.

Adam: But it's not like I would say, "Hold on, no basketball—I'm gonna go read." It's not like that. It's not like I could have nothing to do, like I'd be free, I'd done all my work, and then go, "Well no, instead of watching TV if there's good shows on, I'm gonna read." Can't do that.

Donna: *Sweet Thursday* is another good one, and *Cannery Row*.

DC: I heard of *Cannery Row*. Steinbeck.

Donna: Also, *Mice and Men*. And *East of Eden* I liked.

DC: I thought *East of Eden* was really good, but I don't think he's ready for it.

Donna: It is a lot.

DC: It's a lot. It's thick, it's long. Yeah, I think *Manchild* will be next.

Donna: *Manchild in the Promised Land*, boy. . .well, then there's *Soul on Ice* and all our other. . .so he's gonna do the sixties and civil rights? I guess that's a big issue. I mean a big subject matter, because a lot of parents ask me about civil rights.

DC: You know, what I have been looking for, and maybe you can help me with it, is what was called The Chicago Seven. Remember, the Chicago trial? I'm looking for material on that for him.

Donna: Okay, I'll look.

DC: I know they made a movie, but I don't even remember what year and who was in it or anything to rent it. That's a pretty good piece of history. The documentary I saw on it, and then I saw a movie they did on it years ago, probably like ten years ago. It was excellent. It's the kind of Black history I think he ought to learn about. [Reading:] "What makes you qualified to homeschool your kids?"

Adam: Because you want to.

DC: I'm qualified because I'm his parent. Period. I qualify because I am the head of the household.

Adam: And I say so.

DC: I qualify because I felt like I can do a better job than the school was doing. I have a high school diploma, and that's it. . .Challenges. Did we go over challenges? The biggest challenges starting homeschooling?

Adam: Oh, you said the biggest challenge was knowing where to start.

Donna: You started with junior high school programs, or would you say your adult education type of stuff—like your grammar would be continuing education for adults. The materials you're covering with him are taught in GED classes.

DC: I started with what was called a "Wordly Wise" book. I started with eighth grade level instead of ninth grade level, and that was more of his speed. Adam was behind. Adam was behind in everything. But then he did pre-algebra for a month, just two days a week for a month.

Adam: We covered a whole year's worth.

DC: Matter of fact, she got him through it and even started in Algebra. And then I saw an ad in the paper about someone who could teach math, anywhere from the basics up to physics. I talked to her and she came out, she did it all that first year and then for a few months this year. And then it was just too much. She was sick, she got stuck in law school, and I understand. That was too much. And so, he's got up into about the middle of Algebra II now.

Donna: That's good. He might be able to teach himself a lot of what's in that book.

DC: Yeah, I'm hoping so.

Donna: But you know, I can understand stopping, taking a break and doing other things. So he doesn't like to paint or draw?

DC: He likes to draw. It doesn't mean he's real good at it, but what he does he enjoys. Drawing? On the computer you draw.

Adam: I mess around on my computer, but that's *computer* drawing.

Donna: Do you like computers? Have you tried programming yet?

Adam: No.

Donna: That might do it. The Lego program that my boys have, that's programming.

Adam: Next time I spend about $295, I'll get one.

DC: When and if I put him in a college class, he can do it. For a lot of that stuff, I might just have him take a class. [Reading:] Do I follow an academic plan or schedule, how do I approach the subject? I wing it.

Donna: You don't have a schedule.

DC: Right now we're heavy into the history and the grammar, and he always has to have a book to read. He's reading *Huckleberry Finn* right now. He just read *To Kill a Mockingbird.*

Donna: *Huckleberry Finn's* controversial. It is supposedly based upon a Black kid being the huckleberry or something. They looked at Samuel Clemens' old notes. He was really an excellent American writer, and folks just get too upset over things without becoming literate themselves and knowledgeable of the area and knowledgeable of satire. I think it's very important to cover it.

DC: I think it's got some racism, but for that time—

Donna: But Jim is the only honest person in the entire book. The Black person is the only decent one. [Adam goes outside with Rukiya.] Adam, If we have a question we'll call you back—or we'll just say what we think you would have said [laughter].

DC: What was really good about getting credits for Adam—geography and social studies—I just use Thailand. I mean, living in Thailand that one summer, that's social studies credit right there. I had him write a report on it. I mean, how else would you get as good a geography and social studies credit as by living in a foreign country like that?

Donna: Is he going to go traveling again? Where's his dad now?

DC: I don't know, his dad I think is going to Malaysia next. He thought he was going to Bangladesh and if he went there I said Adam was not going. I said, "You won't see him, sorry."

Donna: Because of India's illnesses and stuff.

DC: Yeah, just the diseases. I mean granted, he can get vaccines, but. . .

Donna: It would be a good experience.

DC: Not for a whole summer. Now if he went for a couple of weeks I wouldn't have a problem with it. But they have political problems there, they have health problems there. And they have catastrophes like you wouldn't believe. But I think overall it's good for him to be exposed.

Donna: But that's what they say about Hilltop.

DC: Yeah, that's true. Can't believe the media. I don't mind him being exposed to it, I don't mind him being exposed to poverty and third worlds, I have no problem with that. But I have friends that are moving to Costa Rica, that built my barn. They've already said he can come and live with them. Why not let him go to Costa Rica? It's a third world country, they speak a foreign language, he'll get that exposure.

Donna: It's what the rich would do if their kids started getting in trouble, send them off to some place like Costa Rica to stay with other friends. How many of us have that opportunity to just send them away?

DC: Yeah. And you know, it would be good for him.

Donna: So which country does he think he's going to now? He's going to go to Malaysia?

DC: His father. . .Malaysia is what's being talked about. Before Adam would go for the whole summer, he might go for half a summer, it just depends.

Donna: Does his dad pay for that?

DC: Yeah, he pays for the flight.

Donna: Well, that's good. And then Adam has to take care of himself once he gets to the place?

DC: Just about. One thing you have to do, you have to wash your own clothes by hand.

Donna: That's good.

DC: So that's about it for the subject stuff. P.E. was easy to do. We're done with P.E. I mean when he plays basketball they have like those all night street kids basketball-type things. He's there till like two o'clock in the morning. So P.E.'s done with.

***

Donna: So, being a Black homeschooler. I think it is different, but I don't think White people can understand our differences.

DC: Well, being Black is different from being White, period. No matter if you're being an athlete, or whatever. . .I think the only difference is there's more Black culture history taught at home than Adam would get in school. Black history month is not just February. It's something that we talk about all the time.

Donna: It's also, I think, a matter of control. We finally have control of *something*, and the one thing we never doubted our control of was the kids who have to live in our house with us. You know, compared to being in school. I think parents lose control. I see parents put their kids in school and they think they're supporting the schools, but to me by the time the child is in fourth or fifth grade you're not just supporting the schools, you're agreeing with everything because you really don't have any say in what goes on. You can't get your kid put back a grade, you can't tell them don't test your kid, you can barely tell them *to* test your kid.

DC: I know. I remember when the kids were in grade school, they had a permission slip to teach sex education in the school. And if you signed it saying yes, then they taught it. But if you signed it saying no, you had to go to the school and see what was being taught, and *then* say no to it. And I had no problems with my child learning about sex, no problem at all. I do think that just because one ten-year old is ready to ask a question about it, that doesn't mean the next ten-year old is ready to ask that question about it. It gets touchy there, a lot of stuff like that gets touchy there.

Donna: And then the fact that parents have to come in if they disagree.

***

DC (reading): Do I have any advice for new homeschoolers of color?

Donna: Call Donna [laughs].

DC: Yep, call Donna. I think the only thing is, just don't be afraid.

Donna: That's true.

DC: Just don't be afraid.

Donna: It's worth a try.

DC: You took on the challenge of being a parent. That was a new experience, unless you already raised a bunch of brothers and sisters. If you can take on that challenge, educating them is just the next step. There's a lot of things out there you may not know anything about, but if you feel like you want your child to learn, that's why we have books.

Not everybody's fortunate enough to have a computer; I homeschooled a whole year without a computer and I know that I can still teach without having a computer. You don't need one. It comes in handy because I'm working and I'm not there at home, but it also comes in handy because of the typing skills that he learns on it.

But what I did that first year—I didn't know anything about astronomy, not enough to teach a child. We went to the library and we rented the Discovery series videos. The Discovery Channel did a whole segment on astronomy, and I had Adam watch them and write papers. Everything he did, he had to write on so that he could practice his writing skills.

One thing I thought was very important that we did—I stopped doing it because of time—is world events. Adam has to watch news everyday. And I've lowered it now to just the evening news and *60 Minutes* most the time. But I think it's very important, and he had to write about it, had to write about everything.

Donna: I like that.

DC: And that's because you want your child, no matter what their age, to blend in with people of all ages and levels. And knowing what's going on in the world, that way when you're in a conversation with whoever you can have something to say and something to back it up with. Instead of just knowing who's the top rock stars. He definitely knows that, I don't have to do anything about that.

"Do I belong to a homeschool support group?" No. There's not enough people around here. And I have reasons why I don't.

Donna: You work.

DC: Yeah, timewise is one of my reasons.

Donna: And you raise two other children.

DC: Yeah, it's like I don't think I need it. I don't feel like I need a support group. I didn't need a support group to help me be a parent.

Donna: Parents without Partners—you'd still be the only Black woman in the group.

DC: Thank you. Everybody has their own reasons why they want to homeschool anyways; it doesn't mean mine are the same as somebody else's. And everybody has different things they want their child to learn. I don't need a support group. If I have a question, I call Donna.

That was the main thing: What can I get my teenager to read that he'll like? I don't want to force Adam to be a bookworm, but loving to read opens up that world to you. And you know, there's a wall there. It could be his age. It could be because he was such a poor reader all those years. He'd have books he had to read in school, and he couldn't read them. He just couldn't grasp it. He could read the words and say the words but he couldn't picture the story going on. And now that he can, I hope that opens up more doors. And if it doesn't, too bad, I'll still make him read [laughs]. I can see him going away to college, coming home for vacation, and I'm gonna say, "Here, read this book. You want a meal, you read." If the book's good enough he'll read. *The Outsiders*, he loved *The Outsiders*. He loved *Of Mice and Men*. He even liked *Interview with a Vampire*.

Donna: He read *Interview with a Vampire*?!

DC: Yeah.

Donna: And wrote a report on it?

DC: He writes a report on everything he reads. Everything. Write about it. He had to do a report on when they had the Pacific Rim conference here. Grandma collected all the newspaper clippings.

Donna: Good, I need someone to sell books in Asia for me, so if he understands all that that would be good. I told my kids that one of the reasons they learn Spanish is because of the Latin American schools I'll be selling to.

DC: Good. "What are the best resources or organizations?" The library.

Donna: The library. Yes. You can be poor and still homeschool for free.

DC: That's right. Those videos were free. All I had to do was go down and get them. Just write down what I wanted and it was great. "Financial sacrifices to homeschool...."

Donna: Well, you don't have to buy school clothes. Oh, your sacrifice is the computer.

DC: The computer. I plan on using it, though, when they leave. I like to play chess on it.

Donna: You do? Khahil does too.

DC: A budget. You know, I was worried about that when I first started. How much is homeschooling going to cost me?

Donna: Especially that first homeschool convention. With that curriculum fair there.

DC: Yeah, how much is this going to cost me? And so that first year I went to a little bookstore in Edmonds that just sold educational stuff, and got that *Wordly Wise* and stuff. I didn't spend much money at all. It was just workbooks.

Donna: Most of the stuff at conventions is a rip-off.

DC: I use the library for a lot of stuff. And we did a lot of ancient history. Astronomy tapes from the library, books he would read. So I was

> *"I don't know why people think that because I homeschool I'm not allowing my child to live in the real world. That I'm not allowing him those temptations that he's going to face sooner or later anyways. People say to me, 'I taught my child the difference between right and wrong, and I put them out there, and they knew not to do wrong,' and all that stuff. I don't even argue with them."*

worried about the budget and I thought that a computer would be good, but I waited a year for that, I wanted to shop around.

People ask kids, "Well, what school do you go to?"

And they get to Adam and I say, "He goes to School a la Home."

"What? Where's that?"

"Ah, it's in Port Orchard. Go to the seventh tree to the left, take a right. You'll find it. You know in the old days, the little school houses? Well, our house is a little school house."

Donna: Yes, how do his friends feel? His contemporaries? Especially the ones who used to be his friends—who wouldn't be anymore anyway, because of the way they are now?

DC: He said he's losing touch with them. You know, he *was* depressed one day. He said he was feeling really low. This was a couple of weeks ago. We sat down and talked for about an hour about it and he said that he was starting to feel like he was missing out, you know, like being invited places, being invited to parties, being invited out on dates, going to movies with friends. And when he does see his friends a lot of times he doesn't have as much in common with them as he used to.

And I was trying to feel sorry for him, but I couldn't. And so I gave him that compassionate look and said, but think of the things you're gaining. I mean, you're getting to know your grandparents, and the time you got to spend with Virginia before she died. You know, there's a lot of things. You can take off for three or four days and go some place. There's things you can do. When I had the barn built, Adam helped, and that was an education. And through that he got to meet Dirk—Dirk is from Germany; he's the one moving with his wife to Costa Rica. So building that barn opened up a door of a friendship that he would not have gotten had he been in school learning how to ridicule other kids. But he feels like he's missing out. So I guess that would be a conflict.

Adam: Yeah, it's a conflict, but—

Donna: We have other things to worry about. And I think that's the lower priority.

DC: Besides the bad grades, the main thing I disliked about him being in school *was* his social life. It took over *everything*. His behavior, his thinking, everything, it just took over it all. And so if it's cut back, it's cut back—but it's not cut back to a negative. It's just cut back to lack of exposure to doing some things that he shouldn't have been doing in the first place.

Donna: Yes, he needs to be exposed to traveling around the world. When I was fifteen I went to Germany by myself and then I met people. I think that's a more important experience than—

DC: Yes, he's been to Thailand three times.

***

DC: Adam says he wants to be a neurosurgeon.

Adam: That's right.

Donna: Oh no. But that's people's brains, what if you find something funny? Oops, there it goes! [Laughter]

DC: What I want Adam to do work-wise for now, we tried to talk about doing it last year and we just ran out of time, is volunteer work for a year.

Adam: That'd be cool.

DC: And it's something he wants to do too. ❖

"I CAN WRAP ANY ADULT AROUND MY FINGER— EXCEPT MY MOM."

A few thoughts on homeschooling by Adam Clough

I was pulled out of public school because I was not excelling. I wasn't paying attention in class, and I was in trouble. The school was going to give me failing grades but pass me on to the next grade anyway. My mom, though, wanted to hold me back. That was the straw that broke the camel's back.

When I was in school, my mom and teachers tried doing all kinds of things to get me to apply myself. They tried progress reports, yellow cards, homework sheets, pink slips, and calling home. It was all too easy for me to get out of. Being home schooled I don't get to get by with slick stuff. My mom knows everything I do, when I do it, and how I do it. Which is both a good thing and a bad thing.

When I first started homeschool I thought it was a bad idea. But the first year my mom stayed laid back and made it fun. The second year she tightened up a bit. I do like homeschool now because of all the free time I get to myself. I've also been able to see more of my family. One particular family member died a little after I started homeschool. I wouldn't have been able to see her if I was in school, so I'm very grateful for that. I also get to spend time with my grandma Pearl. Overall, home schooling is a good thing.

My mom liked homeschool because she could watch me and because she could cover certain subjects. She has me do Black history all year round. I don't mind that a bit. I think you should learn about your culture's past and also about other cultures when given the chance. I'm not going to lie and say I like the work though. She had me read a lot of Maya Angelou, and I do enjoy her writings.

The first year we were really laid back. The results were what we wanted, and I earned more credits than I actually needed at that point. The second year we adjusted ourselves more to the school's curriculum. We hit a lot of areas too hard, which made me short some credits in other areas. This next year my mom is going to help me bring up my low areas to average and my good areas to outstanding.

Differences between Black and White homeschoolers are miniscule. My mom hit Black history hard, though, so I could know what my culture has received from America and what it has contributed to America. I would say that White homeschoolers would cover White history, but that's covered in public schools too. One month out of the year for Black history isn't enough. Schools should also cover Chinese, Japanese, and other ethnic groups' culture.

To sum this up, homeschool is a good thing for some people. It's not for everybody though. Don't pull your kid out if he's doing well in school just to see if he'll do better. That would put you through a lot of hassle. You have to have a good relationship with your child to homeschool. Homeschool is good for me because I'm very conniving and charismatic. I can wrap any adult around my finger—except my mom.

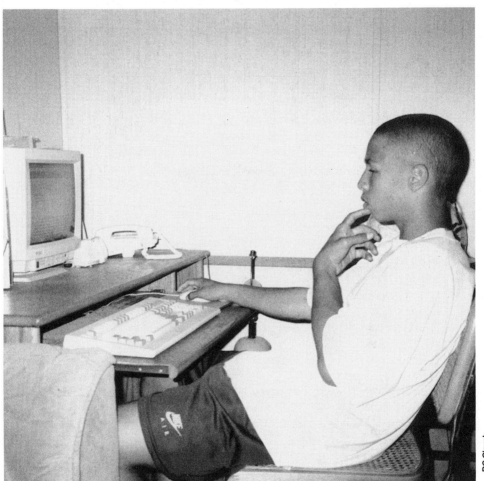

Christina, Jamaal, Cassandra, and Jasmine Pogue

Cheríe Pogue
Detroit, Michigan

THE OKINAWAN SWEDISH COLONIAL GREEK AFRICAN AMERICAN HOMESCHOOLERS QUÉ HABLAN ESPAÑOL

We are a military family of six. My husband Michael, age thirty-three, is a captain in the U.S. Marine Corps. I'll tell you about him first because he will be mentioned the least in our story. He joined the military right after high school and has made it a career. He was an average student at an all-black high school in Pensacola, Florida, and was raised by his mother, a single parent. He has excelled in the military, receiving five meritorious promotions in the same amount of years. He is the epitome of the Marine Corps: "Spit and polished," METICULOUS, physically fit, METICULOUS, organized, METICULOUS, "Felix Unger"—and did I say "meticulous?" He had no aspirations for higher education until the Marine Corps emphasized that it would enhance his career. So he earned his B.S. from National University in San Diego.

College was hard for Michael at first. He had to learn how to learn. He isn't much of a talker. He carefully weighs all sides and then renders his decision. He's much more secure in our decision to homeschool than I. He wants to "know what the children know and know that they know what they should know." (You have to say it out loud to understand it.) He also wants to "influence our children and teach them *our* values and not the teacher's, school's, or state's values." Right now, *he* is being homeschooled. He's getting his masters from City University in Washington via correspondence.

On April third, 1985, I gave birth to the most perfect baby boy in the world, Jamaal Sean. We were living in San Diego and I was earth mother. He was like totally natural birth, like totally breast-fed, like totally organic baby food, like totally cloth diapers. Nothing unnatural touched his body in any way. This probably explains why he had skin allergies as a baby and to this day refuses to eat vegetables. He never slept in his expensive crib. What did I expect? He didn't come with instructions.

Eighteen months later, Jamaal had the pleasure of meeting his sister Jasmine Simone, who arrived after an hour of labor on the first of December, 1986. I have no idea if she was a totally natural birth or not. I didn't care. I made good use of Jamaal's still-new crib. She ate whatever she wanted.

Jamaal was a bright toddler. By the time he was two, he could read short words, and at age three, the newspaper. Now, I did not spend any time trying to teach him to read. He just learned to read. I remember when we were at Safeway and he said, pointing to a sign, "Mom, S-A-F-E-W-A-Y. That says Safeway." Although I was dumbfounded, I coolly replied, "Yeah, you're right," as if this was an everyday occurrence. How did he know his letters? We never talked about them. We never watched any children's programs on television. How did he sound them out? For the next year, I watched Jamaal read more and more. I was still amazed and very proud. However, I gave the credit to Pat and Vanna, because *Wheel of Fortune* was the only show I could think of that would explain this phenomenon. I was so afraid that Jamaal was not developing as a "whole child," that I refused to buy him anything educational for Christmas. It didn't work. He read the boxes, the Christmas cards, the manufacturer's name imprinted on the toys, and the patent information. All true, no exaggeration.

Meanwhile, Jasmine was my refuge. She did everything according to the charts. She was the middle of the bell curve in growth, while Jamaal was in the ninetieth percentile in height and the tenth percentile in weight. She walked and talked at the average age of two. She slept through the night in her crib. And by age two, Jasmine was a two-year-old!

Shortly after having Jasmine, we moved to Poway, about thirty minutes north of San Diego, and integrated the neighborhood. We enrolled Jamaal in Oak Knoll Montessori school after his third birthday, because I figured he needed some intellectual stimulation. He seemed to enjoy school, especially because he could read. He would assist in the story reading and taught his classmates to spell everything. Once during show and tell, Jamaal shared something that I had said to my husband: "Last night my mommy told my daddy, '[expletive].'" Then he proceeded to spell the expletive for the class.

Well, that was the last time I said that word. It was also when I realized that Jamaal was going to have a problem in school—not behavior, but boredom.

When I was in school, I was part of what is now called the "Gifted and Talented" program. We were the first experimental class in our district, and at that time we were called the "Advanced Class." By the time I hit fourth grade, I only had two reasons for going to school: the violin and Spanish. I had been reading for at least eight years and was bored with the needless repetition each year. But I had just started the violin and Spanish, so I was learning something. And we students did form a bond. Instead of looking at each other as peers in some elite group, we were more of a collection of unusual gems, individuals with different strengths and weaknesses. It seemed that the harder our teachers tried to make us alike, the more evident our differences became.

In high school, I was bored to literal tears. I had mastered all of the available Spanish. I couldn't have cared less about math. I wanted out! Out of town and out of school. In the fall of tenth grade, with no preparation, I qualified as a National Merit Scholarship finalist. I took the SAT a year later, and it was a breeze.

Junior High had seemed worthwhile because I was boy crazy and a cheerleader—dangerous combination! I made the Varsity cheer leading squad in the ninth grade, so that and French kept me somewhat happy. I hoped to become an exchange student, but I knew my family could not afford that. By eleventh grade, I was mentally absent. The school orchestra was lame and neglected by the administration. My main motivation was the French club's trip to France in the spring. That is the only thing I remember from that year.

Let me mention that throughout my entire young life I was labeled a "white girl." I spoke standard English, like I was taught at home. I got good grades. (I can't say I earned them because there was no challenge.) I rarely would engage in a fistfight because I was afraid of hurting somebody badly. My peers had no idea how much pent up anger I had inside me. At any moment, I could have snapped and pulverized someone with my bare hands.

Twelfth grade, I only took choir, chorus, English, and phys. ed. The last two were mandatory. I couldn't drop out because I saw my high school diploma as a ticket out of my home town via a college scholarship—my mailbox was overstuffed with offers from various colleges.

My mother was a schoolteacher and had worked as a home tutor for sick children until they could return to school, so I got an idea. I feigned sick starting in February. I researched and found an ailment that could not be detected, so the doctor would have to rely on my description of my pain level. I also knew that if I missed a certain number of days, the school was obligated to supply a tutor for me. Worked like a charm. My time at home was great. I saw my tutor occasionally. I finished the year's English assignments in march. Since the pain "came and went," I managed to still have an active social life. In May, I "recovered" just in time for graduation. I graduated with my class in 1982. The following day I came down with a severe case of red chicken pox. God is fair and just.

In 1989, the military had plans for my husband, and consequently also for my two children and me. I dreaded having to take Jamaal, then four, out of Montessori, and we had planned for Jasmine to start there as soon as she turned three. I was an accountant for a small furniture manufacturing firm at the time. I reported directly to the owner and he had given me virtually free reign over the entire operation. The books were in shambles when I started, and I was elated to have such a challenging job. I had just purchased a computer network and was automating the entire production process. So, hi ho, hi ho, it's off to Quantico.

Quantico, Virginia. An extremely small American town located inside, yes inside, of MCCDC (Marine Corps Combat Development Command). The place where Marine *officers* are made! FBI training! Although I was thrilled that my husband was selected for the Enlisted Commissioning Program, I was unsure about the move. Things had been shaky, and our family was growing apart. Outwardly, we appeared to be the perfect yuppies. My husband was at home full time with the children. (He was earning his full military salary while going to college full time under a special government program similar to ROTC. All his classes were at night.) We had our perfect two children, our two cars, the preppy clothes, we did things together as a family and as a couple, and I loved my accounting job. Everything was fine. Still, I felt that something was missing in my life. The same void that I'd felt in the last years of high school was there again. But how could I drop out this time? This was real life, not school.

So, the military orders brought a welcome escape from my perfect California life. Maybe I could be "fulfilled" in a new location.

In June, my husband took the children from California to his mother's home in Pensacola, Florida, and went on to Officer Candidate School in Virginia. I was to meet him in August after he graduated, and together we would pick up our children. All went smooth as silk, except that "a funny thing happened to me on the way to the fair."

With all those hours to myself, I had plenty of time to think about stuff like "what is life all about," and "why am I here." Somewhere in Utah on Interstate 70, I found the Lord, via Christian radio, among the purple-crimson-orange plateaus illuminated by jagged streaks of lightning. Suddenly everything was different. My world was renewed, alive, and suddenly I realized that I knew nothing. I had wasted my life on meaningless material objectives, and I didn't even know my own family. I felt the necessity to equip myself to reunite and resurrect my family, and tuned to any Christian station I could find, still driving to Virginia. I heard some kooks talking about how "ungodly" the public schools were, and how they were teaching their children at home. Obviously, I thought, these people were taking their religion a little too seriously. Anyway, kids *had* to go to school. Who would want to spend their entire day with their children? Radicals!

Once our family had reunited and settled, the painful yet delightful task of getting to know each other again was underway. My husband became a Christian shortly after our reunion, so we were full of ideas of how God wanted our family to function. I would stay home with the children and maybe start a family day-care center to ease the financial drain. Now, we had to find a school for Jamaal. Montessori was out—too expensive. He was too young for public school. Christian school? Why not?

We soon moved to base housing, which relieved our financial burden, and our membership at Reconciliation Community Church molded us as a family. Reconciliation, the name says it all. It was late September by now and Jamaal, age four, had been out of school for about four months. He needed stimulation and I wanted time to spend with Jasmine—alone. Jamaal was so demanding. "Why is this? What is this? What does that mean? Ha, ha, look, Mom, they spelled something wrong in the newspaper!" He had read all the *Childcraft* books, most of the *Bible*, and zillions of other things. Anything in print. "School," I thought, "He needs school!" *I* needed a break.

We found an excellent Christian school. It was in its second year of operation and the people were so nice. The price was well within our budget—free, in exchange for my services in the early morning. I opened the school and did before-school childcare. The school used the A Beka curriculum, and I was assured that the K4 program would "adequately challenge" Jamaal.

He loved every minute of it. He breezed through his kindergarten work and would listen in on first and second grade activities. During play time, he would flock to his buddies. He did wonder why the teacher repeated lessons and gave tests. He thought she was forgetful and had to remind herself of what she knew.

While Jamaal toiled the day away, Jasmine and I *relaxed*. She was a glorious two-year-old. She played with toys, liked to cuddle, loved to have her hair combed and be all dressed up. Best of all, she had no interest in reading! I was also baby-sitting for Ariana, my neighbor's two-year-old. She and Jasmine loved to play together. I was starting to really enjoy children and I wanted a houseful of them all the time. Baby-fever struck again!

I wanted another one. A boy. A healthy, cuddly, curly-haired, deep-dark skinned, chubby baby boy. Since there were no guarantees in childbirth, I wanted to adopt. One problem: my husband did *not*, under any circumstances, want any more children. Nevertheless, on April twelfth, 1990, we met three-year-old Christina Janae and her five-month-old, five pound, sister Cassandra Joy, our new daughters.

What in the world had I gotten myself into?! Why had God allowed this to happen?! Things weren't going as smoothly as they did on *The Brady Bunch*! I had wanted a healthy baby boy! Within a month of bringing the girls home, I wept daily before the Lord.

Christina was a three-year-old basket case. She suffered from malnutrition after spending the previous eighteen months in foster care. She couldn't walk more than eight steps without falling face-first to the ground. (She has a permanent knot on her forehead.) The unexplained scars on her back haunted me. She could barely talk, and the words she could say were enunciated with a strong drawl. She wasn't adequately potty-trained. She would eat until she would make herself physically sick, and then hide food in her pockets. (Have you ever done laundry and plunged your hand into a spaghetti-filled pocket?) All my plans to just love this child and win her heart went out the window. Reality hit me hard. My new plans were to teach her to put her arms out in order to break her falls. Once she accomplished this, I'd teach her to walk, and then run. Potty training. Table manners. Speaking. Discipline. Love and affection could come later.

And Cassandra. My Cassy Jo. Two pounds, two ounces at birth. High on crack. Heart failure. Respiratory failure. Ventilators. Several blood transfusions. Numerous tubes in her shaved head. This was my baby? At five months, she weighed five pounds. Finally breathing on her own, she was ready to be released to us. I'll never forget when I first laid eyes on her. A social worker came into the office at the same time we were waiting to meet our adoptive children. I glanced at the thin, frail, little thing that she was carrying and I said to myself, "That is the ugliest baby I have ever seen! It looks like a malnourished hairless kitten! I'm glad that's not the one I'm getting." Our worker called us into the visiting room. A few minutes later she brought in Christina and *that* thing. My Cassy.

Cassy proved to be the best baby I ever had. She came with a list of instructions from the hospital, and she followed their exact schedule, never a variation. She was still suffering withdrawal from the drugs she was born addicted to, and would cry uncontrollably and then stare into space, oblivious to her surroundings. My husband and I labeled these episodes the "drug-crazed stares," or DCS. Her eyes were crossed, probably due to lack of oxygen, and this made the DCS somewhat amusing. Her bronchial tubes were damaged so she spent plenty of time at the hospital, and Albuterol, Prednisone, and vaporizer became new words in my vocabulary. Despite her sickly appearance, I fell in love with my baby. She was the ultimate challenge.

Now my days and nights were filled. Four Children Under Five. Get up. Feed the baby. Dress the baby. Feed the children. Dress the children. Get Jamaal ready for school. Leave for school. Buckle the baby in the car seat. Buckle Christina in the car seat. Buckle Jasmine in the car seat. Unbuckle Christina and have Jamaal take her to the bathroom. Thank God for Jamaal. Buckle Christina in the car seat. Make sure Jamaal is in the van. Make sure he's buckled up. Make sure I have my keys to the school. Car keys. Start the van. Pull out of parking space. Pull over to the side of the road. Buckle Jasmine in the car seat again. Buckle Christina because Jasmine has unbuckled her too. Threaten Jasmine. Drive to the school. Thank God it's only eight minutes away. Open the school. Turn on lights. Go back to the car. Tell Jamaal to go inside. No need to unbuckle them thanks to Jasmine. Make coffee and wait for the school children to arrive.

This process took at least forty-five minutes. Two hours later, school would start. Because her mother worked at the school, Ariana, whom I was still baby-sitting, came home in another car seat with me. I was beginning to seriously question the validity of the child safety-seat law. If it wasn't for our naptime, I would have challenged its constitutionality.

Once at home, I was at peace. Jasmine and Ariana played together as usual. Cassy maintained her schedule. Literally, God only knows what was going through Christina's mind then. Although she and Jasmine were exactly one month apart chronologically, they were years apart physically and mentally. I tried to advance Christina mentally by using some of the Montessori methods that I remembered from Jamaal's old school. What a joke! Jamaal hadn't been an average three-year-old, and Christina wasn't Jamaal. I then decided to concentrate on bringing her up to Jasmine's level. Ha, ha, ha! While Jasmine was my center-of-the-bell-curve-breeze, Christina was short, underweight, nonverbal, with the motor skills of an eighteen-month-old. I resigned myself to waiting until she was four, when I would enroll her in special education preschool.

By now, my husband (the lucky one because his training required ten to twelve hours a day and he escaped many of the rigors that Four Children Under Five can cause) was about to complete his last training school. This meant that we would be moving to a new duty station. The school year was almost over. *That* meant Jamaal would be home, Ariana would go to her home, and no more before-school day care!

The coming move frightened me. Jamaal would be legal kindergarten age and I didn't want to send him to a public school. First of all, I knew he would be bored in a regular kindergarten. Secondly, I wasn't pleased with the values being taught. Hopefully, prayerfully, there would be another Christian school with a combined-grade classroom. That way, he would be challenged intellectually and still be with buddies of the same age. But now we had two more children. Yikes! We couldn't afford private school. I hated getting everybody up and dressed.

It would be so nice if I could just keep Jamaal at home and teach him myself. And why not? How hard could first grade be? He could read and write. He understood math. What was there to mess up? Jamaal would be home schooled. Oh no! Just like that, I became one of them: A *radical*. Late in June the orders came: Okinawa, Japan. Yippee! Tropical island! No snow!

My first memory of the Japanese people: flight attendants (all women) doted all over my children. They asked in broken English about the girls' hair, how old were they, and were they twins? I could not explain that the girls were not twins. Language barrier. From that point until this present day, when asked if my daughters are twins, I answer yes, then I mumble, "fake twins." I had been under the impression that the Japanese hated Americans, especially African Americans. Yet we were always warmly received and welcomed. I'll never forget a lady we met at an aquarium. She came up to me and said, as she gently stroked the side of my face and my hair, "You so beautiful. Where you come from?" My reply: "Gushikawa." That was the Okinawa city we were living in at the time. Duh! After realizing my *faux pas*, I replied, "America. United States." I could hear *America the Beautiful* in my mind. I was proud to be an American, and a beautiful American.

OUR FIRST HOMESCHOOLING YEAR:
TEACHER'S MANUALS AND TIDE POOLS

So we began our home school odyssey. In Okinawa, we first settled into the base's "temporary lodging facility" which, in civilian language, meant a hotel on the base. We were under the impression that we would be able to move into housing shortly after we arrived. Wrong! We had to search for an apartment or house off-base. In the United States, given our family size, this would not have been an easy task. In Okinawa, it seemed impossible. Before the search began, we had to adjust to driving on the "wrong" side of the street, and get used to being functionally illiterate. We couldn't speak Japanese nor could we read hiragana. I resigned and left the living arrangements to my husband. In the meantime, I decided to start "school" with the children.

Jamaal and I started working through the A Beka first-grade materials that I had purchased before we left. I followed the teacher's manuals diligently and refused to vary, even though my son was capable of doing the required workbook pages without instruction. As a matter of fact, he could read the teacher's manuals himself! Our schedule worked great for a week, and then the call of the Okinawa wild hit us. What were we doing in such a small, confining space when there was a beautiful, tropical, sun-drenched country awaiting exploration? We went outside just for a break, and never came back to the books. I labeled our time outside "Physical Education" (children ran, jumped, walked, played), "Science" (observed insects, pigeons, fruit bats, and shrews), "Social Studies" (we were in Japan), and "Language Arts" (children communicate with one another, i.e., "Give me that back" and with me, i.e., "Mom, so-and-so is not sharing"). I promised myself that once we moved I would buckle down and really work on school.

After sixty-two days, we moved into our government quarters at Camp Kinser, in the southern part of the island with the East China Sea practically in our front yard. We found a church and met our neighbors. Our household goods arrived from the states. Now it was time to get down to some serious school.

Jamaal and I went back to the books and picked up where we had left off. We fell into a routine where I would teach him for thirty minutes (I cut out a lot of the review that the teaching manuals demanded) and then he would independently work on the corresponding workbook pages. I occupied the girls with coloring, and Cassy slept during the "school" time. We took occasional breaks to explore the tide pools where all types of colorful salt water fishes swam freely. Our neighbor's fish tank became an ever-changing environmental study—our favorite "exhibit' was the octopus that escaped from her tank and hid in the bathroom on the back of the commode. In early spring, we had completed our curriculum and prepared to move to Camp Courtney in the northern part of the island. Naturally, my husband's orders dictated our surroundings.

The time had come to decide what to use for school for our second year. The first year had been smooth, but now I had to think about Jasmine and Christina. They were both four, but so different. While Jasmine exhibited a readiness to learn, Christina was still a baby. She had just become comfortable with her surroundings in our family, but she talked like a two-year-old. I decided that I would push Jasmine into the kindergarten level and let Christina have one more year to grow. I figured that Christina could still be in her "right" grade without competing with Jasmine. I also thought it wouldn't hurt Jasmine to start learning something. After all, Jamaal could read novels when he was her age. After talking to my husband and considering our budget, I plunged full speed ahead into year two.

OUR SECOND YEAR:
CURRICULUM EXPERIMENTS AND GECKOS

Jamaal would be starting second grade. I decided to buy the A Beka second-grade math with the teacher's manual, and their second grade phonics. I saw no need for a spelling book, since he had no trouble spelling. He read all the time so he didn't need a reading book. Science and history posed a more difficult problem. I hated the science and history books that we had used the year before. They were great for reading comprehension but the practical application proved to be difficult.

in Okinawa: Cherie with Christina, Jasmine, Jamaal, and Cassy

For example, in history, an exercise called for the student to talk about his state. We lived in *Japan*, and prior to that the children had lived in four different states and had traveled across the country. The concept of "Your State" was as foreign as the street signs we encountered daily. So we decided to do Social Studies instead. We would accomplish this by meeting Japanese people, learning the language, and absorbing the culture.

Science was even more confusing. Seasons, squirrels, chipmunks, the "birds of North America" were common in the curriculum. They were totally irrelevant to life on Okinawa. The seasons didn't change but there *were* typhoons to track on the map. The island was loaded with habu (poisonous snakes), giant bats, shrews, eight-inch long centipedes, mongoose, gargantuan banana spiders, and tropical sea creatures. In our house there was always a gecko or two. So, we would study these animals.

For Jasmine, I decided to use magnetic letters and teach the sound of each letter. Then I would just put them together and, voíla! She would read. I bought coloring and activity books for Jasmine and Christine. As for Cassy, she was a baby. If she mastered taking a nap when I wanted, I'd be thrilled.

The main drawback in our new quarters was the smell. Instead of overlooking the East China Sea, this backyard was bordered by a pig farm. A few miles away there was a lard factory, and the Okinawans walked bulls along the narrow streets. We had finally attained the Homeschooler's Dream (at least that's what I thought from the magazine articles I'd read on homeschooling)—*farm country*! Can you see me making a happy face?

Eventually, I did get used to the fragrant aroma. One of our favorite pastimes was bringing friends from the southern end of the island up to our farm country. We would wind around the narrow roads and watch their faces when the smell hit them. Then, a young boy would round a corner leading a large beast of burden on a frail piece of rope, and we would pull over to the side of the road beside an open sewer and wait for the boy and the bull, who was usually larger than our Toyota Town Ace van, to pass. Even our black friends would be white-knuckled. Oh, did I mention that our van's air-conditioning didn't work, and that it was usually warmer than eighty degrees? The lard factory, the pig farm, the bull farm, and open sewers! There's no place like home.

The second year of homeschooling was my hardest ever—so far, anyway. I had settled nicely into a routine. We opened our school day with a prayer and then the Pledge of Allegiance—after all, my husband is a Marine and we do love our country. We also said a Pledge to the Holy Bible that Jamaal's old school had used. Next came our school name, "Christian Generation Academy," and our school motto, Joel 1:3: "Tell ye your children of it, and let your children tell their children, and their children another generation." That became the goal for our homeschool. We were teaching our children for our grandchildren's and great-grandchildren's sakes. Together we would read the chapter of Proverbs that corresponded with the date. We'd follow that with a story from *Wisdom and the Millers*, tales of a Mennonite family and their study of Proverbs.

Jamaal moved through his workbooks. I would write his assignments on paper and he would check them off as he completed them. Later we would meet so that I could teach him something new and review what he had completed. Christina colored and played with Cassy while I worked with Jasmine with the sounds of the letters and numeral recognition. After this was completed, the difficulty would arise.

Science and Social Studies. Although the children collected grasshoppers and caterpillars in jars, observed tropical fish, studied pigs and where meat comes from (that's right, the pigs were slaughtered on site), I felt our curriculum was lacking. After all, Jamaal had reached legal school age, and I was sure that no school-age child should be having that much fun.

I opted to buy the *Konos* curriculum. I loathed it. The activities were all right but I was frustrated trying to get the materials and books for the units. The base library wasn't a good resource center for elementary education, nor could we afford to order the materials necessary to complete the *Konos* activities. Buying things on the economy (Japanese market) was not an option because of the language barrier and the poor valuation of the U.S. dollar. Anyway, the children didn't seem too interested in *Konos*. I eventually traded the *Konos* book for the Bob Jones second-grade reading series. My friend hated the Bob Jones reading, and loved the *Konos*. I was quite the contrary. Point being, each homeschooling family must find what works for their own children.

At that time, I was confused and shuffled between curriculums. Too much reading about the different approaches to homeschooling was probably the cause. Our support group got me through that. I met another second-year homeschooling mom who was going through the same uncertainty, and just knowing that carried me to year three.

In the spring, I decided it was time to start Christina's formal education. She would be kindergarten age next September but still acted like a two-year-old toddler. She couldn't remember anything academic, even when she seemed to have mastered something just a few minutes earlier. I was at wit's end as to what to do with her. I needed help and I seriously thought she needed to be in special education. The experts would have to deal with her.

So, out of concern, we decided to have her tested at the local school. The initial testing confirmed my wildest fears: she definitely had developmental delays. Next, we had to sign permission forms to have the school proceed with the testing. I was afraid because I thought this would bring undue attention to our homeschooling endeavors. Up to this point, we had homeschooled freely because the military had a hands-off policy that was established by the Department of Defense Dependent Schools system. Basically, no one was sure who had jurisdiction over homeschooled children and as long as there was no reason to suspect neglect, everybody left us alone.

Now, however, my imagination ran wild and I knew that the school would insist that we enroll our children immediately. After all, I had neglected Christina since she was probably in need of special education. Well, we signed for the testing and after three series of tests it was time to meet with a panel to discuss her educational future. I was on pins and needles when Christina and I went to the meeting. My husband couldn't attend. So, there I was with the principal, the special education preschool teacher, the speech therapist, and a kindergarten teacher. We sat around a table, and it seemed as if they were looking at me with pity and disgust. My imagination shifted into fifth gear. Varoom! They handed me a wad of paperwork and proceeded to explain it in detail.

Bottom line: Christina was eighteen months behind her chronological age. Her fine motor skills were severely delayed. In the other areas, she was two to three points above the level that would make her eligible for special education. The recommendation was that she receive intensive remedial therapy to improve her delays and that "this would be best accomplished by the mother in her home."

That's right. The school told me to work with her at home. Don't send her to school. Keep her home. Praise God. They gave me some suggestions and asked me to consider going into education as a career. The principal even said, "We need more parents like you."

My husband announced that he was being transferred again. The military reassigned him to, of all places, Camp Kinser, the place we had moved from less than a year before—life is never dull with the Marine Corps. This time we convinced the military to allow us to move to the central housing area, specifically Kadena Air Base, which would insure no more moves on the island. We would also have a single family home and a yard without pigs.

Despite the difficulties, I enjoyed that year immensely. Our next-door neighbors and the neighbors across the street were both homeschooling families. With a total of eleven homeschooled children on our cul de sac, we felt secure in our decision and our children had others that were "just like them." For once we were in the majority. When a friend went to the United States for a family emergency, I taught her daughter for two months. I shared homeschooling with several families and helped them get started in the teach-your-own arena. I had become secure in what we were doing, and I was loving it.

OUR THIRD YEAR:
RELAXATION AND A FIELD TRIP TO KOREA

Our last year on the island brought us a relaxing coast in our homeschooling adventure. Jamaal was in third grade and I had chosen Bob Jones English, math, and spelling. For the other subjects, he could do whatever he wanted. His interests were *Hardy Boys*, *Encyclopedia Brown*, computer games and word processing, and bugs. He started producing the *J.S. Pogue Newsletter*, which contained notes from the weekly Bible study at our church, jokes, and observations. He sold his paper for ten cents to the servicemen who attended our church.

Jasmine could read short one-syllable words, so I started her in the A Beka first-grade phonics, reading, and math. She loved the workbooks for phonics and the stories in the readers. I was surprised at how quickly she moved ahead, often decoding words with phonics rules that I hadn't introduced to her yet. On the other hand, she struggled with math. She lacked the motor skills to write neatly, and became frustrated. I decided that since she was only supposed to be in kindergarten, to back off and allow her time to grow. We discontinued the math, decreased her writing requirements, and sailed on for the rest of the year.

Christina had now reached official kindergarten age and I felt as if the eyes of the world were on me. I'd planned on using the same strategy that I had used with Jasmine, and that at the end of the year she would be reading. I should have informed Christina's brain of my plan, because obviously it had other ideas of its own. By May, she had shown no signs of phonics comprehension, and I had failed as a teacher.

Cassandra was three, and that was fine with me. She ran, jumped, played, napped, ate, yelled, whispered, and pretended. She did not have to sit and color during "school time" like her sisters had been forced to do. She was free to be a child and experience the world around her anyway she wanted, as long as she didn't destroy anything.

During that year, we went to the entomology building at least twice a month. There was a collection of dead critters, some preserved in formaldehyde and some petrified. There were live habu and akamata snakes in locked glass enclosures, and numerous bug and rodent charts. Unless the office was extremely busy, there would be an English speaking entomologist there to answer any question that the children might have. This would spark two more weeks of searching, capturing, and releasing back into the wild (my favorite part) of bugs.

We would be returning to the United States in August, and the children and I had not been off the island in three years. We had been content to explore all over the island. Although we couldn't read the signs or communicate efficiently with the Okinawan people, we had no fear of being lost in a strange land. However, we had to do something big before we left the Far East.

The Pogue children with their father, Michael, in Songtan, Korea

Korea, the land of shopping! South Korea actually. All of us, including Dad, left Okinawa on a C-130 military aircraft, and the children were thrilled to fly like combat Marines. Right away, they noticed the similarities and differences between Japan and South Korea. From then on, I didn't regret the time that we'd spent exploring Okinawa and I started to recognize the importance of real life educational experiences.

Korea became our new classroom. Our first lessons included supply and demand economics, capitalism, work ethics, networking, and math. There were shops everywhere and the vendors all tried to entice us with their wares. The supply was plentiful and the vendors openly competed with each other. "Come, I give best price. I custom make," they beckoned, hoping we would consider their shop superior to the competitor across the street. Mr. Kim, the proprietor of our hotel, directed us to his "brothers'" stores for "best deal." We haggled, bargained, and shopped for three days. The trickiest part was trying to figure out how to pay for our purchases. The Koreans are truly capitalists and accepted won (Korean money), American dollars, Visa, and even Japanese yen. The exchange rate took on new meaning, and while haggling we had to be aware of the best method of payment. Often we would agree with the vendor on a price, only to have that price change when we said we would pay with Visa.

After our shopping spree, we headed north to Tong Du Chuon to visit the servicemen and missionaries who were affiliated with our church in Okinawa. We rode the bus from Osan to Seoul, and the children noted the changes in the country's terrain and the stark contrast between the rural and city areas. In Seoul, we changed buses and met a couple we knew, who attended the church at our destination.

In Tong Du Chuon, we attended church services and went sight seeing with the missionaries and the servicemen. We saw farms: chicken farms, cattle farms, and—most interesting—the dog farm. Mixed retriever-type dogs were in open pens, and small, fat pups were in tiny chicken-coop-like cages. These animals were bred for food. While my heart turned to our Lhasa Apso at home, my "foreign" children were genuinely fascinated at the cultural difference. We then rode closer to the Demilitarized Zone, where we saw missiles pointed toward the north and the meager living quarters of the Korean Army. This would later open a discussion of communism, the Korean War, Dad's job, life, and death. All the while the servicemen and missionaries narrated our tour, interjecting their personal views on the Korean situation.

OUR FOURTH YEAR:
OUT OF THE TROPICS AND ACROSS THE STATES

Prior to our Korean trip, we had started our fourth school year. I knew that we would be leaving Okinawa in August and would be displaced for about two months, so I wanted a jump on our academics.

Korea was a field trip, but I didn't dare spoil it by asking the children to write "What I Did on My Korean Vacation." We had hit the confident comfort level of homeschooling. Jamaal would be in fourth grade. He would use Daily Grams for English, Modern Curriculum Press math level D and E. I bought the Bob Jones fourth grade reader for him to use just in case we remained unsettled longer than expected.

Jasmine was now a confident second grader. She begged to use the Bob Jones second grade readers that I had traded for, and she would use the MCP level B math.

Christina should be in first grade but since I had "failed," we would use a kindergarten curriculum until she could read. My plan was to switch her to A Beka first grade in January. I picked *Adventures in Phonics* from Christian Liberty Press for its completeness, cost, and ease of transportation. All the children would use *Understanding Writing*. Cassy would have to just be happy being a child until we were settled in our new location.

As we moved out of our fifth house in five years, I reflected on how different we were from that family who had moved from California to Virginia. We had weathered super typhoons, Desert Shield/Storm, Mt. Pinautaubo's eruption in the Philippines, Somalia, Korean water, a Japanese Encephalitis outbreak, earthquakes, tidal wave threats, driving on the left, and cultural diversity—all part of the backdrop of our homeschool. Each had provided a springboard to formal and informal studies. Our children were alert and acutely aware of the real world. We were pleased with their progress, and enjoying them as people. But what would await us in the United States?

We were slated to leave Okinawa on August eighteenth and after packing, cleaning, and moving—(yes, again)—into temporary lodging, I figured that school could wait until we reached the states. The airplane ride to the U.S. seemed longer than I remembered. The children amused themselves with coloring books and Jamaal's game innovations. We knew quite a few people on the flight who were heading to the States to visit relatives. This caused me some stress, since I did not want to be stuck in an airplane for eighteen hours with some of these children. I like children and would have fifty if we could afford them; however, I cannot tolerate children who act like terrorists. Some of the children on our flight had obviously confused the airplane with a playground and thought that the other passengers were part of the equipment. Their parents must have thought that their children were in school somewhere and that their teacher would handle this unacceptable behavior. Don't get me wrong—I know that eighteen hours is a long time for *anybody*, but I do believe that children should be considerate of others.

So, I grumbled to myself until I decided to take notice of the children individually. The common thread seemed to be boredom. Although the parents had supplied the children with quiet activities, these were not interesting enough to engage the children for any substantial period of time. On the other hand, our children were having a great time with the activities they had in their backpacks.

The real difference, though, was that our children had had plenty of time alone throughout the years to amuse themselves quietly while I'd work with one of their siblings. We had dumped the television three years ago, so they didn't complain on the flight that they were missing their favorite show. They liked playing Jamaal's invented games, and were practically each others' best friends, so they could truly have fun with each other, even now. Also, they had picked out and packed their own activities for the airplane ride.

Bottom line: Our children had been responsible for providing their own entertainment for the past three years, and given the responsibility and freedom to choose, they could occupy themselves peacefully for eighteen hours if necessary. Surprisingly, the "toy" the children used the most was their individual notepads. Each child drew, wrote, copied, scribbled, and colored at will. The work in this notebook, in fact, resulted in some of the best "compositions" that the children had ever written.

This was also when I discovered that Cassy had been learning to write on her own. The only problem was that instead of letters, she wrote Japanese hiragana characters. We were extremely culturally immersed!

We finally landed in Anchorage, Alaska, to clear customs. After some delay we were allowed to roam the airport until our flight was refueled and the flight crew was changed. The airport was like a miniature museum with stuffed Alaskan wildlife and Inuit (Eskimo) cultural exhibits sprinkled throughout it. Of course our family made a "field trip" of it. The children's enthusiasm for spontaneous learning amazed me. It starkly contrasted to the groans, "Do I have to? It's too much like school!" that I overheard from the other children. It seemed as if they had no sense of learning for the fun of it. I couldn't stop wondering how many of these parents had ruined a child's zeal for exploration and discovery by making him or her write "How I Liked my Trip to the U.S." Eventually, we boarded and headed for Los Angeles International Airport, our final frontier.

We would live in the temporary lodging facility on the base. My husband would be temporarily discharged from the military within the next two months and we needed to conserve our cash resources.

Since it would take until the end of September for the discharge to be final, we decided to go visit my husband's ailing great grandmother in the meantime. We set off to Pensacola, Florida via Interstate 10. With our dog and a newly purchased van, we hit the road. I was glad because we could get some school work done. I figured that the work would combat the boredom of our trip.

What was I thinking? Jamaal only vaguely remembered the U.S., and the girls were definitely Okinawan: so, everyone was engulfed in the newness of their surroundings. I didn't quite realize this until we crossed the state line into Arizona. The questions began: is Arizona another island? Are we still in the United States? What time is it here? Do Japanese people live here or is it just all mixed up like in California? When do they (Arizonans) get typhoons? And so forth. My children were foreigners in their own homeland. How was I going to explain America to these Japanese children of mine?

Formal learning would have to wait. During the entire trip, we talked about the states as we drove through them. Dad provided the answers to the children's questions while I searched the AAA book for points of interest that we could visit along the way. Since our budget was tight, we sought attractions off the beaten path and that were low cost or free—and there were plenty! We slept in motels near points of interest that we could see after breakfast and before traveling. This provided a springboard for our daily conversations. We stopped and inhaled our country's diversity and richness.

In order to justify this time "off" from school, I assigned subjects to the trip for my personal satisfaction. Math: We adjusted our watches to the time zones and explained Daylight Savings Time, which we hadn't had in Japan. We constantly calculated how many miles to Grandma's, the next state, the next rest area, etc. Science: We marveled at the stark contrast in the weather (the Okinawan weather hardly changes) as we moved through the states. Geography and more science: We drank in the beauty of the Grand Canyon in Arizona, and the arid desert in Texas, and the pleasantly familiar sticky humidity in Louisiana. More science in Mississippi, probably enough for the whole year—we found ourselves alone in a NASA space center. We zoomed through Alabama and drove over the Gulf of Mexico (Citizenship and Geography) and safely arrived at Grandma's house.

My husband's mother, grandmother, and great grandmother all live in Pensacola and this sparked our history lessons for the week. All of us were amazed that Michael's mother could recall the family history back to slavery. The most interesting part for me was that Michael's great grandmother—whom we all call Big Mama although her name is Corinne Grover—learned to read from her mother, Laura Gibson, at home, and Grandma Gibson also learned the three R's at home from her mother, Neddy, a former slave. *Homeschooling: A Pogue Family Tradition!*

Our visit quickly drew to a close and I still had not used the workbooks we'd brought from Okinawa. The original plan had been to finish them by Christmas and then, after our storage shipment arrived, we would complete the rest of the curriculum. Those goals now seemed unattainable, and I would have to come up with an alternative plan. After all, we were in the States, and no formal education was taking place. I was so glad that we had no permanent address, so that no governmental body would be able to hunt us down and demand to see proof of our homeschooling endeavors. I would figure out a different way to complete the school year by the time we returned to California.

We headed back to California. On the way we saw that autumn had arrived and the trees that were not leafless due to recent flood damage in Missouri were showing off their fall colors. Another new thing for our children! This time we experienced prairie in Kansas, and the mountainous west, prior to reaching Camp Pendleton. *Time for the children to start learning!* No, I really didn't *get it* that they were already obviously learning all the time, even then!

Immediately, I sought a replacement curriculum for the workbooks that we hadn't used. I figured that new ones would refresh our interest in "school." Supermarket-type workbooks to the rescue—"In just ninety pages or less, your child will know everything required for his grade level." I chose math, reading, study skills, and English for Jamaal and Jasmine. Christina would only do phonics since she could barely read.

Michael was now reporting to work daily to complete the discharge process, and the children and I were confined to the Hostage House and its vicinity. Jasmine and Jamaal worked independently on one page per subject each day. Jasmine enjoyed the workbooks, which Jamaal tolerated, but the exercises took approximately fifteen minutes per page to complete, so they were painless. Christina's phonics lessons went smoothly, and Cassy played.

complete, so they were painless.   Christina's phonics lessons went smoothly, and Cassy played.

After our hour of study, we would go out to explore. The base was loaded with wild rabbits (something else the children had never seen), so we observed them in between walks to the exchange. The end of September was quickly approaching, and we would be leaving California and the security of military life for an unknown period of time. Our solace was the church near Camp Pendleton, and the certainty of an eventual reentry into the military. At the end of the month, we would have a van, four children, a lump sum distribution of money, and a dog. No home, and no income.

We knew that Michael would go back on active duty at Selfridge Air National Guard Base in Michigan, near Detroit, so we headed there. Our plan was to find a house and try to etch out a living until Michael's return to the military. Less than two months after leaving Japan, we arrived in Detroit after literally seeing half of the country—twenty-five states. But with no employment and a fixed amount of funds, how long could we continue living decently, let alone homeschooling?

Our first order of business was to find a place to live. It was the beginning of October and was beginning to get cold—freezing to us, after the tropics. We moved temporarily into a two-bedroom, two-bath, furnished suite with a kitchenette.

During our first week in the Detroit area, we contacted two home school support groups which we were referred to by the state organization. Through one of these groups we met a military family who had been in our shoes a year ago. Not long after that, we found a house to rent and my husband found some work with the Marine Corps Reserve.

Our new house was a three bedroom bungalow on Detroit's East side, next door to a bank. The neighborhood, East English Village, was rich in character with its tree-lined streets and mix of unique bungalows, colonials, and flats. The neighbors crossed all economic spectrums and were from all ethnic backgrounds. The yard was fenced, and we had a large basement for playing. Of course, there was a catch. The house was for sale and as a condition of our three month paid-in-advance lease, we had to allow real estate agents to show the house to potential buyers.

By mid November, school was finally in session. We decided to test Jasmine and Jamaal to see where they were. We hadn't taught them in such a long time, we wondered how they would compare to their peers. Using the Iowa Basic Skills Tests, Michael tested each child while I hovered nearby, afraid of the results—I felt the test really assessed my second grader, pleasantly surprised me. I hadn't spent much time with her in math and it showed; she scored at the first grade, sixth month level. However, her spelling and reading levels were at about the fourth grade, and overall she ranked at the second grade, ninth month level. With those results in hand, I resumed teaching, modifying my lessons to the test results.

Jamaal resumed and complete the MCP Math. Jasmine hated math. So, within a week, we ditched her math workbook in favor of Mom's Make Up Math. I would customize a worksheet on a piece of notebook paper. The first part would be our new weekly topic, and the remainder of the page would be review. Soon math was her favorite subject. Christina was now reading! It was choppy, but it was reading. We would continue the phonics lesson and pick up the math later. Cassy played.

Thanks to three Michigan Supreme Court rulings and our membership in the Home School Legal Defense Association (a national organization which fights, when necessary, for members' legal right to homeschool), I felt free to explore during school hours. Thanks to the snow, I didn't drive far. Our local library became our hangout. The children selected titles and read whatever they wanted. I didn't want to ruin a good book for them, so there were no book reports required. I did ask that they rate the book on a scale of one to ten. The children participated in Pizza Hut's Book It! program that autumn and winter. In order to earn their certificates, they had to read and tell me about one book a week. With Pizza Hut directly across the street from our house, redemption was a snap. In late February, the children participated in the "Rev Up To Read" program at the library, which meant they each had to read five books in five different categories and write what they had learned in one or two sentences. They loved it.

The Korean dry-cleaner made us feel at home—we were still bowing as a greeting to people. The tropical fish store made us feel rich when we realized the expensive salt water fish were the same species we used to catch in our "yard," the East China Sea. The bank security guard became a friendly stranger. She reminded us of the Okinawan guards who controlled the gates to the bases. After linking up with the Detroit homeschool support group, I was able to help new homeschoolers get started. I loved doing this since it allowed me to peruse homeschooling catalogs. Catalog window shopping, the greatest hobby!

Shortly after Thanksgiving, we were informed that Michael would be a full-time Marine beginning on the last day of February. All the

Shortly after Thanksgiving, we were informed that Michael would be a full-time Marine beginning on the last day of February. All the while, we were also trying to assist a minister from our church organization in starting a church in Detroit. We began by holding church in our living room, prior to locating a storefront in the neighborhood. This was exciting work and the children became active participants in the ministry behind the scenes. They searched newspapers for buildings for rent or purchase and read the maps for me while I drove to locate the possible church buildings. They also set up the living room for church services. They were (and still are) eager to invite others to the services. In February, another minister arrived and we opened the storefront. The children were quite proud to see the results of their prayers and hard work.

This was also our first dealing with other children (and parents) in the church. Our children had been the only children in the church in Okinawa. Of course other families came, but after they found out that there was no children's church (my translation: babysitting), they left. Although our children had had many friends who attended public school in Okinawa, we had managed to curtail any undesirable mannerisms that they might have picked up during "socialization," i.e. playing. This time, we were cautious about offending anyone and relaxed some of our standards for our children. At that point, they started reciting questionable rhymes and began lacking the zeal for the things of God that they had once had.

We also ran into conflict with some parents about our decision to home school. Although we don't consider homeschooling to be a mandate from God, and nor do we believe that everyone has the desire and/or discipline to homeschool, we do feel that it *is* God's will for *our* family. Other parents felt (and proceeded to tell us) that it would be best if our children faced the "real world," meaning public school. They were concerned that the children would turn eighteen and then face "culture shock" when they found out that the world wasn't a rosy happily-ever-after fairy tale. Of course, these statements were not new to us. Even strangers have felt it their duty to express that sentiment to us. We were just dismayed to face this in the church. After much prayer, we decided to agree to disagree. Looking back over our past homeschooling years, satisfaction came from knowing that our children *did* live in the real world—and not in an artificially created, age-segregated *Lord of the Flies* society.

All of our belongings arrived intact from Okinawa, and I was thrilled to see the textbooks. Jamaal loathed the idea of returning to the

the second grade readers immediately. Christina was thrilled to get in the first grade reader, and Cassy was elated to see her toys.

I decided to go with the children's feelings. They had been working well up to that point, so why change? Jasmine devoured the readers and Christina started her daily math review, formally called Mom's Make Up Math. Jamaal tried the fourth grade reader but quickly discarded it in favor of library books.

We never got around to using *Understanding Writing* like the author intended, but the hints worked well for our Mom's Make Up Writing Challenges, which consisted of writing letters to our homeschooling friends from Okinawa. Of course, I was required to write too. We also made up riddles for other family members to solve. I only had to suggest possible writing assignments and the mail-hungry jokesters would transform into skilled writers. By the end of May, I was satisfied with the progress we had made for the school year.

I promised myself that the next school year would be relaxed. Jamaal had learned how to learn, and I was confident that he could work independently in most areas. For math we would use Saxon but I was unsure which level. After placement tests, we found that Saxon 76, 87, or Algebra 1/2—ranging from approximate grade levels six to nine—would be suitable. I wanted him to use the 76 but he insisted on the Algebra 1/2. I had the Bob Jones fifth grade reader, so that would be used as a standby. Jasmine and Christina were champing at the bit to use the Bob Jones readers and worktext grades three and two respectively. They also requested more Mom's Make Up Math. Cassy wanted to do "real school" so I bought a couple of kindergarten books from A Beka to supplement Mom's Make Up Kindergarten.

The children wanted to learn sign language and Spanish. So I bought *Sign Language for Everyone* and *The Learnables* Level One. *Grammar Songs, Geography Songs,* and some books with science experiments completed our purchases. Once again, the school year would have to wait until we moved—(yes, again!)—into our new suburban house.

We moved in June. School would begin in August. During the time off, the children busied themselves with reading, biking, inventing games, and growing. They enjoyed the newness of Michigan's wildlife; muskrats and raccoons were their favorite sightings. They were also amazed—and still are—by the passing of the seasons.

OUR FIFTH YEAR—
EL ESPAÑOL DE LA MADRE
AND LIFE IN THE NINETEENTH CENTURY

August. Homeschool began a lot like it ended last year. We divided the basement in half: school side/play side. We were confident of what we were doing (fifth year, we should be) and secure with our teaching techniques. *The Learnables* were soon replaced by El Español de La Madre (Mother's Spanish): I give vocabulary and ask questions in Spanish and let the children figure out what I'm saying. This usually works well, but a recurring joke comes from the word for hair, *el pelo*, which Jamaal confused with the word for leg, *la pierna*. Whenever I ask what is done with the hair, the children reply, "You walk on it," and proceed to place their heads on the floor. An uproar of laughter, and a slight blush from Jamaal every time, but even Cassy can tell *el pelo* from *la pierna*.

The girls, Jasmine and Christina, started learning cursive writing together. They were thrilled that they had a "class" together. Instead of rivalry, they constantly encouraged and helped each other. They also loved to read stories from their readers aloud to everybody. This made Jamaal insist on working in his reader so that he could participate in oral reading also.

As for math, Mom's Make Up Math prevailed at first, with Jamaal also requesting it instead of the Saxon.

Cassy started her phonics lessons. It turned out she had been listening to all of the girls' lessons and could sound out several short-vowel words with no instruction. She also knew most of the letters and could spell many words with the short /a/ sound. And all that time I thought she was just playing.

We started the year studying ancient history, but that was soon ancient history. Thanks to the *American Girls* series, Jasmine became a Swedish pioneer and Christina, a spunky Virginian of the Revolutionary War period. Recipes from this time, general cooking, sewing, quilting, and making paper dolls became their history and science. Jamaal picked up Greek myths, space exploration, Spanish phonics, and computer programming. He learned the fundamentals of C, C+, BASIC, and QBASIC (since, as he explains, "You have to do some conversion from BASIC to QBASIC if you want a program to work"). The children agreed that reading the *Little House* series by Laura Ingalls Wilder would be

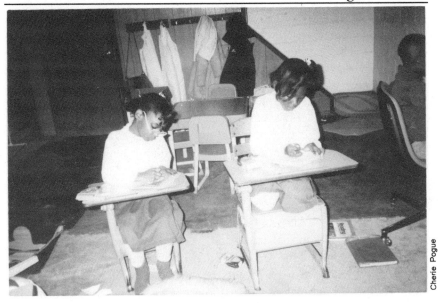

Sometimes it looks like school....
Christina and Jasmine in the basement "classroom"

and sometimes it doesn't.
"On winter days, we shut off the heat, light the fireplace, and work like pioneers."

interesting. From this, we delved completely into that historical period. We even used some folk medicine from the 1800's.

Thank God for the children's independent spirits, their ability to research topics of interest, and their training in household maintenance. In October, asthma had me just one step above bedridden. The children maintained the house, occupied themselves and took care of me while my husband worked. This time of illness made me think about our decision to homeschool with so little structured curriculum. Internally I debated whether to obtain math textbooks for the children.

As if I needed something else to deal with, we also hosted the monthly meetings for a newly-formed homeschool support in our area. "We Are Nuts" (WAN) embarked on its first year as a homeschool support group. We specialized in the "relaxed homeschool family." The main reason we hosted the group was that I gently insisted that children be allowed to come with their parents to the meetings. I hate homeschool activities that do not include those who are homeschooled; it seems ironic to me when people who choose to teach their children exclude them from homeschool events. So, we arranged for a teenager—homeschooled of course—to supervise the children while the adults met upstairs. The children played in small groups while we attempted to "give guidance" to one another. After a few meetings, we discovered that the best part of each meeting was after the formalities, when we ate and chatted. *That* was when the valuable information was exchanged. Next year, in fact, WAN will be simply a fellowship group; we have ditched the formal meetings.

Our fifth year proceeded, and by December it became apparent that I did need help with my math curriculum. I lacked the physical strength to create daily math sheets. I lacked the physical strength to walk up a flight of stairs without getting winded! I chose carefully, because I saw too much progressive and enthusiastic learning to force the children, especially Jasmine and Christina, into the specific mold that some textbooks impose. (As Jasmine put it, "In homeschool you can be any grade instead of the grade you're supposed to be in." That is, although she and Christina are the same age, they can work individually at their own pace.)

Enter Miquon Math and the *Key to Curriculum*. What a Godsend! The "lab sheets" resembled Mom's Make Up Math. They were big, bold, and nonthreatening in appearance. Jasmine, "Miss I-Hate- Math," jumped right into them. Jamaal loved *Key to Decimals* and completed six to eight pages a day. Also, to my surprise and joy, Christina excelled on her own in the workbooks. They all completed much more independently than I would have assigned.

Cassy decided that she no longer wanted to learn to read. She was my first "drop out." My illness didn't help matters, so I left her alone. This was when I discovered her world of imaginary friends. She had approximately ten of them, and they all had distinct personalities, characteristics, and voices. No wonder she had no time for "school!" She had an entourage waiting to play. And so she returned to her carefree days of playing, imagining, loving, thinking, and of course learning.

As the seasons changed, my health seemed to blossom with the first crocuses. I was feeling much better and needed to know where the children were academically. I perused their books, observed their elaborate play patterns, and listened to them chatter endlessly about their lives. They knew so much about the nineteenth century, the winter birds and the new spring arrivals, computers, household maintenance, and Michigan that I was in awe. How could such small children articulate such concepts? It all hit home when we were summarizing the 1800's and I wrote "Henry Ford, 1863 - 1947" on the board. Immediately Jasmine said, "Oh, he was born near the Civil War and died around World War II." Christina chimed in, "Yes, he was alive when the Wright Brothers flew the first airplane." Jamaal added, "His son Edsel lived in that mansion that is in Grosse Pointe. Near us!" Cassy, not to be outdone, supplied, "He had a car."

Satisfied with their knowledge, I felt confident that the year was not a total loss. Field trips were in order to bring our historical immersion to life. They had earned a visit to the Edsel Ford Home, and as a capstone they attended a one-room schoolhouse in full 1870's period dress. By June we called the school year finished, not worrying about where we had left off in our books or where we would begin the next school year.

Of course, as usual, we had other things on our minds. Yes, another move. My husband got a call that he was being transferred to New Orleans, "The Big Easy." So instead of plotting typhoons, we will now plot hurricanes. The Mississippi, the Louisiana Purchase, pirates, Creole, Cajun, food... I think we will be able to find something to study. After we pack, of course. After our Eastern Seaboard Motor Tour. After we find a place to live. After we unpack. By then, he may have orders again anyway. I love it!

What about high school? The common question! For now, we have an answer. After "sixth grade" (I use that term loosely since we no longer care about grade levels), the children will be in command of their high school education. After a required grammar course, algebra course, touch typing, and a part time job (paid or unpaid), they will be free to study things in which they are interested provided they can assign a traditional subject heading to it, much the way I did on our cross country driving. If they want to use textbooks, fine; research from the library, fine; observation, fine. Everything they do will earn credit and after a to-be-determined number of credits, they will graduate from our homeschool. Will it work? Time will tell. If it doesn't, we'll adapt and adjust.

Since we've started homeschooling, we've learned so much academically, and we *know* our children intimately. After being a part of the homeschool support group in Detroit (nearly one hundred black families), we no longer feel like peppercorns in a salt shaker. Still, we miss Asia and race to a local Korean grocery store for kimchee and Japanese candy whenever we feel homesick. Eventually we would like to live abroad again, preferably in a Spanish-speaking country, but we would go anywhere. It saddens me that our country is so preoccupied with race. However, looking at seemingly homogeneous societies I see that there is still the preoccupation with ethnicity—the Japanese and the Okinawans, the Tutsi and the Hutu, the Serbs and the Croats. Only in a foreign country are you known solely by your *nationality*. We had to travel around the world to be seen as Americans. Now that we have returned to the land of the hyphenated, we will properly honor our roots. Just call us the Okinawan-Swedish-Colonial-Greek-African-American-homeschoolers-qué-hablan-español! ❖

Toby Rhue
North Fork, California

ONE FATHER'S PERSPECTIVE

My family consists of three boys—Joshua, nine, Alex, six, and Aric, one—my wife Chris, and me. Chris is chief home maker and knowledgeable in a great many subjects, and I work full time for the Forest Service. We have lived in several communities, each no larger than 4500 people, in Idaho, Utah, Nevada, and California. These communities have ranged from isolated rural hamlets to towns easily within reach of metropolitan areas.

There has never been a question as to whether we would homeschool; it was a given. Chris and I agreed early on homeschooling, even though we knew little about what we had agreed on. We just knew in our hearts that there had to be an alternative to public education and to the high cost of private schooling.

I couldn't remember many good things about my own school experiences. I remembered the mixed emotions and the depression that I often felt at my Southern California high school, where whites hated blacks, blacks hated Chicanos, and other ethnic groups had to keep a low profile. I was not a great student, but I did the required homework and passed most tests. Yet, I didn't do well on my college entrance exams, and I spent my first year of college relearning math and English that I hadn't retained from high school. Of course this did very little for my self esteem, but what kept me going during that time was both my father's wish for me to graduate from college and the memory of a high school counselor who had advised me to forget college, but—if I was really motivated—to consider vocational school, because "they will take almost anyone."

Chris's high school experience centered on another form of oppression: religion. She lived in a rural and predominately Mormon community, where her family was Catholic. She remembers her school experience as a time of being alone, ostracized and ridiculed for being

The Rhue Family (from left): Aric, Chris, Alex, Josh, and Toby

different. So much for the highly praised social opportunities available in traditional schools.

To be honest, although I supported the homeschooling idea, Chris did all the bird dogging. She uncovered great books by Rudolph Steiner and John Holt, and the ideas of these two men opened up a whole new world. A homeschooling friend introduced us to other homeschoolers. Gradually, through books and what we learned from our new friends, we realized that we, too, could do this. And thus we began the journey to allow ourselves to trust our hearts and our boys to guide us as to how to best teach them.

My kids are free to be whatever they want to—maybe explorers, by looking through the pages of *National Geographic* or encyclopedias; maybe chefs, in which case I get the extreme pleasure of sampling their culinary works; or they may dream, inspired by books Chris or I have read to them. If my boys attended public school, it would be impossible to afford them large blocks of time to go deeply into any activity. We have learned that even "doing nothing" is important. "Doing nothing" allows the time needed to assimilate or put meaning to what they have learned during busier moments.

My role in homeschooling is to be as supportive and enthusiastic as I can in challenging the boys to want to learn through having fun—not through the drudgery I experienced in school. Chris and I are always on the lookout for learning opportunities. For instance, we have friends whose daughter was taking karate and doing well. Josh became interested, but at the time we felt he was too young to enroll. Meanwhile I searched, talked with people, and used my limited experience to select the karate style and teacher to focus on the development of students—not for competition, but rather for building physical confidence and learning self-control and self-care. I was lucky to find a teacher who is unassuming, has a relaxed teaching style focusing on what karate teaches you about yourself, and doesn't push too hard. So, this past summer I saw a change in Josh as he became more confident from practicing and from the support he receives from the adults in his class.

We enrolled Joshua and Alex in piano lessons a year and a half ago. Barely able to afford the lessons and the travel time involved, Chris and I had to reevaluate our goals. We had several objectives: to bring live music into our home, to foster Alex's intense interest in music, and to give the boys the opportunity to learn a skill that would be with them the rest of their lives. So, we selected a piano course that would teach several aspects of music in addition to piano, and make it fun too. Josh has enjoyed these classes and plays the piano two to three times a day because he wants to. In fact, he has recently started to ask when I am going to start taking piano lessons from him.

Chris Rhue

We found that Alex's learning style was different; the class situation and assignments stifled him. He preferred to learn musical pieces by ear, and he's interested in playing what he hears on the radio or on a tape. The class style of learning was too structured and slow for him. His interest began to wane, so Chris and I gave him a choice of stopping classes or continuing. He chose to stop, but not if it would have to be forever. We discussed options: we could wait until he was older, or search for another piano teacher. It took about a year, but we are confident that we have finally located a piano instructor who is open to working with Alex's learning style. During the year that he didn't attend classes, we were amazed at the music he was able to learn just from listening to Joshua practice.

The time I spend with Josh and Alex gives me a view into myself-
sometimes a painful view. If only I could just teach them to only mimic
the best in me, and leave the rest! We have a family policy of leaving our
shoes at the door as we enter the house. I sometimes used to stretch this,
wearing my shoes to the kitchen. But then I'd notice two other, smaller
pairs of shoes parked next to mine. So I started taking off my shoes in the
mud room and again, they were joined by the two other pairs. Even when I
changed the location of my shoes *within* the mud room, the boys followed
suit. It's one thing to have someone tell you that everything you do as a
parent is being watched and mimicked. It's another thing altogether to
actually experience it. So, I hope that as I learn to change, Josh, Alex, and
Aric will see my struggles and, equally important, they will see the
benefits from that struggle.

One thing we had to do in the beginning was to collect information on the
legal aspects of homeschooling. This was intriguing, as I learned about
how school districts received their funds, and the authorities granted to
school boards, superintendents, principals, and teachers. I learned that,
depending on which state my work took me to, I would have to deal with
some or all of these representatives of public education. This feeling
overwhelmed us at first, but then we started really using some of our
resources—books, magazines, and our homeschooling friends. In 1991,
we discovered a non-secular private school devoted to supporting home
schoolers nationwide.* It offers suggestions for K-12 curriculum, a
support teacher to bounce ideas off of, and an informative newsletter that
describes, among other things, changes in different states' homeschooling
laws. Possibly the most important reason we decided to enroll with this
school is that they were willing to interface directly with a school district
in any state that we might move to. Since we move often, this would
allow us to devote our attention to the boys themselves, and not spend a
lot of energy on learning about a new state education system every few
years.

My work sometimes requires me to travel to other cities. I like to travel,
and the best way to do this *and* keep my family happy is to include them.
So, our travel planning includes finding a hotel within walking distance to

---

* The Rhues are enrolled with Clonlara, which many homeschoolers find very helpful, flexible, and
reasonably priced. Clonlara also insightfully and creatively awards credits and diplomas based on kids'
real-life experiences. Information available from Clonlara Home Based Education Program, 1289
Jewett St., Ann Arbor, MI 48104, (313) 769-4515.

where my meeting will be, leaving the car for family excursions in the city.   We also make note of places nearby the hotel that are safe for walking to, such as museums, libraries, bookstores, parks.

During a workshop, Chris and the boys explore the city. (Since we live in rural areas, visiting a city is always something to get excited about.) My workshops occupy most of the daylight hours, but I try to compensate by staying either the weekend before or afterwards, to join my family in their discoveries.

The family's travel adventures, while I've attended workshops and meetings, have ranged from hiking Camelback Mountain and visiting the Phoenix Zoo, to visiting the Tracy Bird Aviary and the Salt Lake City Children's Museum. Probably one of the best adventures was a visit to Big Basin Redwood State Park near San Jose, California, where the majesty of the redwoods was almost overshadowed by the boys' discovery of banana slugs. The huge, bright yellow creatures held the boys awe-struck.   Later during that same week I had the opportunity to take the boys to hear the Banana Slug String Band perform.   The amazed expressions on Joshua's and Alex's faces brought me joy on that day and again, now, as I write. It was a magical week of discovery, although *I* did not see the redwoods or the banana slugs. The boys were able to connect with the message in the music of the Banana Slug String Band, connect the music with the people who made it, and connect it all with the forest of grand redwood trees and its creatures.

Homeschooling has helped me to see the importance of being available to both Chris and the boys. My family would like me to be even more involved, and I am improving. My involvement has paid off in calls during the day to find out when I will be home, and a real feeling that I am a part of their lives. However, the best reward is the smiles and the excitement my coming home creates, always having the boys greet me at the door in the afternoon.

I love the fact that my boys can come to my office and walk with me home for lunch. Although the walk is not far, we talk all the way and I learn a lot about their morning. And if I can't leave right away, the boys may get additional insights into my work. They have met many of the office staff, and from time to time I've been able to talk someone into sharing their work with the boys. I might initiate the discussion with, "Here is John; he works in fire management.   John, could you tell the boys what type of work you do?"   The boys have learned about wilderness, archaeology, ecology, and the different vehicles and equipment the Forest Services uses. Often, these experiences lead to lively discussions.

As my sons grow older, I hope they will understand my work and what I stand for. I believe that obtaining this understanding is within their capabilities, and that it will contribute to how they relate to others. I did not understand my Dad's work, or what he stood for. I am only now starting to get a glimpse of what he really values; not knowing has kept our relationship friendly but not close. I want more for my sons. Of course, this kind of involvement and learning takes time—*my* time. But I cannot think of another thing more important to do with my time. I am committed to giving the boys the best learning opportunities that I can find, and I am always looking.

The boys like to visit my office, and sometimes may spend an afternoon or morning there. Also, when I have a work opportunity to visit the forest alone, I like to invite the boys. These days are great. I cherish them because I am not confined by an office, the boys can freely explore, and they can learn more about my work.

As part of my work, I often speak to groups of people, and Joshua and Alex sometimes join me to see what I do. I allow them to make an informed choice about attending a meeting by explaining the type of meeting and how long it may last. Then I ask if they *really* want to go—it's their choice. If they decide to join me, I remind them about acceptable behavior at meetings. When we get there, I show them where they can talk freely, and I allow them to become familiar with the meeting room.

People have commented on how well behaved the boys are, and how it is good to see children at the meeting. This is uplifting, since many people assume that children do not belong in such situations. When someone comments positively, I take the opportunity to point out that the boys behave well because they are *used* to being around adults, and because they are homeschooled. They don't feel compelled to fight for attention, as many traditionally schooled children do.

Public school kids usually are not expected to participate in, or even be around, adult social or work interactions. In most cases the social behavior they learn from other kids is not appropriate in an adult setting—or in *any* setting. Yet, many people I've met feel that kids need a lot of social interaction with their peers. I disagree. Rather, young people need someone to look up to, and a safe environment in which to discover life. Parents should be more involved in planning and participating in activities that include other children.

In the past I've been amazed at how well Josh and Alex could mirror the behavior of adults at meetings. And it has been equally wonderful to see the behavior of some adults improve with the presence of young people. I believe that youth will always strive to meet your expectations, be it behaving or misbehaving, you will not be let down. Respect is a key word to remember around young people—homeschooling has taught me that. I am not close to being a saint; however, when I slip into old behaviors Josh and Alex are there to give me support.

Financially, homeschooling can be a bit taxing; however, I more than feel it is worth it. This is my contribution to my children's future, who will play a part in the future of our country. We don't subscribe to the idea of buying lots of textbooks and having school at home. We do have a large personal library, and we make weekly visits to the public library.

We are often asked to comment on the social handicap that homeschoolers supposedly experience. I remind my questioners of all the "wonderful" social interactions that *we* all had in school, and ask them to try to remember—by counting—the number of positive interactions they could actually recall. Many times they smile and say, "Yeah, school was tough. I'm glad it's history."

Other people say that I am prolonging the inevitable by keeping the boys out of school. I ask what this inevitable is, and they tell me that my kids need to learn how to deal with other kids' joking, the thrill of sports, the game of how the system works, and about pecking orders of things. But much child's play is oppressive and involves put-downs, and this is not the kind of socialization I want for my sons. Oppressive behavior is not natural, even if it is prevalent. Play can and should be supportive and fulfilling.

Many children's psychological development is stunted when they attend school at young ages. Even when a child excels in academics, his psyche may develop poorly. I often recall a phrase I heard or read somewhere— " 'To be smart' doesn't necessarily mean 'to have wisdom.' "

When a person's inner development is stunted, security issues arise, and result in dominating, following, and/or anti-social behavior. A put-down cloaked in a joke, the do-or-die nature of most sports, the dominating nature of pecking orders, and even how society's larger system works—all are essentially based on a system of people creating security for themselves out of someone else's insecurity. In contrast, homeschooling allows my sons safe space and time to develop true security, a strength of character, and confidence.

At any rate, of course the boys are *not* in a bubble, and they *do* interact both with other children and adults. Furthermore, being a bi-racial family means that Chris and I have additional perspectives to offer our boys.

People sometimes inquire whether we homeschool because of racism in the school system, and I find this an interesting admission on their part. However, my first priority is to provide a positive and free-choice learning environment. Chris and I feel a strong sense of responsibility to be available to the needs of our sons, and homeschooling allows us to be there for them. It is really neat to see their growth and to experience what I can with them. I marvel in how they learn.... and in how they *don't* learn. We plan to homeschool as long as the boys want to. ❖

Chris Rhue

Chris Rhue

Josh and Alex working cross-stitch

OLD CROC
AND OTHER NOTES

by Chris Rhue

Being the omnipresent and ever intrusive wife that I am, I must include this note, just to add a few points.

I had a mostly traumatic elementary and secondary school experience. I then went on to become a special education teacher and taught for four years. I sometimes tell people—truthfully—that these experiences, as student and as teacher, caused me to vow that my children would never go to school.

The really wonderful thing is that Toby has always completely supported me and has offered all the help he can. This is what I see as one main difference between us and many other homeschoolers. We often hear that the husbands are skeptical, unsupportive, or downright against it. When I hear this, I am always grateful that we are together in this. Especially as we are unschoolers, and must trust in the children—not in paperwork and test scores.

Our sons' exposure to racism has definitely been cut way down by not attending school. Although I see this as a plus, and if there were no other reason to homeschool this reason alone would be reason enough, it is not the reason we homeschool. It's just another of the many benefits. I homeschool because, after my experiences attending school, teaching school, meeting and getting to know homeschooled kids, and doing some reading, I decided, unequivocally, that school is destructive to children. That school is a very bad place for children to be. Children are born learning; they have an innate desire to learn; they love to learn. School destroys the pure form of that. I also feel that school is a major factor in the breakdown of the family. Children are meant to be with their parents, and extended families, when possible. Their self-concepts, intelligence, moral development, and the way they view the world are most influenced by the people they spend most of their time with. This influence is the responsibility of the parents, not of peers, and not of someone hired to do it for money.

Yes, we have been accused of overprotecting our children. Of isolating them from the "real" world. People tell us that school is useful precisely for finding your niche in the social pecking order. And that no matter how low on the ladder you end up, well, that must be your place; so, good for you to know it as soon as possible. Aside from being balderdash, this is a cruel and abusive attitude. My response to it is this: you may think whatever you want of me. These are my kids, and I'll do what I feel in my heart is best and right for them. Children *should* be protected. That's our job. School teachers don't do it real well.

If there's one thing I've learned through homeschooling, it's how incredibly fast kids can learn something, or grasp an idea (even a negative one) when they are ready, or mature enough. Information about their world comes through all the time, bit by bit. They sort through each tidbit as it comes, mentally and emotionally. They internalize it. Analyze it. They come to terms with it, and they go on.

Much of what children learn about the not-so-positive aspects of our social structure and behaviors is by observing others. They observe other children or adults in social contact with one another. After noticing certain aspects of this behavior, our children ask questions and discuss their observations with us. I am so grateful for this mode of learning. They can sift through and understand behavior before they are a part of it. Kids in school are thrown into social situations and must perform with very little wisdom or experience to fall back on.

I don't think being a bi-racial family makes homeschooling more difficult, except perhaps for the racism among homeschoolers as well. It was perhaps more viable as an option for us because I am white, and because I was a teacher in the public schools. I knew I could do this, and I was very confident and self-assured about it—probably because I have a rebellious, strong-willed nature. I knew I didn't have to follow anybody's rules! I also did not have to grow up dealing with racism. That could wear someone down, make them think you can't fight the system. Sometimes I don't think minority peoples are aware of the alternatives (and their benefits), or of the true freedoms that they do have.

On the other hand, homeschooling probably does affect our experience as a bi-racial family. We don't have to put up with all that school "stuff": lack of equality in teaching materials, teasing between students, racist teachers, stereotypical beliefs among peers and teachers, etc. Of course, we naturally have to deal with some of this anyhow, but on a daily basis it would all be so incredibly stressful.

Homeschooling has made us all more aware of the inequality and "whiteness" of available play and teaching materials. Since we are unschoolers we don't use much in the way of textbooks, but our house is full of other types of books. Since we are free to do as we please and use materials we choose, I try to search out ethnically diverse and balanced materials and activities.

I want to tell about one more thing Toby does with the boys. Several years ago, he began telling stories to Josh and Alex about a crocodile named Old Croc who "sits on his rock, half in, half out of the water." Each Old Croc story begins this way. After that, the story is made up as it goes along. They are all adventures. Old Croc is a hero, of sorts, though not the only hero or heroine in the stories. He is sort of a wise old mentor, friend and guardian to all, master problem solver. His helpers may include the Knights and the Superheros (two of which have very familiar names). Other characters may include the King, Queen, Princess, Village People, various bad guys like monsters, giants, ogres, etc.; a friendly dragon, occasionally Croc's wife and children....well, the cast of characters changes and goes on and on. Some characters are in every story, some only in one. A story may get repeated (although not *exactly* the same way!) by special request; but usually it's a new adventure with each telling.

The best thing about these stories is that Josh and Alex of course get to help direct them, help tell them. They'll holler out, "I think the superheros should come now!" "Let's have the giant go to....," etc., etc. Toby smoothly weaves all of their suggestions into each story.

I can't even begin to describe how valuable I feel these storytelling experiences are for our boys, on so many different levels, in so many different ways. Frequently, when we have a long wait, or a long drive, or before bed, I'll hear, "Tell us an Old Croc story!" And I know we're all in for a treat: a long, rambling, feel-good adventure story interrupted by excited voices chirping out ideas. I only have to look at their beaming, smiling faces to know what a valuable gift Toby gives them through the tradition of these stories.

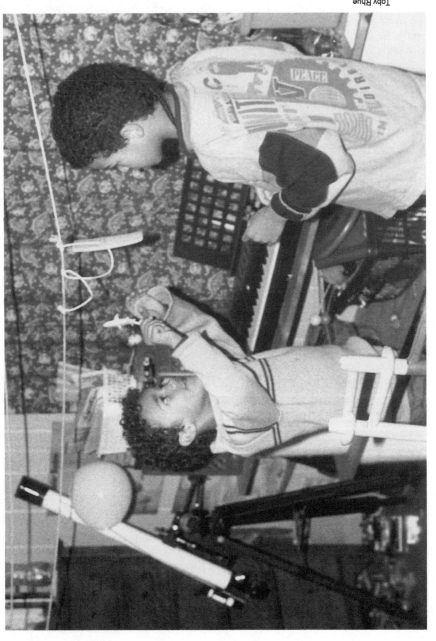

Alex and Josh rig up a pulley system in their room

Josh works on his model airplane; Alex observes.

Josh searches for sea life at Morro Bay, California

Alex meets the waves at Morro Bay, California

Merry Tackoor
Detroit, Michigan

EVOLVING

I've never gone with the status quo. I've never felt you need to go to school every single day. As an institution, I think it's entirely overrated.

I'm a single parent living in a community that's primarily black, with other minorities too. The neighborhood I live in is mostly stable, two-parent families—working people. The economic level ranges from the lower economic status to the middle, with maybe a few upper class families. I have two daughters, twelve and eight. The twelve-year-old is presently temporarily absent from home. So I homeschool my eight-year-old, Erin.

The groundwork for our homeschooling was laid out many years ago. While growing up, I attended approximately thirteen different schools. The whole experience was just generally negative, though I still managed to learn. Also, prior to our homeschooling, I helped raise my two now full-grown nieces. School was not a successful experience for them either, but they weren't my kids. So, although I wanted to keep them at home and try something different with them, I didn't. But on the occasions when they said they didn't want to go, it was fine with me.

When my own two children came along, I didn't want to inflict my negative personal feelings about school on them. So, when my first daughter reached school age, I dutifully sent her to school, although I didn't want to. It was not a successful situation, but that's another story altogether. Anyway, I didn't want to make the same errors with Erin, and so we wound up homeschooling.

I really feel I was led to homeschooling. I don't mean to appear fanatical, but I'm strongly religious and I prayed over this situation and came to believe that homeschooling was our answer. It wasn't an easy choice—it was very scary, and we're still evolving. I've always taught my children things at home, so that in itself was nothing new. My attitude

photo of Merry by Cherie Pogue

has been that even when I sent my children to school, their education was primarily *my* responsibility—not the teacher's, or the institution's. The prospect of having the teachers and institutions go against you, if you keep your children home, is scary. But of course I found out that I could homeschool legally.

We're still evolving as homeschoolers. I've found out that homeschooling brings out both the worst and the best in you. I'm a procrastinator, which makes things difficult at times. But I'm also impulsive, which makes things exciting. Consistency is hard for me, and I need it more than my daughter does. This year I enrolled her in a homeschooling co-op which meets once a week. It gives me a sense of structure, which I need. So Erin will start to learn a musical instrument and take a science class. But I teach her basically everything else. I figure I'm smarter than she is; I know more than she does; so hey, I can teach her. There's a lot she can learn from me.

I do not have a college degree, although I did attend a junior college for a few years. The classes I took in no way would have prepared or equipped me to homeschool my child. Why then do I feel I'm able to teach Erin? From me she learned to count, to print her name, to know her colors, that authors write books, that the sun is a burning ball of gas, and most importantly that God created it all. And, I know how to find and use available resources when I require further information. I have all types of homeschooling materials to choose from. I can select correspondence materials that are not only laid out completely for me and my child, but that will be checked and graded as well. Or, I can choose material that allows me to adapt *it* to *my* program. No homeschooler need ever take the educational journey alone. Help and support are readily available.

Starting out, though, it was scary. I patterned it after what I was already familiar with—school. Erin was basically attending a private school. She got up, put her uniform on, and I was the Teacher. We tried to conduct her education that way.

It didn't last. I was uncomfortable. It was unnatural. We evolved. Now, when she's interested in something, that's what we go with.

Lately we've both been learning about the man-made structures referred to as the "wonders of the world." Her reading relates to the Great Wall of China, the Taj Mahal, Stonehenge, etc. Naturally, from that flows geography lessons and political awareness: Why was the Great Wall erected? What kept Shah Jahan from building a black copy of his wife's tomb? There's nothing like the joy I feel when Erin excitedly recognizes a name or place mentioned on TV. She's so proud and confident. Presently we are planning on building models of a few of these famous structures. We plan to undertake the Great Wall first. Her choice. There's our art project.

I still keep track of what other second graders are doing, and we use some workbooks, and I do give assignments. I use a structured spelling book because *I* need it. But at the same time, I give Erin her own spelling words. The other day she wanted to know how to spell "Aladdin," so that became one of her words.

I never make Erin read anything she doesn't want to read, or that she doesn't enjoy. I don't want to be forced to read something I don't like, and I think children should have their own choice of what to read also. If the story is boring, who wants to read it? Erin is permitted to read anything she wants to. If there's something I want to expose her to—what I consider the classics, like *Little Women* or *Little Men*—and she doesn't want to tackle it herself, then I'll read it *to* her. I read to her quite a bit. She also reads to me, and we make up stories. We do it together.

Usually when we read, we do our spelling at the same time. I tend to approach things as units. I wasn't aware of the unit learning or teaching concept, but someone told me that's what I do. It comes naturally to me; I think of things as complete ideas. If there's anything I want Erin to understand, it's that everything in our world is related. There is nothing separate in the world—*everything* is connected.

Some of the other things I want Erin to obtain from homeschooling are, number one: to acquire a lifelong love of learning. Number two: to realize that learning never stops. Number three: to become a socially well adjusted person. And as far as these goals go, I don't think we can go wrong through our homeschooling.

One of my serious fears when we started homeschooling was how friends and family would react. No one came out and said, "I think this is a bad idea." But people looked at me like, "Is this legal? Are you sure you know what you're doing?" There are *still* people who suggest a good school for her. Never having met any homeschooling children, of course they're dubious about it. When we first started, Erin would perform just to prove to people that yes, she was learning, and yes, I was capable of teaching her. That was a response to my insecurity, and I've since outgrown that. I don't care what people think anymore. *I* know what she's doing, and *I* know she's learning, and *I* know that she's adjusting.

As far as the social opportunities of homeschooling are concerned, I'm pretty satisfied. Erin does have a social life, partly through our church. Right now she's also on a soccer team. At first she was apprehensive about it, because she wanted to do a good job. But after the first practice, she waved me away and now she doesn't like me to come. When it came time for her first city championship, she was very unsure about going. I told her, "Erin, it's up to you. You do as you choose. If you go, that's fine. If you don't go, that's all right too." And she decided to go and play. She is becoming stronger, more secure, more self-assured. I can see her blossoming in front of my very eyes, and other people notice it too.

We've gone to a homeschool support group, which has helped us meet others. This homeschool co-op will be good, too, because Erin will meet more homeschooled children. Making and keeping friends isn't too much of a problem, actually. But it was one of the concerns I had at first. My older daughter had picked up some really bad social habits at school, and some ways of interacting, that I didn't want my youngest contaminated with. When you send a child to a public school—or even a private school—it's like playing Russian roulette. You never know which children are inclined to follow and to be easily manipulated and swayed, or to absorb negative influences and behaviors like a sponge. There are some kids who can be around kids who are disruptive, rude, and antisocial, and they won't pick that up. But other children are overwhelmed by it, and I didn't want to take that risk again. Erin is never forced to socialize with anyone she feels uncomfortable with, and one nice thing happened this summer that reinforced that what I was doing was right.

We had received a scholarship to attend the YWCA for their summer program. Erin didn't care to go, but I had a few friends who said her opinion didn't matter; I should *make* her go "for the social interaction." Well, Erin would come home and tell how somebody bullied her, or threatened her, about money and things like that. She quickly started to get very clingy. So I told her that after the first week, I wouldn't make her go anymore if she didn't want to. The next day she came home and told me a girl was arguing with her and said, "Your mama." I looked at my daughter, and she said, "Mom, she didn't even finish her sentence. Your mama *what*? And she called *me* stupid?" Well, I realized right then that number one, my daughter knew what a complete sentence was. But number two, she had no awareness of "Your mama" being a challenge. That's just not part of her vocabulary. And so she was completely unthreatened.

Now, I know some people who would say that's sheltering a kid. But my feeling is that she doesn't need that kind of interaction right now. I'm afraid kids do need to be sheltered, there's too much hostility out there. So, yes, I believe in sheltering my child—giving her the nurturing, secure environment she needs to grow up in, and allowing her to *have* a childhood. Do I believe in keeping her *ignorant?* No.

Our schedule is completely different from a school schedule now. Erin and I are basically night people; that's when we become active. We're nocturnal. So our homeschooling doesn't take place early in the day, but in the afternoon and well into the evening. We read every night (and first thing in the morning, too). Also, we homeschool wherever we happen to be. The back of my car has books, paper, a clipboard, and crayons. If I'm in the drive-through for the bank, Erin is doing something or we're talking or we're spelling together. Any place we go is an educational opportunity. For example, before I took her to see *The Lion*

King, I found some animal cards, and picked out the ones that related to characters in the movie and other African animals. While we sat waiting for the movie to start, we talked about those animals. Anything leads to learning, because life *is* learning. Every day is a learning experience.

We had a problem getting Erin to understand the concepts of country and state. So we went out onto the street, and she marked it "United States—country." Then we assigned every house the name of a state, and so she got the idea. We also make up poems, special poems just for Erin. Things are tailored just for her.

Erin also learns cooking and manners from her aunt every Tuesday. They have class together, and Erin has her little booklet and such, and she gets certificates and things like that. I will be having her take the California Achievement Test just because I want to know where she's at. I like to have some type of standard to give me guidelines to go by, but that's the only reason.

What are my future goals and dreams for Erin? I want to have a well-adjusted, happy child. If she wants to go to college, that's fine. If she doesn't want to, that's fine too. My goal is to have her prepare to earn her own living in this world, and I'd like to get an apprenticeship started for her in some area that she really loves. Right now she tends to be athletically inclined and gifted, and we're headed into gymnastics. If we stay with that, maybe she'll be able to support herself by teaching gymnastics. That's one option we're considering. She also likes to cook. So I'm allowing her to cook, and buying her utensils and encouraging her to keep making stuff. Maybe that will become a way she'll be able to support herself. By the time she's sixteen, I hope she'll have a well-developed money-earning skill that she enjoys, instead of just being a high-school graduate with no way to support herself. I'm also trying to raise a good Christian child, a good citizen, a happy and secure person who's confident, well-adjusted, family oriented, and who can take care of herself and support herself and be an independent woman in this world. And I don't think we can go wrong through our homeschooling. ❖

Sunshine Lewis, age 13
Pensacola, Florida

HANDS ON

What is homeschooling? People ask me that all the time. I think every kid should be exposed to homeschooling. If they're not actually homeschooled, they should at least get to know someone who is. Contrary to popular belief, homeschoolers generally get a *better* education—because of individual attention, hands-on experiences, and a better and broader learning environment. Here are some of the learning experiences I've had:

WORKING WITH PLANTS AND PEOPLE

Fine Herbs and Such is a local herb nursery that sells not only herbs, but also unusual plants. I have a job there where I help out one day a week for three hours. Miss Penny, the owner, explains how to identify, grow, maintain, and use different herbs and plants. (Just in case you didn't know, an herb is a plant that is mainly used as a spice in cooking, but can also be used for skin care, herbal shampoos, lotions, and medicine.) She also has other helpers. Her mother—Mrs. Spence—and another elderly lady that everyone calls Miss Lefty are always at Fine Herbs, and they have wonderful stories to share. Mrs. Spence has lived in Asia, North Africa, and many other places. She told me that once when she lived in India they would buy fruits and vegetables at a big open air market place, but they had to send out of the country for other things. One day her husband asked if she needed anything, and she told him that she needed bread pans. He told her to get the measurements and the shape that she wanted. Thinking she was pretty smart, she cut a picture out of a

Sears catalog and wrote the measurements on the picture. When she got the pans back, their sides were slanted, just like they had been in the picture, because of the camera's perspective!

Another thing all of us helpers do is share reading material, and for a time Mrs. Spence even gave me knitting lessons.

Miss Penny and I have developed a schedule that includes sweeping, transplanting, planting, weeding, washing and rinsing pots, filling mulch buckets, pruning plants, emptying pots, and more. She says that I have a good hand for plants and that I could probably get a good job at a garden shop. Before I knew Miss Penny, my dad knew her. She sells some of her herbs at the Farmers Market, and my parents bought fresh vegetables there. My dad is really into organic gardening, so they got to talking, and somehow or another Miss Penny told my dad that she and her mother had a large tract of land to the back of Fine Herbs and Such. They didn't use the land, and they were interested in finding someone to grow organic vegetables on it so that the soil could be developed. Daddy told her we were interested. So, for two years we farmed the land, growing peas, carrots, greens (kale, collards, mustards, and turnips), melons (watermelon, cantaloupe, and honeydew), rutabaga, dikon (a spicy oriental radish-like vegetable), broccoli, brussels sprouts, peppers, cabbage, onions, cauliflower, squash, lima beans, okra, radishes, beets, tomatoes, and even potatoes and corn! We ate what we grew, but we grew so much that even after giving some away we still had plenty. So, my mom and I started going with Miss Penny to the Farmers Market to sell our vegetables. Sometimes I got to sell the vegetables by myself.

Later, Miss Penny asked me to come help her sell the herbs. When we stopped farming Miss Penny's land, she offered me a paying job at her nursery.

I'm also in a garden club. I've won several first and second place ribbons for horticulture and plant design at the Pensacola Interstate Fair, and other shows—including a statewide show—with the help of Mrs. Reasoner and Mrs. White, who help direct our junior and intermediate gardening groups. Mrs. White helps us with our plant arrangements and we also enter our potted plants, dish gardens, and terrariums. Recently I won the Intermediate Achievement Award, two cut glass vases, and a blue ribbon in the Florida State Garden Show in Tampa.

WORKING WITH YOUNGER KIDS
THROUGH JOBS AND VOLUNTEER POSITIONS

I never got paid to baby-sit until last summer, 1994. Before that, as a mother's helper, I watched the homeschool moms' toddlers and babies while my brothers were on the homeschool soccer team and when we were at swim meets. (We belong to a homeschool swim team.) Helping in this way led to paying baby-sitting jobs.

I also volunteer to do things for other people. I've been helping out at the library ever since I was six, helping set up for story hour. At nine, I read to three- to five-year-olds during story hour. Now, I help stack the easy books, help kids on the computer, help people find things, and watch the children's desk. Next year I'll be old enough to volunteer for the library's summer program.

The summer program is something the library does every year for kids in P-cola. It starts around the end of May, and each year there's a different theme. Last year the theme was C.O.L.O.R., or Celebrate Our Love Of Reading. They did story hours and films having to do with color, such as *The Red Balloon*, and the mascot for the summer was a chameleon. The best part of the program, as far as I'm concerned, isn't the videos—it's the game. When you register, they give you a bookbag with a schedule for the videos and story hours for the different age groups, a pencil, a coloring sheet and/or word search puzzle, a bookmark, and a game card. The game card has a path printed on brightly colored paper. Some of the spaces on this path name a subject for a book (such as funny story, mystery, Non-fiction 000-508, etc.). Other spaces say, "Go back two spaces," "Go forward one space," or "Surprise, your choice"—which means that you get to choose your own book subject. Whenever you go to the library, you can roll the die. Whichever space you land on, you read a book of that description and write it down on the back of the game sheet. When you get to the end of the game sheet, you get a certificate and a prize.

The volunteer job isn't such a big deal considering it's more or less the same thing I've been doing the past couple of years. It will involve helping kids find books, supervising the rolling of the die, stamping kids' places on the game sheet, making displays, assembling program packets, running film reels, handing out snacks at the last program of the summer, and helping the head librarian. It may sound pretty easy, but it will probably be very challenging, and I'm looking forward to it.

Another volunteer job I did, around October of last year, was to read to second, third, fourth, and fifth graders at Hallmark, a nearby elementary school. The younger kids loved it, and the fifth graders adopted me and my family, letting us use the classroom computers. (As it turned out, although we had the teacher's permission, we didn't have permission from the principal. I got the idea that the principal didn't like me reading to the kids. What she said was that school-age children were not allowed to participate in school volunteer activities during school hours. However, the School District Volunteer Handbook states that volunteers can be of any age.)

While there, I not only got to read to the kids, but I also learned how to write haiku and got to work on the computer, and the kids and I had a good time. Most of the kids from Hallmark live in my neighborhood, so I see them around home or at the library. Most of them wave and say, "Oh yeah, I remember, you came to read to us. I really enjoyed that, thanks for coming."

HELPING WILD ANIMALS

Just recently, my mom got together with another homeschooling family, the Clarks, who have two daughters: Amy, twelve, and Caroline, eight. Our moms took us over to the wildlife rescue center. The center was founded by a lady named Nancy Treiber, and it's funded by donations from the public. People bring in sick or injured wildlife. Or, they call and let the center know about a hurt animal, and then whoever is capable of going on a "rescue" goes out and picks the animal up. We also do "pelican roundups" and other things to help Pensacola wildlife.

Our families registered to volunteer, even though we're not supposed to work directly with the animals. They need us to help with fundraisers and gardening, to grow food for some of the animals, like Sheba the sheep. We've planned a garden and a compost site, and we'll also be growing sprouts for the iguanas. Working at the center is really fun, and I enjoy being around the animals. I've also learned a lot. For example, I've watched veterinarians at work.

DANCING—AND DREAMING

Another thing I do with my time is dance. I had never danced in my life before I joined a free dance class two years ago. It was free for a month, but if you liked it you stayed on and started paying. About three months after I started, Miss Charnette, the teacher, suggested that instead of just being a class we should be a performing arts company. Everyone agreed and we decided to call ourselves Dare To Dream Dance and Performing Arts Company. About four months later we made our debut at a Fourth of July show on Pensacola Beach. We danced on a metal stage in the burning hot summer sun, in black unitards and white canvas shoes. Since then, we've danced in hospitals, schools, and nursing homes, at festivals, ceremonies, and Universal studios in Orlando. In September, we'll even dance at Miss Charnette's wedding! Besides teaching me how to dance, being a part of Dare to Dream from the beginning has taught me a lot about getting along with people, and has also helped me to realize that dreams and goals are important if you want to get anywhere in life.

YES, I DO "ACADEMICS" TOO!

By now you're probably thinking, "Wow, homeschooling sounds great! I think I'll ask my parents to take me out of school." Well, it's not that easy. In the state of Florida, parents have to contact their local school board and let them know that they will be homeschooling—and then the kids have a test or a yearly evaluation. Besides, homeschooling isn't *all* fun and games. I do some academic work through classes and at home.

FRIDAY CLASSES FOR HOMESCHOOLERS

I take lessons that our local homeschool support group provides. They change what they offer every six weeks, so if you start out (for instance) taking a beginning pencil drawing class, you could switch to a colored pencil, or a watercolor pencil, or even a chalk drawing class after six weeks. Most of the classes last an hour on Fridays at a community center. I've taken classes in water-color painting, drawing, science (physics and general), and algebra. There are also classes in tennis, German, Spanish, basic math, reading, and writing. From what I've seen of public school, these classes are much different. Some of the main differences: we have a better learning environment, classes are only once a week on Fridays, you get to choose what you want to take, and the teachers are often experts in their fields.

My art teacher, Mr. Fuller Brown, is a really good artist. He also teaches at a community college, and he sells his art throughout the South. My science/algebra teacher, Mr. Kent Hovind, has written books on science, and he travels all over the country giving lectures and teaching classes. He makes his classes fun with experiments and stories about situations he's experienced. One of the things he loves to ask us is, "Do you think you understand? Do you think?" Depending on the teacher, class might be held outside, with hands-on science experiments—such as figuring out how many pulleys it might take for a single person to tow a car, or art projects like painting your view of Escambia Bay.

LEARNING FROM OTHER CLASSES

In addition to these classes, which are organized specifically for homeschoolers, I also take classes where I might be the only homeschooler, such as my dance class. I remember well a Yamaha keyboard class, which I started when I was nine years old. I stopped taking keyboard classes when Ms. Donna Emanuel, my teacher, moved away, but she taught some helpful things in a fun way. We used to play musical forms of Bingo and Mother May I—and one of the things that made the class so fun was the fact that we were learning.

LEARNING AT HOME

I also do academic work at home. I study reading, writing, and arithmetic, plus geography, botany, and music. We don't really follow a particular schedule, except that every Monday we get a spelling test and review what we learned or observed the week before. My parents were both teachers previously, but I do most of my work myself. They tell me what workbooks to use, and help me when I have problems. So, depending on what your parents and *you* feel you are capable of doing on your own, or what they feel they are qualified to teach, or what other people you can find to learn from, you can set your own pace and decide what subjects and methods are best for you.

As for curriculum, we must have tried about six different kinds of math books—math is not my strong point—before we settled on one that worked for me. So don't worry if you can't find the right curriculum right away. Some people use the local school's curriculum, but sometimes the school curriculum isn't very good. Parents can also trade and share ideas and information; a homeschool newsletter is a good idea. How much a child learns in homeschooling depends greatly on the parent. My parents are very supportive of me and my brothers, so we naturally learn more than if they weren't. But your parents don't have to teach you. We learn many things from different people.

LEARNING FROM FAMILY FRIENDS

We have a close family friend whose name is Derrick Ames. He's a doctor who lives in Baton Rouge, Louisiana. Whenever he comes over, he teaches us juggling, history, and other things, and brings us books and videos. One time when we went to visit him, he showed us his collection of chess sets and different strategies you can use to win the game. (He has won chess tournaments.) Another friend, James Williams, is an ex-college teacher, and he teaches us Spanish. A friend who's an architect, Larry Grantham, teaches us about ancient buildings and took us on a tour of his office and houses he'd designed. He lives in Foley, Alabama, and he also brings us books and videos on architecture. He is from Frank Lloyd Wright's school, and has designed and built a Wright-style house here in Pensacola that has no right angles.

EVERY KID SHOULD BE EXPOSED TO HOMESCHOOLING!

We get a lot of freedom as far as planning our own education. Our parents give us choices, such as do we want to work on world history or Spanish history for this year, and we get to choose what Bayview classes we want to take.

Once a year we are given the Iowa Test of Basic Skills. I usually do pretty well on that, and that way I also meet other homeschooling kids outside my league group.

"Well, that's not so bad," you're probably thinking. No, it's not. But even though I really do want you to start homeschooling, it's only fair to warn you that we have run into some racism. Mainly from some of the so-called Christians, who wanted an all-white Christian homeschool league. One lady was really mean. She would rather her family and friends drop out than be in the league with us. It doesn't really bother me much, though. That's the way she was raised and even though it's wrong, *I* know the truth, and not everyone is like her. It's much better now, anyway. There's even another black family in the league, although they don't participate in league activities. And, there are still some rotten apples, but they stay out of our way and we try to stay out of theirs.

I seem to make and keep friends fairly easily. Since I'm not exposed to many *homeschoolers* of color, I'm part of several groups so I can meet *kids* of color. Three fourths of my dance class is people of color, and I also belong to a Mentoring Club which is just for people of color.

Now, even though I love homeschooling, and I think it's better in some ways than public school, that doesn't mean it's what I want to do for the rest of my pre-college life. I would like to go to a public school for high school, if only for one semester, so that I could add that experience to my life.

I love homeschooling and I'm very glad that my parents decided to homeschool me. Again, it's something I think every kid should be exposed to. Not only because of the good it will do for the kids themselves, *now*, but also because of the good it will do for *the world* in the future. It's very important for kids now to get a good education, so they can stay off the streets, stay out of jail, and grow up to take proper care of the world before it's not fit to live in anymore. ❖

John, Fela, and Sunshine Lewis at the wildlife sanctuary where they volunteer.
In the background, bald eagles Athena and Apollo, and Sheba the sheep.

John Lewis

Miss Penny and Sunshine working together at Fine Herbs and Such

Mrs. Spence, Fela Lewis, and Sunshine clean up and trim rosemary at Fine Herbs and Such.

Sunshine and friends on the way to a homeschoolers' swim team
practice and then a garden club meeting: Eli Born, John Lewis,
Terry Lewis, Fela Lewis, Sunshine Lewis, Caroline Clark, and Amy Clark.

Detra Rose Hood
Pasadena, California

LEARNING TO TRUST OURSELVES AS BLACK HOMESCHOOLERS

After my husband, MTunu, and I married in 1976 in Chicago, we planned to move to Mexico to continue our educations at the Universidad de Guadalajara. So the next July we packed our green Toyota, said good-bye to family and friends, and headed for south of the border. It was scary leaving behind everything I had been so familiar with, but I knew this venture would allow me to break out of the narrow box I had been living in.

I was definitely a little fearful not knowing what was ahead, as we traveled from state to state. But at the same time it was a kind of freedom to know we could decide our own destination, and it was quite an experience to observe the beauty of the land as we drove. In Guadalajara, we found an apartment and got settled in. We then went to the university to get information about registering. There were many things to go through, but we did finally get accepted. My husband began his studies in sculpturing, and I began mine in dance with a famous teacher, Onesimo Gonzalez. We started classes at eight o'clock in the morning, and by noon each day we were finished.

During the afternoon we would prepare our meals and visit with our neighbors. My husband spoke Spanish fluently, and although I couldn't speak a speck to begin with, I knew at some point I would have to utter a few broken words just to get used to pronouncing and hearing the sounds. Our neighbors were helpful and patient, and we became close. My husband taught the neighbor's son chess. He would come visit often to play and talk.

The Hood Family
(Tunu, Tiye, Detra Rose, and MTunu)
at the 1993 John Coltrane
Jazz Festival, at which Tunu performed

Even though I felt out of place sometimes, I enjoyed my new environment, and everyone was so friendly—sometimes people approached us and invited us into their homes. We made many friends. There was a family of African American brothers who were studying at the Universidad Autonoma in Guadalajara, and there were two African Panamanian sisters, one graduated from the Autonoma.   Onesimo and his family became close to us. There were so many people in Guadalajara—Africans from Africa, Africans from Brazil, and Africans from other places in Central America. It's like that in the States too, but it seems you are closer to people in Mexico.

I guess you may be wondering what Mexico and my travels have to do with homeschooling. Well, I think they have much to do with how I view people and things today, and we have faced parallel challenges and rewards in our homeschooling path. My experience in dealing with a different culture helped me in the challenges I would later face; in Mexico it was like *I* was being reschooled. I learned from that experience the value of treating people with kindness and making friends for life, the value of sharing and exchanging ideas about other cultures, and I also learned to overcome fears of uncertainty.

Our stay in Mexico would later be echoed by many aspects of our homeschooling adventure. In homeschooling, too, we would face the fear of leaving behind familiar territory, the excitement of exploring foreign ideas, the rewards of learning new things along with our children, the value of community interchange, and the importance of giving and receiving support from friends. We continue to seek outstanding teachers, and our children even finish their schooling each day by noon, just as we did in Mexico!

After two years we returned to Chicago and enrolled in Columbia College. I conceived my first child, and my husband and I started planning to move to California where the weather is a little less harsh. Two months after I graduated we packed up the car again, and after saying good-bye to our families and friends once more we headed west. We settled in Pasadena, not far from where we live now, and our son Tunu was born two months later in October. We now had the responsibility of sharing our combined knowledge to raise our son to the best of our ability.

DECIDING TO HOMESCHOOL

After settling in our new apartment with our new son, it became clear what our main responsibility would be from this day forth. When you are single, or married without children, your intellectual focus is not directed on the rearing of children, even though you may have many young nieces and nephews and cousins around. As soon as you have your own, you become acutely aware of what other children around you are doing. I began noticing the behavior of school age children, and how aggressive they were in their conversation and presence. I am certainly not talking about just African American children; I also noticed that their white counterparts were quite hostile with their parents. This set off an alarm in me and I began to see that a lot of young people were walking around angry and hostile. Sometimes the girls seemed even angrier than the boys.

I didn't quite understand where all this anger and hostility was coming from. So whenever I took Tunu to the park or other places where children played, I would try to talk to young people and ask them questions about school and about what they liked to do. When I'd give them the benefit of the doubt, assuming they were not bad children, they would open up.

One day all three of us met a young boy in the park, ten or twelve years of age. The park was rather empty and Tunu played by himself. While we sat and ate some fruit, the boy came over. We asked his name and about school and so on, and somehow the conversation led to television and the programs he liked to watch. He told us he liked the Playboy channel and some other adult programs. We asked him, "Well, what about homework?" and, "Do you have a curfew?" He explained that he watched every night when everyone else was in bed, and that he enjoyed seeing "white women" with blond hair do their thing. I was sort of shocked as I listened to such a young person describing this to us with a smile on his face. So I said, "If you are up that late, how are you doing in your school work?" That didn't seem important to him. What was important, he exclaimed, was watching his white teacher in her short dresses.

That incident gave me a lot to think about, and we started discussing what was really going on in the school system. I didn't blame the school system for that boy's attitude; that kind of problem obviously starts in the home. But I was concerned about what some children—of all races—bring from their homes and then present to others on the school's playground. The peer pressure is harsh and real on the campus, and no school is immune. Even though I knew a lot of Black male students made it through the school system, some even becoming high achievers, it bothered me to hear and see the negative things children were saying and doing. I began asking myself whether I wanted to leave my child's education to chance in this system that seemed out of control.

For a number of reasons, we eventually made the decision not to send Tunu to school. Our main reason at first was our fruitarian diet and lifestyle. But other issues concerned us too. The news reported that many kids graduated from school incapable of reading well. We saw school children get off their buses in the afternoon, cursing to each other and to adults. We knew school violence was increasing, and that many teachers were afraid of their own students—even *kindergarten* students. And we saw that the most common problem of the school system was thinking all children should learn at the same pace, study the same thing, and retain information the same way. That produced a lot of frustrated parents and confused young students who wanted to understand and learn, but who had no base to hold on to and no one to slow down and show them the way. Eventually, these issues became our main reasons for homeschooling, more important than our vegetarian lifestyle.

HOMESCHOOLING THROUGH PRESCHOOL

At around age three, Tunu started showing signs of his artistic inclinations. He started talking early and when something struck his interest he would begin calling out its name. For instance, just riding in the car would bring on an outburst of, "Lights! Lights! Lights!" as he pointed to street and traffic lights. When he saw clocks, the same thing would happen. When we returned home he would go straight to a big blackboard in the hallway and draw what he had just seen. From then on, we kept drawing pads and pencils in the car. My husband is an artist, so Tunu had many opportunities to watch and help with projects.

Also during this time, we introduced him to different artistic activities. Those were the nice relaxing days of no pressure. We'd wake up, eat breakfast, clean up, read stories, and do an art project such as working with clay. Some days we would paint, and for special projects we'd put together solar windmill kits or do solar art. In the afternoon we'd listen to story tapes while eating lunch. Then we'd go for a nature walk around the neighborhood or to the park. We would discover different shapes of leaves, feed the squirrels, see if we could identify the different fruit trees, and collect pine cones to begin another art project.

Tunu began writing, learning his alphabet, and reading at an early age. I was content for him to lead the way to what he wanted to learn. Some days he liked to write more, other days he liked to listen to stories or try to read simple ones. He received his first library card at age four, and wrote his name on the card and application. One of the first books he borrowed was about a duck named Paling who lived on the Yangtze river in China. I had to read that book to him about twenty times, and I was glad when the due date came! But the next time we returned to the library he found the same book, and I couldn't persuade him to get another. So I read it about twenty more times.

PLANNING AND CHOOSING A CURRICULUM

These early years of learning gave me time to organize and plan for the future. It was not necessary to have a special room for class—living in an apartment didn't allow that. I think organization, though, is the key to success in this venture of homeschooling. In the beginning, I think a filing system of some type is necessary. If you plan to start homeschooling, you will probably collect a lot of materials and catalogs that you may not use right away but would like to get back to later. One of the early resources I contacted was the *World Book* encyclopedia, and they sent me useful, free kindergarten through third grade materials: posters on various subjects, parts of speech posters, and the "Scope and Sequence" on what subjects were taught in the public school systems.

Investigating what type of things are happening in your community can also make you aware of valuable resources. Keep a list of what kind of classes are being offered at the Boys Club, community centers, etc. Even private organizations sometime offer African-centered programs.

I didn't start off following any particular curriculum. I hoped to find a Black publisher that offered some type of curriculum in reading or social studies, but that didn't happen. My main two focal points were math and reading. In teaching Tunu reading I did use a phonics method, and let me stress that it worked for him.

As time went on I knew I had to decide whether to follow a formal curriculum or make up one of my own. I made the decision to use a formal curriculum for math and language arts only. For social studies, science, music, art, and physical education, I would construct my own. This meant I had two things to work on. First, to find the right curriculum for math and language arts I would have to go through hundreds of catalogs. Second, I'd start building my library with information I would need for the other subjects.

(Yes, all this sounds like it takes a lot of time, and it does. To be a successful homeschooler, you do need total commitment. I notice that a lot of parents have limitations about how far they want to interact with their children's education. When my son was in a gymnastics class a group of parents were talking about their children's school. They turned around and asked me about my son's school, and I told them we homeschooled. One of the parents declared adamantly that she would never try to teach her children curriculum. I replied that it was easy to send your children to a stranger and let her or him teach them, but much harder to undo the negative attitudes about learning that children picked up in school.)

Sending off for catalogs and looking through them can get kind of confusing, and you can't really decide from catalogs if particular materials are exactly right for you. You do take chances this way. I chose carefully, because I didn't want to have to keep changing down the road to a different curriculum. Besides, most homeschoolers are on a fixed budget, so it pays to do the right research.

Another ingredient to successful homeschooling is perseverance, being able to move forward against all odds. There were times when I had reservations about not sending my son to school. The fears came, perhaps, from a lack of confidence in myself. Coming from a background in the public school system, that mentality gets imbedded in you, and if you are not careful, homeschooling becomes a mental conflict. When I began preparing Tunu's academic work, I'd sometimes wonder, "Are they doing this in school?" "Am I keeping him behind?" "Should I be teaching this subject now or later?" In other words, my mind had not become totally independent of the system's influences. But even though I was a little apprehensive about my undertaking, I also knew that throwing him into a system that didn't care about a Black boychild's progress or success was *not* the solution. That kept me steadfast on my vision of independence.

Tunu was about four years old when I made a friend who shared my interest in vegetarianism and fruitarianism. We often talked about food preparation, and in our conversations, homeschooling came up. She was interested in taking her five children out of school, and she had been doing her own research. She'd had many problems communicating with her children's teachers—I don't know exactly what the situation was, but she was tired of it. Together, my friend and I continued to research. I still had some time to think about what type of formal information I wanted to give Tunu, to acquire information about homeschooling support groups, and to learn about the California laws on keeping a child out of school.

My newfound friend had so much energy I wondered where she got it all. She had to take care of a husband, a home, and five children—and then she wanted to take them out of school! That was a commitment I was glad I didn't have to face. She inspired me to pursue my own goals with vigor. Having someone around with a common interest helped me to stay focused on the road I wanted to take. My friend was very much a Christian, but open to new ideas.

One day my friend told me she knew of a homeschool parent in the area who wanted to invite us over so we could look at the curriculum she was using and to talk about the "Umbrella," a homeschooling support service that helps parents get their children's records from school, helps with curriculum planning, informs parents about changing laws, and has a newsletter and field trips for children. So we met at this person's home one day, and she turned out to be Caucasian and Christian. As we entered her home I noticed how she used all the rooms to display samples of her children's schoolwork. She led us to a table in her dining room where the books she wanted to show us were spread out. She had two different types of curriculum, both Christian. I wasn't enthusiastic, but wanted her to go on and share whatever she needed to tell us. She talked about the pros and cons she had experienced in using these books.

I picked up the A Beka math book—about second grade level—and began to go through it carefully. I had noticed that many private schools used A Beka books, but I felt, at the time, that by using a Christian curriculum I would be pushing religion, and I didn't want to do that. At first glance the math book seemed interesting, though, so I continued to look. It was presented in a colorful fashion, but the majority of the images of people were white; the few people of color were illustrated in a caricature kind of way. As I focused on the way the math itself was presented, though, I was impressed with how they explained different topics. I also looked at the A Beka language arts book and its sequence, too, was easy and interesting enough for a child to keep focused. So I decided not to rule out A Beka.

Our hostess began to tell us about a reader she was using on the life of George Washington Carver. She went on about how he was a happy slave and had a good master and if it wasn't for his Christian belief he would not have become the genius, scientist, and inventor that he was. I became agitated because she was trying to convince me of the good master/happy slave theory. I asked her how could a person who owned another be "good," and how could a person who was stripped of his land, language, and freedom be happy? We went back and forth with this until I realized there was no end. I said thanks once again and left.

So what did I accomplish from that meeting? I became even more aware of how some Caucasian Christian people think they are doing "good" by teaching children what they think is African American history, when in fact they are doing an injustice. It would be better not to teach the history of another people if you are not going to tell the truth.

At that point, my task of searching out a curriculum became twofold: to make sure it had all the necessary elements to accelerate my child's learning abilities, and to make sure it was not culturally biased. It was a long and difficult search, and my quest to find the perfect math and language arts book did not succeed. I didn't see many curriculums that didn't have at least some biases. So I picked the lesser of the evils: A Beka for math and language, even though it was a Christian publication.

A Beka's selling point was its ability to present and explain the problems in an orderly and easy to understand way. And even in the early grades, it challenged the students with a variety of math concepts. But one of the complaints I and other A Beka users have is the repetition of certain concepts. If you're not careful, you can spend a lot of time repeating and getting caught up. I had to learn to determine when my child had mastered a concept and the right time to move on to another. If he later forgot anything, we could always go back to review.

Another thing about following a certain curriculum is that you tend to simply follow what's between the pages. But I began incorporating the history of mathematics, beginning with the ancient numerical systems. Finding the right information was no easy matter even though there are a lot of books dealing with that aspect of history. Almost all avoided the question of the African foundations of mathematics, by starting the history of mathematics in Greece.

After some persistent research, I came across the *African-American Baseline Essays*. This is a series of essays that give information about the history, culture, and contributions of a specific geocultural group—art, language, language arts, mathematics, science, social studies and music. The essays were done for the Portland, Oregon public schools. They offer a holistic and thematic history of the culture and contributions of each specific geocultural group, from ancient times to the present. These essays have helped me in preparing a study plan for any particular subject we were studying, especially in African history. Also, they have excellent references and bibliographies to facilitate follow up reading and library-building. Another thing I like about the essays is that you can use their information for any grade level, since they have a curriculum outline for kindergarten through sixth grade. In fact, my son is now at ninth grade level and I still use the essays.

My daughter was born at home on February 14, 1986 on a stormy morning. We'd planned for her home birth, and my son got a chance to participate in the coming of his sister. It was an exciting morning for all of us, not knowing whether it was a girl or boy. I know my family was kind of skeptical about me not going into the hospital, but none of them really voiced their concerns until after she was born. We named Tiye after the Nubian queen, mother of Tutankhamen.

It took a little doing to get my footing after that. With all the middle-of-the-night feedings and the piles of diapers, I had to find a different approach to homeschooling. It took a while to establish a working routine, with one child breastfeeding and the other child asking questions and needing more attention and guidance. I have listened to the stories of one of my neighbors, who has four boys and also homeschools. Whenever I see them all together it amazes me how she can do it. But I know if you have a good support system you have won half the battle. That means your husband, soulmate, family members, church, etc.—whatever works for you.

(Since we have no relatives in California, MTunu has been my main support system. Even before we decided to homeschool, we made plans together for our family's growth, researched the local public schools, sat in on classrooms, and visited Black private schools. Even they didn't offer what we really wanted, though one of them did have an Afro-centric curriculum. When we started homeschooling, my husband taught Tunu calligraphy and art, and read him history and geography. He hasn't always had time to formally prepare lessons, but he has shared a lot, and his involvement inspired Tunu to read history and geography on his own. MTunu has consistently encouraged me in this homeschooling effort, and his support has helped greatly.)

This brings me back to the friend I mentioned earlier, who took her five children out of school. With all her enthusiasm and energy, it ended up not working for her. If your mate doesn't have faith in what you are doing and is not there to help build up your confidence, or feels it's all your responsibility to educate the children, it can become overwhelming. That's the way it was for my friend, unfortunately. The natural disagreements and misunderstandings that occur in any relationship, coupled with the politics of having your children at home with you much of the time, can put wear and tear on a marriage especially if one of the partners is not in it for the long haul. I felt badly that my friend had to abandon her dreams and hopes of educating her children, and had to return them to the system.

After a couple of years passed, things got a little easier to manage. My son got more involved in outside activities. We enrolled him in his first gymnastics classes around the age of six. He also had a strong interest in basketball and would run around the court trying to make baskets for hours.

When Tunu was about seven, we visited a piano store just to look around. He was so fascinated with the pianos that we couldn't get him out of the store. His father decided to buy one; I looked and said, "Is that in our budget?!" Well, we bought the piano and I coughed it up as our first major investment in Tunu's education. I soon enrolled him in a music conservatory offered in the Pasadena City College where they had a music program for young children. Then one morning my husband read me a newspaper article about a jazz pianist who taught at the community center. I was excited to know there was this person who was interested in sharing his wealth of knowledge with children in the neighborhood. So, the next day we went to Jackie Robinson's park where the community classes were being held. We met Mr. Sonny Phillips, the teacher, and he explained to us what the classes would be about. I was exhilarated and somehow during the conversation I realized he was talking about *me* taking the class also. Tunu continued his semester with the conservatory, and at the first of the year we enrolled him and me in Mr. Phillips' class. Sonny Phillips is an accomplished musician who has a number of credits to his name as a recording artist and is well known as a blues organist. We felt privileged to be in the company of such a master.

Tunu took to the classes right away and I was—well, let's just say I was *there* and eager to learn. Tunu and I became study partners. It was fun and challenging for me and I cherished those days that we played together. Sometimes our study time got combative—like many young boys, Tunu often seemed motivated by competition. I'd sit down at the piano and he'd tell me what I was doing wrong, and show me how he could play better and faster. Though I'm not a competitive person, I didn't mind; the sense of friendly competition helped get him to really focus on technique and to go beyond his assigned lessons. And on many days we would sit and play together peacefully, and the sound would come together, and it would all be good.

I soon became known as the "back-up mother." I accompanied my son at recitals for a number of years. Then there came a time when I suddenly noticed my son's progress and realized he needed to venture out into his own space. So I started setting him up to play at neighborhood events and festivals, and later contacted the Alice Coltrane Organization. He was a guest artist for two years at the Coltrane Festival. Later, at the age of thirteen, he entered the John Coltrane Youth Competition and won first prize, a five hundred dollar scholarship. He also entered the Downbeat Jazz Competition, and the next year was picked as Best Performing Artist in their youth competition.

Homeschooling has definitely helped Tunu to develop his musical talents. Often he plays early in the morning, with fresh, renewed energy. It's good to be able to devote your "prime time," or the part of the day when you focus best, to your most important interests. I've also noticed that when he plays in the morning, it sets a calm, centered tone for the whole day. Homeschooling allows children to really develop their strengths, and to give them their full, undistracted attention.

I am proud of the accomplishments Tunu has made in his music, and Tunu is pleased too. He often wonders why people only talk to him about his music, though; he would prefer talking about his drawings and the buildings he has done on his train layout, or about electronics, or building a remote control car, or becoming an architectural engineer. I have to remind him that people respect his talent, that he is admired for his musical accomplishments, and that he does not have to feel embarrassed about any of this. Tunu continues to study piano, and we are glad to be able to teach our children about the great artists and musicians who came before them.

We are also eager to tell them about the great African civilizations and leaders who died and left a legacy of information for us to study. We try to instill in Tunu and Tiye that they can master as many talents as they like. We often refer to Imhotep, the great thinker of ancient Egypt—philosopher, master builder, architect, healer, father of medicine, and master of all learning. Knowing the history of our people empowers our children with self-esteem that will build the confidence and skills they'll need to make it in this world.

Detra Rose Hood

Tiye has grown up watching her brother do many things, which has encouraged her also to forge forward in whatever she feels inclined to do. She enjoys reading and is a very physical person. We've enrolled her in gymnastic classes; she feels she'd like to compete. She is also a dancer who studies ballet and tap, and when she performs on stage she displays tremendous confidence.

I've started Tiye with A Beka math, but have also invented a lot of math curriculum with her. She is a different type of learner, more into hands-on activities, than her brother. She likes to work all kinds of puzzles and has became a great chess player, often beating her father and brother. I had bought the Mortensen's Math (an activity that teaches basic and higher math skills) for her brother to use, but Tiye has found it more interesting.

Tiye's favorite pastime is drawing and writing stories about her drawings. Our bonding time is when we sit for hours together making dolls and jewelry. She is quite an entrepreneur, and has sold many of her children's jewelry designs. Somehow, though, she can't let go of the dolls she makes. She wants to be a actress and a lawyer. Truly nature's child, she enjoys gardening and discovering the variety of bugs and insects in our backyard.

Tiye informed me recently that she would like a pet turtle and that she wanted to find out about the different types of turtles. So we went to a pet store and bought a book on turtle care. After reading that, she decided to take care of a green worm she found in the vegetables to see how it feels to feed and clean out the cage every day. She told me that was her experiment before she'd decide to commit to a real pet. After several days, she decided it was hard work and a lot of responsibility to remember to take care of a pet, but she still wanted to try.

Again and again, my children show me how homeschooling helps develop independent thinking and promotes independent action. It allows children to expand their minds and to think things through to the fullest. I say this because I often hear that in classroom situations, children depend on the teachers to give them all the answers. Several parents of school children have spoken to me about their concerns, and I suggest they try working with their children at home. Children get used to being spoon-fed education, and passivity soon becomes a habit. Habits are hard to break.

Tiye is nine years old presently, and doing third grade work. She likes the challenge of math but says she enjoys language and writing more. She has a pen-pal she enjoys writing to and sharing her drawing with.

I didn't start off in the early years keeping records on my children; I began at about third grade. Over time, keeping records gives you some idea of children's progress. With them, you are able to determine his or her weaknesses and provide the necessary help. Also, if you are approached by any school official, instead of just verbalizing what your child can do, you have something on paper to show. You will have to come up with some creative ways of keeping your own records. If you believe in tests or quizzes, they can cover more than just simple facts. Assessing the lessons you teach, and looking for new ways to improve, is something else to look into.

My preparation for lessons includes many things: setting time aside to review the materials needed, reading about the subject, choosing objectives, forming a plan, gathering materials, and planning quizzes and tests. I feel enthusiastic when my children and I are researching, investigating, and discovering new concepts—whether in science, math, language arts, or history. I get more excited about some subjects than others, but try to give a balance. Variety comes into play when we use hands-on activities, discussions, and lectures as well as reading assignments and field trips. There are a number of television programs—PBS, The Learning Channel, and The Discovery Channel—that offer free Network Educator's Guides to homeschoolers as well as classroom teachers. Being involved in my children's studies by asking questions, allowing them to discuss their activities and subjects, and helping them discover new approaches to learning has been one of our goals. I have also taken classes *with* my children—piano, dance, history—and my children have no problem with this.

THE NEW OLMECS (TI-TU ACADEMY)

Most homeschoolers I have met have given their school a name, usually derived from their political and/or religious ideology. We have formulated our own values and doctrines that guide us in our everyday life and our African culture. Ti-Tu Academy belongs to Tiye and Tunu, as the name suggests. Our school is centered around them and the things they are involved in; therefore, they are allowed some freedom to define what they would like to pursue in their studies.

The other part of our name, "The New Olmecs," stands for "Natural Environment Wherein Optimum Learning Motivates Excellent, Courageous Students." It came from another visit we made to Mexico some years ago. We visited with Onesimo, his wife Sonia, and their family, and they took us on a tour around Veracruz—Sonia is a anthropologist and dancer who had studied the ruins there. We drove to Xapala, where a museum houses some of the giant stone Olmec heads found around that area. (The Olmecs dated back to around 800 BC, and were the first people of Mexico.) When we saw one of the heads, we were amazed at what African features it had; none of the native people came close to having features like that. It was clearly a separate colony of people, with a distinct culture, that carved this work of art. I won't go into the historical background of the heads, but a good reference is Ivan Van Sertima's *They Came Before Columbus*.

Anyway, our reason for naming our school "The New Olmecs" was that we wanted to keep the connection between our African forefathers and our Mexican brothers. As African people in the new world, we have the right and responsibility to identify with Africans who came before slavery. We feel these African people left a legacy of cooperative work with the indigenous people, and created the first true civilization in Mexico. The historical records show these Africans pioneered the way for other Africans to come to the so-called "new world." African Americans often think of our history as only coming from the mother continent, but we also need to develop new and different relationships with our brothers and sisters across the Texas border. Of course, the media and politics do a good job of keeping the Mexican people and African Americans at odds with each other.

THE POLITICS OF SCHOOLING—AND SOCIALIZATION

As we all realize by now, our school system has a history of not giving the necessary attention to our young people. Our young Black children end up disillusioned about the system and drop out. Why is there no solution for the overwhelming growing problems in our schools? School officials claim it is because of the lack of funds that our children are not equipped with tools for success. I say it is because their priorities are simply not centered around the health and welfare of our children. So, we continue to keep our children at home, because we are troubled by the politics and racism of the educational system, and we don't care to get our children caught up and lost in the shuffle. We see the politics of whether or not morality should be taught in the schools; the politics of socialization; the politics of which schools should be getting up-to-date books, supplies, computers etc.; the politics of conforming to the System. The School System disseminates education in an imbalanced way, and it ignores our African children, especially boys.

When MTunu and I continue to hear outcries about things happening to young people in school, it reinforces our faith in what we are doing for Tunu and Tiye. Even the question of socialization comes only from those who don't wholly understand homeschooling. I am often approached with the question, "What about learning how to play with other children?" I usually respond, "How can you be concerned about my children's socialization, given what school socialization is like?" The schools can only do their best to reinforce good behavior, because they don't have enough time to teach or reteach moral behavior. But in many homes, children don't learn to respect one another or to not hurt each other by name calling or making fun of each other. Teachers are overburdened with bad social behaviors in the classroom, and there is bound to be a fallout of aggression on the playground.

I personally feel that kind of social behavior is *not* a necessary ingredient to learning. In fact, it is non-essential for the mental well being of any child. After a parent has approached me with their concern about homeschoolers' socialization, and then I see their little Oscar giving another child a blow upside the head with joy, and I hear all kinds of cursing and disrespectful languages coming out of the mouths of babes or young adults, I know these parents' socialization theory is definitely not working. I have to ask myself, is it *socialization* we see on the campuses, or is it peer pressure and chaos? I'm not promoting homeschooling as the answer for everyone, and it cannot solve all our problems, but certainly, homeschooling parents can see problems germinating in their children and at least give direct and early attention to them.

EXPLORING HOMESCHOOLING WITH OTHERS

One of the things available to us as homeschoolers in the Pasadena area was an electricity workshop offered by a Caucasian Christian lady. The classes were held at a Christian school where she rented space for her workshops, and were held three days a week for two weeks. Her curriculum was geared to third through eighth graders; it was informative and she presented hands-on activities to work on, such as conductors, making a doorbell, and finally wiring a light socket for a lamp. My son and the other students were excited about what they were learning and I felt this was just another harmless opportunity for contact with other homeschool families. There were two other Black families who participated.

The class went smoothly, I thought, up until the last day. I had to go to the farmers' market, and one of the other Black parents stayed with the children. When I returned, the lesson was over, but all the children except mine and my friend's were in a circle with the teacher praying over them. She asked one of the students to hold out his legs, and told him half of his body was uneven but she could heal him if he believed. She started praying and holding his legs, and as everyone watched she said, "Now your body is even." She then did this to a number of students. One student's legs didn't respond and she told him he had to pray harder. Now, I didn't have a problem with her being Caucasian, and I didn't have a problem with her being a Christian as long as the classes didn't have religious overtones. What I *did* have a problem with at the end was the fact that she imposed her views on the children. They did not understand where she was coming from, and anyway, I had paid for an electricity class, not a class in religious healing. I was upset, though glad my children had not directly participated. We didn't return to any of her other sessions.

Since homeschoolers believe each family has the right to choose their own individualized life style and philosophy, when we open up workshops and classes to the homeschooling public we should consider and respect the fact that homeschoolers' views may differ. I thought this teacher should have just dismissed those students who were not interested, instead of holding the whole class captive.

There were other workshops we attended with my friend Penny Wright, a homeschooler with two daughters. She introduced me to another homeschool organization that presented a variety of one-day science workshops, taught by a retired schoolteacher. The workshops covered subjects from earth sciences to biology to chemistry, introducing basic concepts and presenting hands-on experiments. When we began taking the classes, they were being held in San Bernardino—quite a distance away from us. The hour and half ride was a serious outing. My children enjoyed the sessions we chose, which most times were related to our home curriculum. This gave them a different outlet to express themselves. The teacher, again, was a Christian, but she didn't make us feel uncomfortable. We got the information she presented to the class, and that was enough.

WE START OUR OWN AFRICAN AMERICAN HOMESCHOOLING NETWORK

We participated in many of these workshops and I was thankful to Penny for sharing them with us. I was also grateful for the opportunity to be involved in the workshops, and for the chance for my children to receive valuable information in a non-competitive way. But since we had to travel so far and on the days we attended the workshop, my friend's and my families were the only Black people, I was still unsatisfied. I had been coming into contact with other African American homeschooling families in the area, and exchanging ideas about education and other things we had in common. I noticed that in our conversations there was a consensus that we needed to expand what we were teaching in the area of science.

Eventually I felt there were enough of us to try to start workshops for our children, who were around the same age. Our children had been getting to know each other, and I thought, well, why not come together and network? We were all doing that informally in one form or another anyway. I was excited about the thought of coming together for a common cause and started making calls to other African American homeschoolers who were not in the immediate area. My purpose was to bring together our children—first to give them an opportunity to socialize and form a common bond, and second to develop workshops in subjects that challenged us in our individual homeschool situations.

Penny and I had been discussing the prospect of forming an African American homeschooling network, and she thought it was a good idea. One day she told me about a woman from NASA's Jet Propulsion Laboratory who had spoken at her church about an outreach science program offered in the neighboring public schools. Penny gave me the details and right away I made contact with this woman, Dr. Yvonne Freeman. I told her who we were and that as a group we were interested in starting some type of tutoring program.

I must admit I was kind of apprehensive about discussing homeschooling with her, because you never know what kind of backlash you may receive from exposing yourself to others, and even after my descriptions strangers still don't fully understand what I'm talking about. Anyway, in trying to find out what kind of services we could tap into, I gave her a list of things we were interested in—field trips to JPL, use of their science resource center information, a tutor, Space Camp information, etc. I think in my excitement I sort of overwhelmed her, but to my surprise she told me whom to contact for a tour of JPL, the location of the resource center open to all teachers, space camp information, and the name of her associate who ran a tutoring/mentoring program made up of African American workers who were concerned about children's progress in school.

The next morning I gave her associate, Mr. Clint Simmons, a phone call. I introduced myself and once again approached the conversation with caution, not knowing what his response would be. After my brief description of homeschooling, we talked about the number of parents and children who would be involved. There were eight families and about twenty children interested in the program in the beginning. He

The families met first with each other to talk about their concerns. Most were Christian. I encouraged them to bring their religious beliefs with them to our class, but I also explained that our actual class time was limited. Certainly, they were welcome to pray *before* class. I knew their home science curriculums were based on creation theory, and wanted to give them the opportunity to voice their opinions. From the start, I wanted them to feel comfortable about bringing their ideas to our network. Essentially, I hoped that together we could implement services that would benefit all of our children, regardless of our differences. And they seemed open to this possibility.

Next, about five families met with Mr. Simmons and we all were curious about him and his volunteer organization, Alpha Association. Its purpose was to provide orientation, through networking, for Black employees at NASA's Jet Propulsion Laboratory. Members set up programs in local elementary and high schools, and volunteered lunch times, evenings, and weekends to tutor. The organization helped students reach their goal of attending college, even giving scholarships to help make this possible. As Mr. Simmons spoke about his dedication to pass on positive images so that young people could see Black professionals in science, engineering, and related fields, I knew we needed that for our homeschooling children too.

One or two families were concerned about the fact that Mr. Simmons concentrated solely on Black children, but it didn't bother me one bit. In fact, I was happy to hear it. Mr. Simmons explained to us how he would approach the curriculum using hands-on and visual aides. He also made it clear that he was interested in just teaching the facts, and not in discussing religion. This seemed all right with everyone, but I later realized that everyone hadn't honestly communicated their true feelings in the beginning. Well, Mr. Simmons decided to adopt our program and we began in October 1991 with our first classes, which were free of charge to all of our African American students. I found a place for us to hold our classes at the park recreation center. Penny and I knew that we would have to collaborate with Mr. Simmons, to help him in the presentation of his materials and in doing research.

About twenty children participated in our first session. We all came from different backgrounds and beliefs, but nevertheless our common ground was homeschooling and we could build from that, or so I thought. The classes met once a week for about a hour and a half for ten weeks. When the first class started, the parents also met and we formulated ideas to keep the program running smoothly. We decided what weeks. When the first class started, the parents also met and we formulated ideas to keep the program running smoothly. We decided what extra research the children would do, and then homework and assigned reading material were prepared by Mr. Simmons. We set up guidelines to evaluate how the program could be more effective, and rules on how the students should behave in class. We definitely didn't see ourselves as a private school, because not all of our curriculum was dependent on the network—just our shared science classes.

Mr. Simmons also had an assistant, an Ethiopian woman, which gave our class another dimension. The children were excited with the first class. It started out with the earth sciences—the planets, what makes the weather and chemistry of the earth. Written quizzes and tests were given to the older children, and the younger ones were given oral tests. These tests were not to classify the students in any way, but rather to help them understand the information that was given to them. The second semester they studied electronics and simple chemistry. Our network was working together on a common goal and our children were getting valuable information.

The network continued to meet regularly to discuss the format of the classes. We collected dues for materials we needed, and one of the mothers was always available to help Mr. Simmons and his assistant. All parents were responsible for their own children's behavior. Places had to be found to hold our classes, and I usually did that research. Penny and other parents shared other tasks. This was good because we all felt responsible for the success of the program.

At the end of our first year we planned a commencement banquet. The children displayed their science projects and talents such as music, singing, and readings. We gave Mr. Simmons an appreciation gift and he gave the children certificates of achievement. Some homeschooling families attended who were not in our network. All in all, we were pleased with our first year. Still, though, we had to come to terms with the idea that we had to meet on a regular basis, which felt regimented to some people. And some families traveled from a long distance, which could be a problem. Even I felt a sense of intrusion on my time, since I'd had to plan and organize people and places.

The next school year we opened with some new families attending the program, and a few of the last year's families deciding not to return. We decided to plan a more detailed class on electronics—some of the students showed interest in robotics and we thought that it would be challenging for them. We also did an eight-week chemistry class that taught facts about the atom, the state of matter, molecules and compounds, and understanding the table of elements. The class was advanced for some of our younger students, but they grasped the information because parents got involved in giving them resources pertaining to their individual levels. Also, each family brought in experiments related to the subject at hand.

One parent who was instrumental to the success of the chemistry class was Valinda De Cohen, who assisted Mr. Simmons in giving both the younger children and some adults a basic understanding of the subject. The sharing and involvement she exemplified was the core of what our network was all about. She was quiet, but would bring all kinds of stuff to the class, and come in and set up experiments. She really helped and encouraged our kids to go over and beyond the basics.

Another person who was involved in the program almost from the beginning was Mrs. Dorothy Brown, a retired teacher interested in finding out about homeschooling. She realized she could use some of our techniques in tutoring her granddaughter, though she was enrolled in public school. So, Dorothy tutored younger students who had trouble following the classes. She was an invaluable part of the network, always there and ready to work. Her knowledge and insight helped me in many ways and we still maintain a close relationship.

Mr. Brown, Dorothy's husband, is a retired chemistry and biology teacher. He presented many workshops for our children, bringing with him a wisdom I hope they will remember. Our first meeting with him gave us insight into the way the system works with our children— both the school system and also the larger system of society, which determines many aspects of the school system. He adamantly explained what we as parents needed to do to prepare our children for college. We had to instill a sense of responsibility to their parents and to themselves, to teach them to care for their bodies and to respect others. We discussed techniques for developing positive attitudes toward math and science; some of the things he felt were needed to be a successful student were understanding methods of inquiry, observation skills, reading comprehension, language and speaking skills, problem solving skills, note taking, pre-algebra, and applied math. Mr. Brown was like an advisor and counselor to me.

The children were inspired by Mr. Brown's classes too. He presented information informally, allowing them to formulate conclusions and bring in ideas and their own projects to share. His workshops dealt mainly with biology, and he also devised a series of math problems to see how good the students' computation skills were. Once he gave a session on worms, describing all the body parts. (We learned that a worm has five hearts!) His workshops were a hit.

Not only did our network present science classes and field trips, but it also allowed us to do other things as a group. For one thing, we attained access to the Jet Propulsion Laboratory's resource center for teachers. They offered information on a variety of science topics, classroom posters, stickers, science videos, and allowed us to use their curriculum outline if necessary—all for free. Some of us attended a teachers' workshop at JPL which certified us to use their treasured MoonRock—yes, a rock from the moon, one of few housed in this part of the country.

We also had a one-day heart workshop presented by the American Heart Association School Site Program, and a workshop with a noted African artist. And, some of our children were picked to be extras in a major TV production, *Men Don't Tell*, starring Jessica Lange. (We happened to be holding a class at the Boys' Club when agents came in scouting.) The children enjoyed themselves tremendously, despite the attitude of the on-site tutor employed by the production company; she seemed rather put out that they brought their own projects, kept themselves busy, and didn't need her services.

As a group, some of the parents volunteered to tutor during one summer at the neighborhood Boys Club. So, we suddenly found ourselves surrounded by a group of young public school students, from second to eighth grades. Our first important task was to simply get the attention of the students, and then to supply them with helpful tutoring. This was not one-on-one; it was more like ten- or fifteen-on-one. Personal coaching was impossible, so we devised a curriculum that enabled each grade level to learn something. Another difficult thing we had to break through were the attitudes these kids had about learning. They didn't want to take an active part in learning, and they were afraid of trying new concepts. We struggled before the boys were able to open up and accept learning for that short time. I am not quite sure if we made any permanent changes in their attitudes, but I like to think we did.

This tutoring session surely proved to be a challenge for us—not just because of the students, but also because of some of the staff, who didn't understand our commitment and our sense of working together. We also got some insight into what goes on in school classrooms, and I guess you can say we sympathized with teachers' difficult position.

Another event we did together as a homeschool networking group was a public radio show called *The Family Tree*. A friend of mine contacted me because she was producing a series of shows on the educational system and educational alternatives. I invited some of the network families to participate, because each family had knowledge in different areas to share with the general public. On the air, we discussed issues such the legal aspect, curriculum, support groups 'and umbrellas, working while homeschooling, and single parent homeschooling. The show was informative and we were satisfied in general, but we did feel the producer could have done more research, instead of assuming she already knew about homeschooling. After all, it's an extremely diverse topic.

One disturbing thing happened in our network one year.

Our problem arose when a new Black family entered the group. At a regular meeting, we informed the mother about the purpose of the network, and then began our discussion about future workshops and other things. She agreed with the idea of having the robotics classes, but she wanted to have some other friends participate, and they were Asian. I didn't see anything wrong with that; we had opened up field trips to other people in the past. As long as she understood that the body of the network was Black parents who wanted to plan and make decisions for their Black children, fine. We discussed it among ourselves and then with Mr. Simmons, who didn't feel it was a big deal as long as everyone understood the reasons for his dedication to mentoring Black children. But I guess none of this was good enough for our new member. She apparently felt she needed to come in and change things without respecting those of us who had formulated the network. I ended up feeling that we were being spied upon and criticized by someone who had false intentions and wanted to change the ideas and conceptions of the network. She even called me a racist.

At this point, it was hard to stay focused on the positive—which was presenting the actual classes. We tried hard, though, to keep a smooth and pleasant atmosphere for our children. I tried to avoid, as much as possible, the negativity that this new family displayed. In retrospect, I guess what I could have done was to not let her child participate, and allow just the two Asian families in instead. They understood our purpose, and they weren't interested in becoming members anyway. They knew they had the opportunity to be involved in any Asian center, and the whole thing just wasn't an issue to them. For some reason, though, it was an issue for this Black family.

I wanted to form alliances where we as Black homeschoolers could be in control of information pertaining to ourselves and our children, collecting and sharing information, setting up a support group and eventually forming a strong organizational base to provide some of the things our children needed. At the beginning everyone was supportive of this idea, but as time went on and we began working toward those things, some of the network parents started to show their fears of becoming an independent group of Black people. The conclusion I've deduced is that we as Black people have become comfortable in letting other people outside of ourselves dictate how we should homeschool. While Christian, Caucasian homeschool organizations have apparently flourished without the assistance of any outside groups, Black homeschoolers find it easier to be followers than leaders. Somehow, we will have to learn to trust ourselves, and to grow comfortable and secure despite our differences.

I learned some valuable lessons from our network. I made long-lasting friendships, and the group experience was positive most of the time. I gained organizational experience, and I learned to be open to, and work with, people's ideological differences. I used to think Christianity taught people to be tolerant of others, but unfortunately, I learned that many Christians aren't nearly as tolerant and open as non-Christians. I guess I learned to be tolerant despite others' intolerances. I learned some lessons the hard way—perhaps I was a little naive in the beginning in my vision of people working together and sharing ideas even if they disagreed in some respects. I felt every person's own identity was important and that their opinion was important to the group, and I often would state this in meetings. But if people are not honest with you about their beliefs, or if they feel other beliefs are a threat to their existence and they are not honest enough to communicate this, then problems will soon develop.

I eventually left the network largely because I wanted to focus more on my own family, and on Tunu's educational needs. But I haven't given up on it; in fact, since Tiye is getting older and needs to be around her peers, I look forward to organizing more network activities for the coming year.

LOOKING TOWARD OUR FUTURE

Because I hear that fewer African American students enter college every year, I am concerned about how I, as a homeschooling parent, can make college available to my children. Tunu is presently around the ninth grade, which brings a new dimension to the school year. Making him aware of what his responsibilities will be and preparing the background he will need is no easy matter. Since he desires to become an architectural engineer, my role is to make him aware of resources available in the community that will help him acquire skills he'll need before college. We've looked into the Pasadena City College, the High School of the Arts, and also the Art Center College of Design Saturday High School, which he presently attends. His first class there was an environmental design class, which is one of the curriculum requirements for the architecture department.

Like all parents, we want our children to succeed in their dreams. As a homeschool parent, I know I have to be an effective teacher. So I think about ways to be that while also allowing my children freedom to study fields they are interested in. I do have certain goals I want them to accomplish, along with incorporating their own interests. My husband and I are the most important ingredients in our children's education outside of themselves.

Our philosophy behind our own homeschooling is that we believe each individual should have the opportunity to study in an environment that is not harmful to the way he or she learns. Being at home allows us the time and space to focus on special projects and interests, and to devote time to the outdoors, for the world is our classroom. We also want to exercise the right to educate our children in an African-Centric way of thinking, because they too have a past. With an understanding of their heritage, they can more powerfully create their own future, and can become more conscious, independent thinkers.

Homeschooling parents wear many hats. We provide the necessary funds to keep the house running smoothly; we take care of everyday house-chores and errands; we keep abreast of our children's progress but also pursue information that can help them in their future. I am not personally equipped to give my children all of the higher learning they need. MTunu and I know our limitations, but we also know we are qualified to help Tunu and Tiye *find* valuable, available information and resources.

I hope I have shared enough information so that African American families can see they do have alternatives if the public or private school system isn't working for them. There *is* a way to keep our children on track. They do not have to become lost souls. We can help them become productive, caring human beings. ❖

Detra Rose Hood

Tunu and Raymond Carr busy in
homeschoolers' robotics class, with teacher Clint Simmons

Tiye and friends busy at a homeschoolers' dollmaking workshop

Detra Rose Hood

Tunu with one of his architectural design projects

Mr. Simmons and homeschoolers at the African American homeschoolers' network 1992 culmination program.

Tunu Hood
Pasadena, California

CLASSES WITHOUT SCHOOL

I am fourteen years old, and I have a sister named Tiye who is eight years old. As long as I can remember I've been homeschooled. What I like to do best is race a radio-controlled car that I built, play basketball, and work on my model train layout. I also play the piano a lot, and when I grow up I want to be an architect.

A typical day begins around 7:30 a.m. I get up and eat, and we start working around 8:30. My first subject is math, followed by English and music. The workbooks my sister and I use the most are published by A Beka; they are fairly easy to understand. The math subject I studied first this school year was algebra—I learned about equations, solving word problems, and extracting square roots (which is very hard). I am currently working on graphs, statistics, and probability, which I am doing well in. After I finish that section we will start on solid and analytical geometry. In English I'm diagramming sentences and also writing and working on my spelling. After that I eat lunch, and then practice the piano for an hour or two, finishing around two or three o'clock. Occasionally I'll have "homework" later in the day, but not usually.

In my free time after school work I enjoy many recreational activities, including running that radio-controlled car, working on my model train layout, playing basketball (I've been on a team twice before), and swimming. And, if I'm taking a class, I might spend some time working on a science, history, or art project.

Though I don't go to school, I do often take classes. But there are important differences between school classes and the kind of classes I take. For one thing, my classes don't meet every day. Science classes, for example, meet once a week for an hour or an hour and half. This means that I have plenty of time to work at home on related projects. Instead of spending an hour in science *class* each day, I often spend an hour each day working on a science *project*.

For another thing, I've had a lot more say in what I wanted to learn in these classes. Each time a class ends, we have the chance to tell our teacher what we'd like to study next time, and whether there are any particular ways we'd like to learn. In one science class I said I'd like to have a volcano building contest—and so we did.

Also, my classes aren't determined by people who don't know me. My parents usually help plan and choose them, and they definitely know me and what I need a lot better than a school district could.

I don't get grades in my classes, and when I take tests it's more to help me understand the material than to label me. If I don't do well on a test, I can always learn what I missed and take it again.

I can remember what I learn in my classes, because my attention is focused on just a few subjects. I don't take six different classes every day.

My teachers are not *school* teachers—instead, they're experts in their fields.

And, most of my classes focus in depth on a particular subject like electronics or the civil rights movement, instead of on a general school subject like science or history.

SCIENCE

Four years ago my mom organized a science class for African American homeschoolers, which proved to be the first of many. Our volunteer teacher was Clint Simmons, an engineer who works for NASA's Jet Propulsion Laboratory, which designs rockets and spacecraft. We held class once a week at Loma Alta Park in Altadena, and first we learned about the solar system and earth science. During that semester Mr. Simmons brought in models demonstrating the position of earth in relation to other planets, and so on.

The next semester focused on electronics and how to wire circuits, using Radio Shack 100-in-one electronics labs. One of the first circuits we built was a crystal radio that did not work on batteries or electricity. Instead, it used a large wire antenna to pick up a radio signal. It worked O.K. but some of the kids who lived in different areas had trouble getting good reception because of being too far from a radio station, or because of interference from power lines or buildings. Later we built another radio that used batteries, and it worked much better. Our radios taught us about amplification, and how the different parts of circuits work together with other components. We also had the volcano building contest I mentioned earlier. Everyone who wanted to participate built a model volcano out of household products like clay or plaster. One student made a volcano that shot sparks out into the air—he had mixed a chemical with baking soda and vinegar.

On the last day of class we had a science exhibit and banquet celebrating the end of the year. Many people came; most were families of the students, and many of them brought projects. I had gotten a book from the library and used it to figure out how to build a solar-powered car out of aluminum foil and coffee cans. I never completely finished that car, but I have built others since. One thing about homeschooling is that it gives me time to follow up later when I'm interested in a subject. Two years after my electronics class, I built my radio-controlled car.

The next year my mom continued the science classes, this time at the Boys and Girls Club in Pasadena. We studied electronics that semester also, focusing on robots and how they work. There were about eight students; some people from the previous year didn't show up but there were some new ones. In this class we built model robots that worked just like real ones. They were very hard to build, and several kids broke some of the small plastic parts during construction. It took about six weeks to finish the robots, and during this semester we took a field trip to the Jet Propulsion Laboratory. We visited their robotics lab, where engineers design and build robots, and there we saw models of robots, and a lab where NASA tested and built robots for space missions.

The next science class I took with Mr. Simmons was last spring at Villa Park. It dealt with simple machines and how we use them in everyday life. We learned about the earliest simple machines and how people used and invented them, and we built a wooden wall clock. It was fun—there was a lot of cutting and sanding involved. The clock was powered by a small pendulum, which turned the gears and the hands when it was wound up. My mom also brought in household items that were simple machines, such as potato peelers, nutcrackers, and other tools. We were encouraged to do projects using simple machines on our own time. I made a car powered by a mousetrap, with model airplane wheels and a balsa wood body. The simple machines class was the easiest science class I've taken, but it had more projects.

FIELD TRIPS

I've been on many field trips both on my own and with other homeschoolers, besides going to JPL with my science class. Once a group of us went to the town of Hesperia, in the Mojave desert, and went on a walk to see what lived in the desert. On the next trip we learned about earthquakes and volcanoes as we hiked to the San Andreas fault, the largest earthquake fault in California.

A couple years ago we had a chemistry field trip. We conducted experiments, including making a balloon, which we then filled with gas by mixing baking soda and vinegar. My most interesting field trip was last year when we went to Lake Arrowhead in the San Bernardino mountains, where we learned about safety outdoors and around the house. We also learned about distilling water, what to bring with you when camping, and a lot of other useful things.

AFRICAN HISTORY

I started taking African history classes four years ago, and my sister has participated in similar classes for younger students. Our classes were organized by the African American Cultural Institute, and they dealt with the beginning of African civilization to the present. The first semester was about Egypt and its dynasties, and the teacher was Asar John Pope, a historian who traveled to Egypt. That class was really helpful in learning about ancient civilizations. The next group of classes was taught by Wenonah Wells, and I learned about later civilizations like the Ghanaian Kingdom in West Africa and Benin, which lasted until the 1850's. We made posters of Africa and of what different African countries produce. At the end of the semester we got prizes and presented our posters.

Two years ago I took my last African History classes. That year we started the civil rights movement. We kept notebooks of newspaper articles, and did a lot of writing and looking up definitions, which wasn't as fun as making posters.

AND OTHER CLASSES

Last summer my sister and I attended classes at Polytechnic, which is a private school in Pasadena that we got into by means of a scholarship. The classes my sister took were drama and gymnastics, and I took geometry and computer art. Geometry was hard because our teacher gave us tons of homework and we did a whole school year's amount of work in ten weeks. I did not do very well in the class, my average test score in the class was sixty percent although my average homework grade was eighty percent. The computer art class was much easier. We worked on Aldus Freehand, which is a computer art program. I did many projects using that program; the first was a simulated amusement park. Later on in the class we used Playmation, which is an animation 3D drawing program. I used that program to animate many still drawings, including a short movie of a city with a freeway with moving cars on it. My most interesting animated drawing started with cars on a street, and then the demolition of a building at the end of the sequence.

The latest class I've taken is environmental design, at Art Center college where they have a design program for high school students. My class dealt with scale drawings, floor plans, making models, and lots of other design-related procedures. The first project was to design a playground incorporating a hill and a dip, making a model with foam core and anything else you could find around the house. Building the model was challenging and it took about four weeks to finish. The next project was to design the interior and exterior of a restaurant or coffee shop, and build a model. I built mine entirely out of foam core and it had small electric lights that illuminated the whole thing. That class was very helpful in learning about designing structures and architecture, which is the career I want to be in. I have researched what it takes to become an

one of Tunu's environmental design projects

architectural engineer. Some of the things it takes are skills in math, drawing, English, and earth science. I plan to take classes again at Art Center. The next time, though, I will take industrial design or a graphics course.

MY LIFE AS A MUSICIAN

I've been taking piano lessons for seven years, ever since I first went into a music store when I was seven years old and banged on the keys. My Dad decided to buy a piano, and I started taking lessons at Pasadena City College. A few months later I started studying with Mr. Sonny Phillips, a jazz musician. That was also the year I had my first recital. Me and my mom played a song—she had joined the class too. Since then, I have been in recitals continuously except for last year, when I took a much needed break.

During my piano studies, I've learned a lot about music. I've played songs by Scott Joplin, Duke Ellington, Charlie Parker, Tad Dameron, and many other jazz musicians. My favorite pieces include Scott Joplin's *Maple Leaf Rag* and Quincy Jones' *Secret Garden*.

I have played not only in recitals, but also in many other performances. The first was in the John Coltrane festival four years ago in 1991. I played at that festival again the next year, and in 1993 I entered and won the Coltrane Festival youth competition. Last year, I played as a guest artist during the competition. The winners of the adult and youth competitions performed at the Wiltern theater along with the other performers, including Carlos Santana and Alice Coltrane. The performance was good, and it lasted until late at night. I really enjoy performing once in a while, but not too often, because after all there are other things I like doing even better. ❖

Fahiym Basiyr Acuay, age 14
Camas, Washington

IT'S NORMAL TO ME

Well, I suppose the questions at hand are: How do I learn? What do I learn? *Do* I learn? So I'm going to answer, starting with the last question. But first, I'd like to clarify the difference between homeschooling and unschooling. Homeschooling can be like going to elementary school at home. You have only one or two teachers—your parents—who teach you as if you were in school. Unschooling, on the other hand, is learning "by any means necessary," to quote a famous African American. Can you guess who?

I am an unschooler, although I started out as a homeschooler. My mom got sick of teaching me everything and decided that I was capable of learning many things on my own. And, I am.

So, do I learn? Duhh. I learn just as much as anybody else.

What do I learn? Well, I basically learn the same things as any "schooling" student, if not more. You know: math, vocabulary, reading, social studies, art and science. I even exercise.

How do I learn? Whew!!! That's a tough one. But I can handle it. I spend about a half hour, every other day or so, studying algebra, using Key Curriculum Press workbooks. That's all the textbook work I do. But I also hold a job as a paperboy, which involves collecting money—plenty of math there! I have to keep track of who paid and who didn't, and at the end of the month I add up my collections, fill out the deposit slip, sign all the checks and deposit it all in the bank. Besides this, I have a personal bank account. I use it to deposit the money I am saving.

Being a noticeable stutterer (you know, saying stuff like "b-b-bird" and "w-w-w-w-what," kinda like Porky Pig) has gotten me into several speech therapy programs, which involves *lots* of vocabulary. Besides, my sister Hafidha is virtually a human dictionary, and is constantly correcting the family. As a matter of fact, she's correcting me now.

How do I cover reading? By reading, of course. My sister used to play reading games with me and read to me. She used to make up games and plays which we acted out for our parents. I learned to read from her when I was about four. Historical fiction is one of my favorite areas. I have enjoyed Johnny Tremain and most of Lloyd Alexander's work. Being a paperboy involves lots of reading too. I mostly read the sports section and the local news. Stuff like that. Even my comic books. The library is probably the greatest resource we use.

My dad's a CNN fan, and we watch it with him a lot. I learn a lot about geography/social studies from the news. Not to mention the fact that our computer has lots of educational programs, including a world atlas. We've got this really cool board game called *On Assignment with National Geographic*, in which you travel the world as a photographer. It's a very fun and "educational" game. Another good board game we sometimes play is African American Bingo. It has brief biographical notes on various African Americans, some of whom are often overlooked.

Art is no doubt my favorite subject. I *love* to draw. I basically taught myself how to draw. Just years and years of drawing. Most of my drawing consists of comic book-like stuff and game maps. In fact, I'm working on developing a Dungeons and Dragons-type game map now. I also took an art course last year which helped too. I'd like to say that I dream about becoming a famous artist.

Truth is, I don't do very much science, though I really wish I did. It's my second favorite subject. But every so often, me, my mom and sometimes my little brother, will watch a couple of science programs on *The Learning Channel*. I also took a science course and a course in technical education last year at a junior high school. I would like to make a terrarium containing a collection of insects to study their living habits. I like life sciences.

Exercise? I'm a fourteen-year-old boy, I do nothing all day but play and work (besides schoolwork and watching that cable TV). Anyway I love basketball, football, rollerblading, bicycling and swimming.

That's basically how I learn. But, of course, I'd know nothing if it weren't for my mom and dad and sister. But especially my mom, because she spent so much time (when I was little) teaching me while my dad was at work. I don't really think of my family as my teachers but as people who help me to learn. But of course I do more than just schoolwork and sports. Oh yeah, cable helps too!

I constantly find myself glued to my video games, on the computer or the Super Nintendo. I also (if you haven't already caught onto the idea) have a paper route. Yes, I have a job. A small, annoying job, for which I'm moderately paid. Every week day I load an average of fifty papers into double sided bags, which I put over my shoulders, and carry around half of a large apartment complex. Then at the beginning of every month I go around to almost very customer, and try to collect money from them. I've learned trying to get people to spend money is not easy. I've also learned how to deal with people, that people are different in many ways and that being nice gets you further with some people. Now that I'm fourteen I'll try to get a job somewhere else such as a pet store, the car wash, or flipping burgers.

My major unschooling challenge is the feeling of being sheltered from other people my own age. I could somewhat relieve this problem by joining some group activities such as the YMCA, martial arts, BMX racing and the NBA!!! Another job where I don't work alone might also help. School does offer more social opportunities which has its pros and cons. I had a taste of this last year when I went to school part-time to study art and science, my two favorite subjects.

Part-time school? Many kids ask, is that possible? How do you only go to school part time? One kid joked, "What—do you go to school for two or three periods than go home?" I just laughed and said, "Exactly."

Even though two periods may seem like a very short time, being an unschooler, it seemed long enough. I got to meet a lot of people I enjoyed being with and talking to. But then I was also forced to be exposed to people that I didn't want to be around. School also offered the after-school activities that I really enjoyed (basketball, track, and an easy-to-access library). The only reason that I would go to school is for the social life and sports activities. I think that I can learn more on my own though.

If I went to school full-time, and had never homeschooled, I'd probably be one of those kids who hated school. I don't enjoy sitting down for hours doing one thing or not having any choices. School doesn't have the flexibility that I feel comfortable with. As an unschooler, I get to do more things on my own terms but I have help when I need it. That help is more individualized than in school. By unschooling I always have a teacher who likes me, most of the time!

I am very interested in going to college. I would like to study medicine but I'm not quite sure which field yet. I am interested in naturopathic medicine and dentistry. College could lead me to a chance to play professional basketball. Most likely I'll get a high school diploma instead of the GED. I think a diploma will improve my chances of getting into a good college, or the college of my choice. I have a lot of options: continue unschooling, go to high school part time, or go to school full time. Either way I can still play on the school basketball team. I have another year to decide.

It's already tough being black, especially living in a place where you are a small percentage of the population. Everywhere you go, people are looking at you, making sure you're not doing anything wrong, because of what they see on TV and the news. It seems that people are afraid of being called a racist and so they are superficially nice to you all the time. It's hard to tell what people really feel or what they are thinking. Then, being an unschooler on top of that makes you totally different from everyone else. The only people that I can relate to or who can relate to me are the ones who are open-minded. You just have to ignore what the other people say—or just take the good from what they say and leave the rest. I just have to be myself regardless of what others think.

Schooled kids are already set in how they are *supposed* to think, according to other people. After a while, they begin to really believe this stuff. In school, from my experience, the kids who believe it the most become the popular ones. I haven't been pressured much to be like everyone else. So, when I talk to schooled kids, they see me as being different.

Un-/homeschoolers, of all colors, haven't had that pressure either so it's easier to be myself when I'm with them. I haven't run into any homeschoolers who are prejudiced against me—or against anyone, really.

Un-/homeschooling certainly is not for everyone. But if you think that school is long and boring, I'd consider it. Talk about it with your parents, because (although it may not seem like it) they generally know what's best. At first people (even your friends) may be a little skeptical of the idea. But hold on, they'll get used to it. (And if they don't, who needs 'em anyway?) Some people might call you a dropout. In this case just remember, there is a distinction. Dropping out means that you left school, got a bum job, and aren't doing anything educationally worthwhile. Un-/homeschooling means you left school, got a bum job, but are still pursuing learning, instead of just giving up.

Every time I look at the lives of schooled kids I see what I don't want to become. I don't want to be "normal." I want to be me. Some kids have been in school all their lives. Some kids have been homeschooled all their lives. I've done both. I've even gone to school part-time while still unschooling. I wouldn't call my experience incredible or unique, it's just the way I live. It's normal to me. ❖

Doreen Burnett Gounard
Galilee Harbor, Sausalito, California

OUR DREAM IS ALIVE

It's 4:30 p.m. The sky is more dark than light on this cool November afternoon. I'm just putting the diced onions in the skillet as I begin preparing dinner. The baby, Tristan, is happily at my feet, pounding together two small pots that he pulled out of the cupboard under the stove. The galley begins to smell of yellow curry and tomatoes. While the sauce simmers, I step out into the cockpit and holler, "Maya!" I listen. The air is full of the scent of woodstoves burning. The only sound is a seagull atop a neighbor's mast, calling back. The lack of response from Maya means she's on a neighbor's boat.

"Marc?" I say to my husband, who is working in his studio, "Check on Tristan while I go find Maya." I step off our boat onto the pier as I look for my daughter, a rambunctious seven year-old mulatto child—"full of pepper," as my grandmother would have surely described her. Since we moved onto our boat, *Imani*, and into Galilee Harbor in Sausalito just six months ago, Maya has truly enjoyed the freedom of movement and adventure this maritime neighborhood has afforded her.

Galilee Harbor is located in Sausalito, California, which lies just north of San Francisco's Golden Gate Bridge. Galilee is a cooperative community, where we all share duties, maintaining the harbor, showers, gardening, etc. The harbor includes seniors and teenagers, singles and families. Its majority is white, yet I am the third African American woman here. This harbor is a microcosm of people who all share a love for the sea. Some boats never leave the harbor, while others have been in and out over the years, exploring the world and bringing back tales and vitality to the community. There are many artists here—painters, photographers, apparel designers, and maritime artisans; and there are also amongst us a commercial fisherman, a retired fireman, and two nurses.

Maya has made many wonderful friends here, and I know, as I walk down the dock, that she is with one of them right now. I stop at Richard's boat, *Solent*, only to be told that yes, she *was* here, until just a little while ago. She was last seen with Karen, helping Cass—the oldest member of our community at a young eighty-one—carry some supplies back to his boat. I stop at Cass's *Yo Ho Ho*, only to find out that Maya had dropped off his things and gone with Karen back to her boat. Luckily Karen's barge is next, and I peer inside the glass door to see my very grown-up-looking daughter curled up with a cup of hot chocolate, head to head with Karen, a big-hearted, sailboat-racing yachtswoman. As they both peer over an Usborne puzzle book, *The Emerald Conspiracy*, I stand and watch their interaction. They're sharing the fun of finding out the clues, solving the mystery together, and I realize that this moment is what homeschooling for us is all about: sharing the fun of finding out the clues of this life and solving the mystery together with our family and with our community and friends. "Homeschooling" is virtually a misnomer since so much of Maya's learning happens not only at home but also in the world, in *her* world, in her community, amongst people she cares about and who in turn care for her. For Maya, this is all normal, for she has never been to school.

We decided to homeschool when Maya was almost two, which was also the year we began building our home, a thirty-three foot catamaran sailboat. My husband Marc, thirty-nine, a Frenchman of European descent, is a jewelry designer and manufacturer. Prior to his jewelry career, he had many years of sailing experience, working as a charter skipper in the Mediterranean, Atlantic, and Indian oceans. I am a thirty-six-year-old African American woman, originally born and raised in Springfield, Massachusetts. I received my B.A. in Visual Media Studies from American University in Washington, DC. For the next eight years, I worked within the advertising, film, and dance communities, prior to meeting and marrying Marc, and moving to the San Francisco Bay Area to build our boat. Our future plans are to embark on a multi-year journey through the South Pacific, staying months and maybe years in various countries, learning different arts, customs, and languages. Given this lifestyle, we have long known we would have to take on the responsibility of educating our children ourselves. Reading books and publications regarding cruising with kids, I came to the conclusion that we would utilize a curriculum such as Calvert's, which reproduces the subject-oriented approach of most modern schools. That was until my dear friend

Francesca gave me a book for my thirty-first birthday, John Holt's *Teach Your Own*. It hit me like a ton of bricks. I read:

> You may expect too much from yourself. Your children's learning is not all going to come from you, but from *them*, and their interaction with the world around them, which of course includes you. You do not have to know everything they want to know, or be interested in everything they are interested in.

I kept finding myself nodding my head in agreement, almost murmuring a small *amen*.

> Even though many and perhaps most adults today dislike and distrust children, there is, at the same time, a growing minority of people who like, understand, trust, respect and value children in a way rarely known until now. Many of these people are *choosing* to have children as few people before did. They don't have children just because that is what married people are supposed to do, or because they don't know how not to have them. On the contrary, knowing well what it may mean in time, energy, money, thought and worry, they undertake the heavy responsibility of having and bringing up children because they deeply want to spend a part of their life living with them. Having chosen to have children, they feel very strongly that it is *their* responsibility to help these children grow into good, smart, capable, loving, trustworthy human beings.

John Holt's book spoke to my soul, the soul of a woman whose own mother died when she was ten. It spoke to my need and desire to directly experience my children's lives, for no one knows how long I will have the privilege to walk this earth with them.

So although we began homeschooling to prepare for our future travels, we now know that we would continue even if we stayed here. Child-led learning has proven a very effective method for Maya. She's not taken out of the world to pass her days in a building called school; instead she remains rooted in the world: observing, questioning, and most importantly, conquering the obstacles that life sets before her.

It was a crisp autumn day. Maya woke up with a start and ran into our cabin. "Mommy! Poppa! I want to learn to row a dinghy!" Dinghies are small boats with oars, sometimes equipped with sails and an outboard motor. They are plentiful here on the waterfront. She continued: "If I knew how to row, I could get to the other dock so much easier! I could just row right over and get Max to come out and play. It would be so cool!"

I laughed heartily as I imagined that this must be what it will feel like when she asks for the keys to the car. But Marc the sailor responded seriously. "Maya, how would you go about learning how to row? We don't have a dinghy yet." Maya thought out loud: "We don't, but so many people here in the harbor do. Maybe Richard or Karen will show me how and let me try."

So that began Maya's rowing lessons with Richard and Karen. Rowing is a skill she will need to know as we visit different places and anchor our boat away from the shore. The dinghy will be our water taxi. I was so pleased that *she* saw the need and elected to begin to learn, not because *we* insisted, but because she feels compelled to know. This is also how she learned to read.

When Maya was three months shy of her sixth birthday, she and I embarked on a mother-daughter train trip across the United States. I was several months pregnant and thought this would be a terrific time for Maya to learn to read, especially since she was easily playing spontaneous reading-readiness games, such as: "I'm thinking of a word in this room that begins with the letter P....", and she already understood a lot of basic phonics. But on the train her response to my prodding was, "I don't want to read by myself now. I have to be at least six, and anyway, I don't want to learn that. I like it when *you* read the stories to me!" Well, of course, I reassured her that learning to read would not end the stories that we shared together. But she didn't buy it. So, I dropped the issue.

Three months later, her brother Tristan was born, and four months after that she decided to get a book from the library to read to him. She chose an "I Can Read" book, *The Small Pig*, which she subsequently deciphered with both Marc's and my help. We learned not to offer this help, but to merely respond to her questions. This was difficult for us to do at first, but in this way we were able to give her just what she needed to move forward, and to keep the learning *hers*. Consequently, she grasped the concept of reading very quickly. She's been reading for nine months now, and her reading vocabulary continues to grow day by day. She now reads at least two hours per day, of her own volition. And lovingly, we end each day in bed. She reads a story to the family, and then I read from a chapter book until both Maya and Tristan are asleep.

"I'm the green ranger!" Alex shouts. "I'm the red ranger!" bellows Ryland. Maya screams—"I'm pink!" Marika goes for yellow, and Aidan white. Thus begins a serious game of Power Rangers in a San Francisco Park. These children and many more are part of the San Francisco Homeschoolers, a group of more than thirty families. From this group, we have become close with several families, and Maya has found peers she likes and relates to. Many of the children are bi-racial and/or bi-cultural, which is an added bonus. She is not the only child whose parents don't "match."

The group has also been wonderful for me. Being the primary parent in our homeschooling effort, I feel blessed to have met such wonderful men and women whom I can relate to and with whom I can share my homeschooling experiences. We are each other's sounding boards and advice columnists. As a result, our world extends out to all of the Bay Area, as we field-trip, ice-skate, and explore the wilds together. We are living such rich lives.

Yet, economically, we are hardly rich, for we live on one income. In fact, we live on very little. For years, our mantra has been, "We can make more from less." Subsequently, we have become smarter and smarter at bringing our monthly expenses down, yet living an increasingly full and rich life: shopping at farmers' markets instead of grocery stores, learning to make our favorite Thai, French, and Indian dishes at home, swapping clothes and sharing museum and zoo memberships with other families, and not buying into the "American dream" house mortgage game. We built our boat over the past four and a half years with $10,000 down and then every spare dollar we could put aside. So, now we own the boat outright, living in Marin County, one of the most affluent counties in California. Our current docking fees are one half of our former rent for the West Oakland flat we lived in while building the boat. (West Oakland was and remains one of the least affluent communities in all the Bay Area.) Boat living is one real way around the renting or home owning dilemma.

One year ago, when Maya was not in first grade, and the boat was under construction behind our rented house, she entered the West Oakland Library, skipping and singing, at 1:15 in the afternoon. The local library was our treasure trove, full of good finds (the books) and good friends (the staff). But this day, as we entered the building we noticed a new security guard, a slim African American woman. She asked Maya why she wasn't at school.

Maya responded, "Because I'm free!" The woman gave me a quizzical look. I explained, "The state knows I'm doing this. I filed an affidavit." She stood back, contemplating the idea, and then responded. "Go on, girl," she said, "Do it yourself, because we know those schools are never going to treat our children equally. I don't care who they happen to be sittin' next to!"

With that heard and digested, I walked into the library, nodding my head in agreement. The stranger had hit upon something that I know to be true. Being able to sit in the same room as white children has *not* been the panacea that our beloved mothers and fathers hoped it would be. There are still too many black and brown children whom the school system does not serve, whose individual learning styles are not empowered and who consequently are labeled "unable to learn" and ultimately abandoned.

When I let my extended family know that Marc and I were definitely going to homeschool, the general reaction was shock, surprise, and lots of disappointment. They didn't understand why we wouldn't even try the local schools. I pointed out that our agenda was different, given our plans to travel worldwide. "But still," they said, "Maya should go to school until you leave. Otherwise she'll be odd!" I pointed out that she was already odd, given her mixed heritage, and that anyway, school was no guarantee against oddness. "But you're abandoning the public schools," they went on. "Instead, you should get involved and help change things."

Well, I'm sorry, but I don't see the public school hierarchy willing to accept anything but faddish change. I lived through the reforms of the seventies, in junior and senior high school. I experienced several innovative and creative courses and educationally I flourished. Yet, by the time I graduated, most of the reforms were gone and students were left stranded, never allowed to complete what they had started years before. Instead, they were thrust towards the "new" approach, called "Back to Basics." The pendulum had swung again.

The kind of change that schools say they are ready for is just not enough change for me. I've worked hard to keep my daughter's natural learning ability intact, and I know there is not a public school yet formed that would truly honor that. Trying to change those schools into what I want for my children and others seems futile to me.

Moreover, I will not subject my children to the fickleness of local politics when it comes to their educations. No, I will keep the power and pass it on to them directly.

> The Negro will never be able to show all of his originality as long as his efforts are directed from without by those who socially proscribe him. Such "friends" will unconsciously keep him in the ghetto...No systematic effort toward change has been possible, for taught the same economics, history, philosophy, literature and religion, which have established the present code of morals, the Negro's mind has been brought under the control of his oppressor. The problem of holding the Negro down, therefore, is easily solved. When you control a man's thinking, you do not have to worry about his actions.
> —Carter G. Woodson, *The Mis-Education of the Negro* (Africa World Press, 1990, first published in 1933)

By homeschooling our children, Marc and I are preparing them to think for themselves, to question the status quo, and to come up with new solutions. That's the gift we will give back. In honor of all those who have come before, all those who have fought the good fight, we continue the struggle, this time in our own way.

Our children deserve to know that they each have a gift to share with their family and community, and that it is up to each of them, with the support of family and community, to identify that gift and develop it. Then, maybe this country can begin to walk its talk, and many more of our children can live full and rewarding lives. This is one very important reason we homeschool Maya and Tristan. We want them to find their gift and follow their bliss. Life's dreams can be lived. Living here on *Imani*, we are proving it every day. Our dream is alive. And that's our most important lesson to our children: don't just dream dreams—live them. ❖

Maya and Marc designing together in the jewelry studio

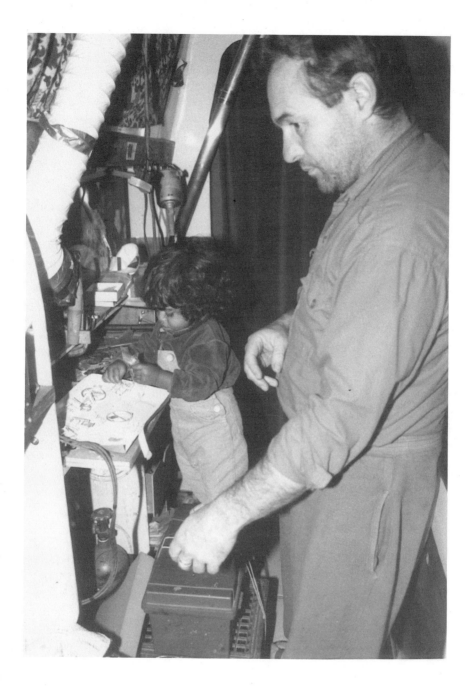

Marc and Tristan at Marc's studio workbench

Doreen Gounard

homeschoolers at play: (left to right)
Maya Gounard, Marika Cifor, Alex Schotz, and Tristan Gounard

Maya reading to Tristan and Doreen

Maya Gounard and Richard Bowen rowing in Galilee Channel

Doreen Gounard

Maya feeding her friends the seagulls

FORUM FOR HOMESCHOOLERS OF COLOR*

Kevin McDonald: Good morning, I'm Kevin McDonald and it's my privilege to introduce today's speakers.   Lenore Colacion Hayes** is a marriage, family and child counselor trainee at Cal State Long Beach, where she's currently completing her thesis project for a Masters of Science degree in community clinical psychology. Her area of specialty is working with families of color.   She has worked as an assistant counselor in a public elementary school and also as a counselor for learning disabled college students. She and her husband have homeschooled their nine-year old son Nigel, since 1989. They also run BayShore school, a private ISP [Independent Study Program]. Welcome, Lenore....

Also on our panel, Reed Colfax.*** Reed's also been in published form.   He hails from the mid part of the state, Boonville.   He's now completed college and on his way to law school. Welcome, Reed.

Why don't I pass the microphone and we'll start.

---

* This is a partial transcript of a session which took place during the HomeSchool Association of California's 1993 Conference. It is slightly edited for clarity. The HSC is one of the largest, best organized, and most active statewide homeschooling organizations in this country. It publishes an excellent newsletter and sponsors a large conference each year--information available on request: The HomeSchool Association of California, P.O. Box 2442, Atascadero, CA 93423, (805) 462-0726.

** Lenore Colacion Hayes holds an M.S. in community/clinical psychology. Her area of research and applied interest is in the development/prevention of racism in young children. She is a homeschooler and operates a private independent study program for homeschoolers in Southern California. You can contact her at BayShore Educational, P.O. Box 13038, Long Beach, CA 90803-0038, or (310) 434-3940.

*** Homeschooled all his life, at the time of this forum Reed had just graduated from Harvard and was about to enter Yale Law School. His parents, David and Micki Colfax, are the authors of the homeschooling classics *Homeschooling For Excellence* and *Hard Times in Paradise* (see Appendix III).

Lenore: It's good to see so many homeschoolers of color because when I first proposed this, the conference coordinator said, "Oh, we don't have very many people of color that come to our conference." And I said, "Well, maybe that will change if we have a workshop, or a couple of workshops discussing the needs and differences of homeschoolers of color, as well as a workshop to help people who are not so aware of color issues, to help their children and to stop perpetuating racism." And that will be our second workshop later this afternoon, but it's great to see so many people here now.

Essentially what we want to do is to just open up dialogue, to have everyone discuss what their issues are, if they have any issues that were different when they became homeschoolers, why they started to homeschool, if it had to do with race or if it was other things. What kind of welcome have you received from the mainstream of homeschooling? And, what are you doing to try and get other people of color in here too? Is there anybody that would like to offer anything?

Woman #1: I'm here because I have five sons that I've been homeschooling [audience laughter], and having sons makes me have a particular concern because, for one thing I don't know *how* to educate them and the system *doesn't* educate them....I have one son that I really firmly believe has a slight form of dyslexia. But the system wouldn't help me prove that, and then I also believe that he has a slight form of Tourette's; at this point I see him all the time and he always has to make a noise or something. He said, "It just feels better when I do it." The boy is eighteen years old now and he learned how to read by me teaching him from the Bible. Other than knowing how to read, he's failing in every course.... He probably would not have failed if I had taught him at home. Now my oldest son who's twenty, he is now at TSU. He was gifted all his life, so I had no problems. And now I have this eighteen-year-old that is pitted against this gifted child.

Lenore: Were you ever questioned because your child was Black and gifted? They have problems with that.

Woman #1: Nobody, nobody, not even other Black peers of mine wanted me to have him in those gifted programs....They questioned it. "Why do that to him when he can make straight A's in regular school, just let him be an A student." I wanted him to be able to reach far beyond that A, that boring A—even if you get B's and C's, just grasp way far out. Now he's having a good time down at TSU, he's doing pretty good, he's going for mechanical engineering.

Pamela Sparks* : How old are your other sons?

Woman #1: Four, two...[audience laughter] I did take my eighteen-year-old out of the regular school system for one year and I had him at home. But by this time it was hard for me to reach him. It was almost too late, but something that he did learn from it was that he had to take responsibility at some point. He did learn that, and he did go back to regular high school......They wanted me to put my other son on drugs for hyperactivity. And I couldn't get any counseling because he was just *this* far from—when they tested him he *was* learning disabled, he was just like—like you're maybe five dollars short of being eligible for financial aid [audience laughter].

Lenore: Is this your child who has Tourette's? Did he take Ritalin?

Woman #1: He is not known to have Tourette's.

Lenore: Did he take Ritalin?

Woman #1: No. I did not allow that.

Lenore: OK. Because there is a slight percentage of children who take Ritalin and it turns into Tourette's. If they have any kind of idiosyncratic motions, if they take Ritalin, many times it will bring upon full-blown Tourette's. The problem is when they get rid of the Ritalin, the Tourette's stays.

Woman #1: Well, I took him off of sugar for three years. I cooked without sugar, we had nothing but raw sugar in the house, period. And I put him on herbs and foods with high vitamins. It did help, but once they get in high school and you give them all the lunch money and they go to the store, you know. It's very tragic. I've had two marriages, so he's living with his dad, and his dad is very wealthy. And so now he's learning to live off his dad's wealth. It's very scary to me. I don't know how to reach him anymore. But I'm still trying, trying. I go to the high school twice a week to have lunch with him, so I can tell him something, I don't care if it's just, "Hi, I'm here."

Pamela: So you're going to homeschool your other three?

Woman #1: I'm going to homeschool my other three because I've got to give them a better break than my other son.

Lenore: Reed, I'd like to hear what you've encountered.

---

* See Pamela's essay, "The Daily Rhythm of Life," in this book.

Reed: Right. Well, I've obviously got a very different perspective because I grew up in a white family. I have one younger brother who's Native American, but the rest of my family is white. The town where I live is also completely white. There are a few Blacks who are in group homes, they've either come from troubled families or have some sort of learning disability, and so they're in group homes. That maybe accounts for two or three Blacks. And the only other Black within ten miles is Alice Walker [audience laughter]. So there are the two of us and then like three group home kids [more laughter]. That was to a large extent, where I lived, all my exposure to any minorities. Of course we had friends in the Bay area, but would only contact them fairly rarely.

And so when I went to college, that's where I got most of my experience and an education as to how Blacks are educated relative to other students. I decided to major in Afro-American Studies when I went to college. Afro-American Studies is not highly regarded at Harvard. When I got there, in my sophomore year I decided to major in it. And they began to close down the department, just because....

Woman #2: It's Harvard.

Reed: Exactly. It's Harvard. The Afro-American Studies department was created under huge political action in the late sixties, early seventies, and its mere existence was a critique of the other departments at Harvard saying, "Look, you're not teaching Black history, you're not teaching sociology of Blacks, you're not teaching Black literature." And they said, "Well, we'll give one survey course, that'll take care of it." Finally, in the early seventies, late sixties, a lot of Black students said, "Forget it. We're going to create our own department where we can learn." And I think that's obviously something that's also happening at the lower levels, below college, in high school and junior high you're getting no teaching of anything that's been done by Blacks. I don't know how many times I'd run into students at Harvard, some even majoring in Afro-American Studies, who would say that they'd never read a novel by a Black. To me it was just shocking because I read all the time. Richard Wright, Ralph Ellison, etc., etc..... Alice Walker, of course [audience laughter]. So that was a real shock.

Harvard went through the process of starting to shut down the Afro-American Studies Department while I was there. Again, we had to organize and we had sit-ins and protests and marches and strikes. Finally they gave in just to avoid the publicity. It was much easier for them to just hire the number one scholar in Afro-American Studies in the country,

Henry Lewis Gates, and make him the head of the department and everyone's happy again. But the same thing's happening—there are not enough courses offered in the department, and very few students wanted to major in it, because they see it as a dead end, there's not a lot of places you can go out of Afro-American Studies. I'm going to law school, which is certainly one avenue, and some people go to business school, but, if you go into the graduate studies program in Afro-American Studies there are very few positions and there's very little you can do with it.

That's really my experience with education for Blacks, since what little I know about high school, where I would have gone to school, it was entirely white.

Pamela: What did you encounter socially? How was that experience for you socially, having more Black people to socialize with?

Reed: Well, it was very interesting. I thought that I would get involved in the Black Students Association, which was very socially oriented. I thought originally that it had a political bent to it, but it was very social. And what I found at Harvard was that the Black students, almost across the board, were extremely driven for money. They were just on the fast track. And that was perfectly reasonable, I felt. This is their chance to offer themselves some protection for the rest of their lives, and so they might as well just load up with everything they can. A *huge* number of Blacks major in government and economics and go to business school and law school, where the money is.

So actually, socially, most of my friends were not Black, they were white. About fifty percent of the people who major in Afro-American Studies were white and I tended to get along better with them because they weren't on this driven, fast track—which I wasn't either. Things like the Black Students Association were *entirely* about making connections, just setting up networks so you could make a lot of money. That's all it was. It was disappointing for me, but reasonable, certainly. I can understand why they were doing it.

Lenore: I think another issue that I personally face is bi-racial. I am Latina from my mother, and my father's Anglo. My husband is Anglo, so my son is very fair. And when we tell him that he's part Mexican, that frightens him. He's nine, but he doesn't know any other Mexicans outside of my family. And he looks very mainstream. Donna Nichols-White is always getting on me because I said, "But he's so white, I can't put him on the cover of your publication!" [Audience laughter] ...But my son almost rejects anything that isn't mainstream and that's a real problem for us because that's what I went through. I went through kindergarten in 1960. My parents moved from Los Angeles to Orange County because they felt I'd get a better education. Well, I was the darkest thing those people had ever seen! [Audience laughter] And what happened was, I went to school, this was in the sixties... And I had a lot of children call me "nigger," because they thought that was what I was; I was the darkest thing they'd ever seen in Orange County. It was frightening because I thought they were going to turn the hoses and the dogs and the whole thing on me. And, I spent most of my life pretending—because I was bi-racial and I could say, "Oh, this is just a good tan"—I spent most of my life saying, "Yeah, this *is* just a good tan. I'm *not* anything but white."

I went back to college when my son was two and I got into a wonderful program at Cal State Long Beach. In the psychology department we have all different colors of professors, and it's encouraged. We would take those African-American Studies and put them in the counseling; it's a community clinical program where you have to go out, and not just learn how to solve people's problems. But these professors encouraged me to start looking back at my own roots and where I came from, and not to deny them. The time was up, they knew, they weren't going to let me get through with it.

And so I'm noticing this with my own son, even though he doesn't go to school, he's never gone to school, but he doesn't have that ethnic pride that I lost.

Woman #3: How old is your son?

Lenore: He's nine. And so we do do a lot of reading, and we do spend more time at my grandmother's house where it is more Mexican, for him to see that. I think it's important because bi-racial children need to be proud of *both* of their cultures instead of just taking one and saying, "This is the easier one to get through life." They need to know both of them.

Man #1: I'm not homeschooling. I have a four-year old boy and I live with two other people, so we co-parent each other's children. Their two-year-old is part Asian and we're trying to figure out what we're going to do. So I'm here to understand what homeschooling is about.

Woman #3: Is that what his parents are? Asian?

Man #1: His father is.

Woman #4: But he doesn't live with him?

Man #1: Yes, we all live together in the same house. We live in the flats of Oakland, so we live in a very diverse neighborhood. And one of my concerns is, I mean, I looked around this conference—and here *we* are [audience laughter]. It's a white phenomenon, at least the part that's surfaced in our area. So if I go ahead and we start homeschooling this child, Cory, I'm pulling him out of the most diverse institutions I can. I'm pulling him out of a diverse school, I'm pulling him out of where the kids in the neighborhood during the day are at school. Certainly he's going to be involved in other associations of people, but nine to five those associations of people are elsewhere. So that's one of the concerns I have.

And I've thought of other ways around it, I'm not real interested in homeschooling me, myself. I would love to cooperatively homeschool and pull people from the neighborhoods that are getting the same kind of experiences that you're talking about and say, "Hey, we can do better than this."

That's one issue, and the other issue is with Dana, my two-year old. I'm sort of relating to what you were saying about your children. Again, if I pull her out of the general milieu of school or other institutions like that, where's her role models, you know?

Lenore: I think that having worked in schools—and I worked as a counselor, I was going to be a school counselor—I thought I could impart all of this wonderful homeschool knowledge on them, so I was going to be a counselor. But what I noticed is we were in an area that was upper-middle class—and *we* were overflow. So we had all sorts of children coming in. They were not treated well, specifically the children that did not speak English or were not fluent in English. They were taken out of their classrooms, much like the stigma that we remember for special ed, "Oh, there he goes for the dummy class." So there's that.

I wanted to do my thesis project there, which was developing pride in children by telling different folk tales. And they would not let me do it because they felt that it was excluding white children. And my response was, "But everything else here is for white children, can't we make something for the children of color?" So I don't think that you're really going to lose a lot by not putting him in that environment.

Man #1: I'm not really worried about the education....

Lenore: No, but the socialization. But since you live in Oakland....

Doreen Gounard* : I was just going to say, I live in Oakland.

---

* See Doreen's essay, "Our Dream is Alive," in this book.

Lenore: Yeah, it's so diverse.

Doreen: I live in *West* Oakland. And I've gone through the first year of homeschooling with my daughter. She's going to be six in October. And it's been very interesting. She's bi-racial; my husband is French. By not taking her *out* of the world, we have allowed her to have a very diverse world, actually. Her relationship with Ruby at the corner store, the Chinese lady and her husband—that's where she's learned how to count, and that's where she's learned how to do a lot of things. And they understand that she's home, being homeschooled, and that that's okay. That's part of it.

The other part of it is that she interacts with neighbor children when they get home from school. During the day we interact with homeschooled children, not only in Oakland but also in San Francisco. I found that what I was looking for for her was just what you were talking about, that mirror image. She needed to know more bi-racial children so that she could understand that everybody doesn't match.

Woman #2: And that's fine.

Doreen: And that's fine, you know, some people match and some people don't match. But just so that she would have that and I realized that I had to make that community for her, that that was my job. The rest of it she takes care of herself. But my job was to go out and make sure that I made those kinds of contacts. And thus, she's been able to establish friendships with one boy who's half Chinese and half Irish, and others. Kids are very color conscious, I think, especially around five and six years old. I think children are really trying to figure it out, you know. We went back East just recently and she was explaining to my family in Massachusetts about all her friends.... And she put all the colors out. She says, "One friend, he looks just like me. His mama is *this* color and his daddy is *that* color, but *we* look a lot alike" [audience laughter]. They begin to see that it doesn't always make sense, but that's the way it is. And it stops being weird, and I think she's feeling more grounded in her sense of self, and that she fits in a couple of worlds. We've got lots of French relatives this summer—it's August, they've come. So she's really getting that too. I think that the reality is that to homeschool, to take that initiative, you have to take on the responsibility of making sure that the children are able to see the mirror but also able to see—
Lenore: I think that's something that every homeschool family should be doing, regardless of their color, so that children see that there are others

out there. And I think the other thing I wanted to say is that a lot of it is, they pick up our own—what's going on with us. If Mom or Dad is uncomfortable being around a certain color or a certain eye shape or a certain size, they're going to feel that as well. I think research has shown that children start noticing color differences as young as two.

Pamela: I have a couple of issues with my children. I have four, my oldest is eight. First thing, they were in preschool. I also went back to school when my children were tiny. We had a preschool experience that turned out okay for the first couple of years, but at one point we encountered a lot of my daughter trying to find her place and trying to imitate what she saw, and asking why she couldn't wear her hair in the same way, a lot of appearance things. We had decided to homeschool, and once I'd finished my schooling it was nice to take them out and embark upon that.

I think one thing we can do is like you said, creating the kinds of communities we want for our children and helping them see diversity and not always thinking you're different. Also, outside of community issues, just their place in the family is so important. Their having better family relationships and stronger families makes them stronger people and makes them so much more emotionally secure. So whatever they encounter, even if they continue to encounter that "I'm different" thing, they're more emotionally secure.

And they're *brighter* people. I think my children are so much freer to embrace the world, they're not afraid of those things. I was thinking this when Reed was speaking, that at the very least, by taking them out of school and sort of nurturing them as whole human beings and emotionally and spiritually and all that, they will be secure, bright, strong individuals.

Now there is a second point though, and that is, it is a community that we create. On the one hand I find it easier to find this sort of diversity and encounter diversity, and read a lot of literature and study other cultures and meet a variety of people and that's fine and that's one aspect that I think is good for their education. Also just knowing how to get along, the world being a raw place.

But then there's the other—I want them to have a strong Black community. I want them to have a sense of themselves in the African-American communities that, that—

Woman #2: Tradition.

Pamela: Tradition, exactly. And that is harder. That's my biggest challenge. When I grew up, my world was Black. Everybody around me, in school, in the neighborhood. I don't know, I just grapple with raising my children where nobody's Black.*

Woman #1: In my neighborhood, growing up, if you did something you *got it*. It didn't matter *who* saw you....

Pamela: But everybody cared about you, everybody knew your mother....It's like that saying: It takes a village to raise a man. I just want them to feel at ease and at home. Every summer we go home, we spend a month in Chicago and we spend some time in Mississippi where my husband's extended family is. And when we're there, we're just *home* and I think that's good and that allows them to develop those relationships with the extended family that I like for them, and help them develop relationships with the neighborhood kids. Again, that's something I was thinking about when Reed was speaking. I want them to recognize some of the bullshit that goes on.

Woman #2: Exactly! That's true.

Pamela: But by recognizing it you don't have to necessarily distance yourself from it. You don't have to be apart, you don't have to feel superior. You can have real healthy and nurturing relationships so that you're building each other, so that you can help call out each other's bullshit and ground each other. And so they need to be able to have those relationships, because all of our children are going to need to heal our communities—

Woman #5: That's right.

Pamela: And develop our communities, not just find their *own* place in the world. And not just economically. So I'm counting on my children to be instrumental in building Black community.

Lenore: I have a question. One of the things that a lot of people are saying now is that when Blacks want to live in the same community, or Hispanics want to live in the same community as Hispanics, that that's separatism. That if we want to be diverse, we have to mix. That's sort of what happened with this workshop, actually.

Woman #5: And it's harder, I think, in California. I'm from here, I've never lived anywhere else. And there just aren't enough of us. My mother lives in Atlanta now, and when I go down *there*...

---

* At the time of this forum, Pamela and her family lived in Saratoga, California--not in the Houston, Texas area as stated at the beginning of her essay.

***

Man #2: Spending time in both sets of worlds, I sit on a local school board of which I'm the first Anglo member in about twenty years. The community I live in started out as a white community, middle class, and now it is a very diverse community. And over the six years or so that I've served on that board, I've found that yes, it's very lonely.

Lenore: It's very lonely.

Man #2: The idea of being the only person that's different by color of your skin in a room is something that I've gotten very used to, but it doesn't make it any more comfortable. The idea of reaching out and all that, I think, is a message that needs to be *universally* recognized. Because I have found that that has been the dilemma for our family, that we've learned the bitterness of racism, not only intellectually, but by experiencing it also. And the inadvertentness of it, often.

Lenore: Do you have a bi-racial child?

Man #2: No, no. It just happens that we live in a community where, um...

Woman #6: *You're* the minority.

Man #2: Right. Our school district is 85% minority. Minority-majority [audience laughter]. And most of the community where I live has taken other routes to education. The other part of course is the fact that the community that the district serves is very poor—and guess what, I think the educational programs match that poverty. So I've found it very troubling no matter where I sit. It seems that most of us haven't learned the lesson that it doesn't matter what color you are, there are still certain aspects of human behavior you've got to deal with, about inclusion and that.

So as I sit here, one of the things that—this is my first time in this conference, and I looked out at the crowd and I wasn't surprised... But I find it frustrating, I've not found a good answer to it.

Lenore: I think as homeschoolers we're going to be faced with the problem, you know, are you really smart enough to teach your own kids? Aren't you putting them at a disadvantage? Shouldn't you put them in the school? I mean, they're Black or Hispanic or Asian, they're already at a disadvantage, and you're keeping them *home*?

Woman #7: I wanted to speak a little from an Asian perspective because there aren't a lot of us around. I've only met one other in my area, so maybe they're around, but I don't know.....One of the things I came up against when I started thinking about homeschooling was that all my life I did great in school, and my kids did great in school. I went to private schools, I sent my kids to private schools, and we all were at the top of our classes, and all of that. Part of the problem I came up against in my mind was that if I didn't keep them in school, would they be able to still get jobs and make a living?

But one of the things that really bothered me about going through school with all white people, since it was such a private school and stuff—at least in their school I think there were two or three other kids of color, but it was mainly white. But one of the things that bothered me when I was going through school and then watching my kids go through, is that it's really strange to be mostly Asian.

First of all, it's really easy to ignore Asian kids in school because they're usually—well, to perpetuate a stereotype, they're usually well-behaved and quiet and very smart. And they sit and they do their work, they turn it in, you know? I felt really neglected, a lot, by my teachers. Not by the other students, they all thought I was Black too [audience laughter]. I was confused for a long time. My kids thought they were Black for a while too, but that's another story. It was really frustrating to watch that in their schools. They pretty much took them for granted and didn't give them any kind of special attention.

Pamela: So why'd you take them out? *Did* you take them out?

Woman #7: Yeah, I did. And part of it was that that way I did feel like they were being seen, and that they could escape through....

Woman #2: Invisible, like Ralph Ellison.

Woman #7: And my younger son is pretty quiet by nature anyway, and I felt like he was going more and more into himself being in these schools, being oh, "This cute little Ben, he does so well, and isn't he nice?" One of the last things that really got to me was when they got their first report cards. They were first and second grade I guess. They got identical grades. My children got *identical grades*—and I *know* they are not the same people. But the school could never keep their names straight. They didn't have big public school classes. There were only eight children in each of their classes, and they could not keep my children straight, and that really bothered me. I thought, I'm paying $850 a month—

Several audience members: No!

Woman #5: Then they're supposed to know your kids' names! [Audience laughter]

Woman #8: We had a problem similar to that in private school. While they spoke of wanting to be a culturally diverse environment, they didn't do anything, they just paid lip service to it. And I spoke to the teacher about not seeing the child, she totally did not see my daughter. It was a school where they don't give typical report cards. They like, tell a story and draw a picture at the end of each grade, blah blah blah. But the picture that my daughter got was a *blonde* child. The teacher did the same picture for all the children. And when I pointed it out to her I said, "This is not my daughter. How could you put that in her notebook?" She said, "Well, that's how I think of Erin" [audience laughter and exclamation].

Woman #7: I think we're listed as white on the school roster, since we're bi-racial....It *really* bothers me.

Woman #8: Exactly. You know, I had found the best school that I thought I could find. I really liked the curriculum. But the Eurocentricism that they were pushing on my children was going to kill them. And the problem that I found was that the teacher couldn't even admit her bias, and you can't deal with it if you can't see it.

Woman #2: But they don't know they're biased. They don't know.

Woman #8: But when you're confronted with something that blatant, how could you say there's no bias? And that was just like my final straw. I had found the best school I thought I could find, and it wasn't going to serve my kids.

Woman #5: There's no room for them.

Woman #8: Yeah, no room whatsoever.

***

Woman #2: Lots of Black families take their boys out of school at twelve. Even in the religious schools, twelve is a dangerous age for a Black boy.

Woman #9: That's a dangerous age for any minority.

David Colfax: I think a problem you have in the homeschooling community, nationwide—we've spoken at conferences all over the country—is that there will be two or three Black families at the conference, and afterwards the conference organizers will ask us about them, "Can you meet so and so?" Because Reed's our son.....The thing here that I find disconcerting is the way they say, "We have a Black family!" It's very condescending. "They're going to be like us, they're going to come into the homeschooling community." Many of the things that we see in the homeschooling communities are problematic too. I mean there's a lot of racism, there's a lot of anti-Semitism.... I'm talking about the white dominance in the homeschooling movement. I'm not talking about California, this is by far the most....But there's a problem with that kind of thing, "Have you met so and so? They're homeschooling, isn't that wonderful? And they're doing it very well." And there's all the racist....

Woman #2: It's very condescending.

David: It's *very* condescending and yet at the same time what is kind of frightening about it is you feel that Black person or family is kind of being drawn into that ethos, which is very repressive, very white dominant.

Woman #2: And they forget all their problems. They forget why they came to homeschooling.

David: I think it's really useful to have this kind of group, coming not out of some other part of the country, but coming out of California, the West Coast here. In the rest of the country, the level of this kind of workshop is unimaginable. They're good people. They're interested in homeschooling, and well-meaning, but the race thing is a problem.

Man #1: If you institutionalize the Eurocentric position just because of the nature of people who have gotten together for homeschooling, I would assume that it's very uninviting....Here's what my question is: Number one, are there lots of other people of color that anybody's aware of that are doing homeschooling, probably on the side, and aren't organized?

Woman #2: The more affluent we become, the further apart we are. And the same with the Asian communities. You know there is not the impetus to be in an all-Japanese community anymore. You're always isolated. So you just never get together. You don't even see each other.

Doreen: That's one perspective of it. There's also what I've experienced in Oakland. I met a family in the library who have been homeschooling. Their children are twelve and ten years old, Black boys who have been homeschooled all their lives, except for one year of school. Total isolation. Absolutely. Those children are in the house all day long.

Lenore: Do they say why?

Doreen: Actually, the thing is, her feeling is that as a Black family they do not want to be questioned. They don't want to be hassled. They understand how the establishment works, and they're not interested.

Man #1: As I start going around my neighborhood and asking mothers and fathers with kids that are my kid's age saying, hey, what do you think about getting together? There's always a lot of resistance around that issue. What I'm wondering is, is anybody having success countering that resistance?

Lenore: That's what newsletters are really good for.

Micki Colfax: I'd just like to say, as so-called pioneers in homeschooling, back in the early seventies when we were homeschooling a racially mixed family, we just never *asked* anybody's permission. We never asked anything; we just did it.

Woman #2: But you have more freedom than a Black person would have in the same situation.

Micki: Well that's true, that's true. But back in the early seventies it wasn't as—there was no networking, there wasn't even the term "homeschooling," we were just, you know, not sending our children to school.

Man #1: You were underground.

Woman #2: Yeah, but there's still more freedom even after that. We couldn't do that.

Micki: Oh, I agree. I absolutely agree. But the fewer questions we asked, the fewer they could answer.

Pamela: I disagree. I disagree with you saying that we couldn't do that. I think the problem is that we don't *feel* as free. When you grow up, you have a psyche that confines you. But I don't know, I think we can. We just have to make that choice. And we have to break our own barriers.

Lenore: Well, think of all of us coming here today to do this, and for them even *letting* us put this out there.

Woman #10: I was a part of the whole sixties and seventies student radical movement at San Francisco State, and very much involved in starting the ethnic studies there that went on to all the other state colleges. So my kids have grown up in that environment. We were fortunate in that we grew up in San Francisco which is very diverse and always has all kinds of things that go on in the community that you can be involved in.

And you can see that even over in the East Bay, which is where we now live. Five years ago San Leandro was a retired white community. We were the only Asians there in our neighborhood for a five block radius. The kids couldn't stand it for the first two years. They called San Leandro "Clorox City." If they wanted something interesting to do we had to hop in the car and go to San Francisco. But we never lost touch with our ethnicity and with our culture and with other cultures, and being involved in the community, and the kids could always do something. The poetry, we go to poetry meetings.

My son was the only non-Black in an all-Black Boy Scout troop for years, for whatever reason he chose, even from three years old. It wasn't from any influence on my part or his father's part, at least not that I could see. All his best friends were Black. And I looked at that kind of like, "What's wrong with your own ethnicity and when are you going to learn that there are other people in this world?"

And then when he hit college it all changed around. All of a sudden it was Filipino this, Filipino that, and "I'm Filipino now." Now he goes to San Francisco State, which is where I went. And the Filipino group that we started there through the years became more socially oriented—party this and party that. Last year was its twenty-fifth year anniversary and it came around full circle. The students then became politically oriented again, and nationalistic, and my son became involved in that.

And I have a sixteen-year-old daughter who started homeschooling last year. Most of her friends in elementary school were white and she had one ethnic friend who was Korean and they've been best friends. Junior high I saw a gradual change. She started to have less and less to do with her white friends and wanting more and more to do with her ethnic friends, "ethnic" meaning people of color. Then she got in high school and she had maybe one white friend left. And this summer she turned around, and I looked at her, and it was interesting because she made a comment to me, she said, "Mom, I know I'm racist."

Pamela: What did she mean?

Woman #10: She doesn't like white people. White people and Mexicans. She's not comfortable with them and with the white people, she didn't like white people because of what she has read in history and what she's gotten in the schools. Unlike your kids who became part of the woodwork, my daughter stood out because she's outspoken and so she was looked at as being a troublemaker. She actually got into an argument with one of her teachers over how do you spell the word Filipino.

Woman #2: Yeah, how do you?

Woman #10: If you're going to be nationalistic, there is no "f" or f sound in the Filipino alphabet. It's a "p." .....

Pamela: I want to say something about this *reverse racism* as they call it. My husband is sometimes racist. And it is a struggle for me because he doesn't even appreciate.....he doesn't like us being involved in the homeschooling support group that we are involved in. He doesn't understand those friendships, he doesn't understand why we encourage those friendships. I think, on the one hand, that's a little insecurity on our part. We're afraid that because our own community isn't strong enough, and because our own connections aren't strong enough, we have to make sure that *at least*, at the very least, we don't get too white. My husband doesn't want to see his children adopt certain mannerisms, whatever.

Woman #10: Well, with my kids I don't really say, "What, you're racist? Then you'll never be able to go anywhere again." They have to really identify who they are and what their background is. And with me, I am really multicultural. I'm Filipino, I'm Yugoslavian, Spanish, Basque, Chinese and Indian. My daughter is all of that, plus some Italian on her father's side. And I look at my kids and I say: Appreciate everything that you are. The good and the bad, you know, meaning in personality. And also in all of the ethnicity, because there's beauty to be enjoyed in all of that. And one of the things that really has stayed with me from my experiences at San Francisco State and the student strike was the professor that was the whole cause of the student strike back then. He had made this comment about it's really important to know who you are and to have a love for your background, but at some point you can let that go and just be another human being.

Woman #11: You know, one thing I teach my children is that we all are descendants from Noah. Noah's wife had three children, and one of them was Black, one of them was Oriental, and one of them was white, and they came from the same womb. The Bible teaches that and I teach my children that, and because of that we all came from the same family. We're all the human race. And we all need to love what each other is. But at the same time, learn to love what we are too. Not discount what we are, but not discount what someone else is, and not let what people have done in the past make us hate where we are today. Because what people have done in the past with their own ignorance, they've paid for it. They've died and paid wages for sin. They paid for that. We have to go on now and teach our children how to love everybody, but also love yourself. That's why we're here, right? That's what we need to learn to teach them: to love themselves, but not to push our way on anyone else.

Pamela: And when we love ourselves securely, we are free to love others and not feel threatened by it or whatever. And I think this also speaks to what you brought up earlier, about how do we respond when people object to separation. You know, like let's make this workshop only for families of color, or you know, have the African American community living here, and the Latino community here. I think there is a lot to be gained by this sort of gathering and by culturally homogeneous gatherings, if you want to call it that, like the Black churches, or whatever. You know, you read all kinds of studies about Black universities and women's colleges; there is a lot to be gained from separation....

Woman #12: Getting your strength from....

Pamela: For getting your strength, and then you are freer to embrace the world and you feel secure and you know who you are.

Woman #13: I'd just like to make a comment about that, because I think sometimes you don't know who a person is when they walk in the room. I identify my self as part of a multi-racial family. Our children are adopted and our daughters are African-Brazilian, and our son is from El Salvador. So when we step out into the world, we are a multi-racial family. We are a family of color, and we are proud of that. And we feel that that has opened up doors that would never be open to us otherwise. So if a door shuts and says you cannot enter because you are not a particular race, people don't necessarily know what we are.

It's been a very hard decision to decide to homeschool in our family. But the saving grace for us has been the fact that we are part of an organization called Parenting African American Children and it's led by the African American community. And what is very clear to me is that I can do a lot to teach my daughters how to be women and the organization can teach them a lot that I cannot teach, how to be Black women in this society. And if we can come together and feel that part of us, then we can help each other and be a support system and see that. I couldn't homeschool my children if I did not have mentors, other women and men in the Black community to take them on and give them what I cannot give them. I can give them love, but I cannot give them that.

Reed: One thing I think we should keep in mind in all this discussion, sort of what's missing, is that sure, there is a Black culture, possibly an overarching Black culture, but we're ignoring a lot of economics. There's a huge amount of stratification within the Black community divided by economics. And they're very different cultures at different levels. I was in college, it reminded me, you said your daughter was racist, well I didn't get along with any *rich* people [audience laughter].

Woman #5: Nobody does.

Reed: It didn't matter if you were Black, white, Asian, just if you were rich, okay, you be over there I'll go talk with these people. But I think that that's another level that is not often addressed.

Woman #10: The awareness of it is a big step though. Because if you're not even aware how can you even deal with it? And so to me, to hear my daughter come out and *say* that she was racist—I'd been aware of it for a little while already. But for her to come out and say it to me was a big step. Well, one of the things she did this summer was she met two new friends, both of them from Europe. One of them is here for the summer. And she found the two of them to be so fascinating that she had to step back and say, now wait a minute, what's going on here?!

Reed: You're not supposed to like white people [audience laughter].

Woman #10: And I was just pleased as punch. It's sort of the same thing when our son decided to go to this Boy Scout troop and it was an all-Black one, and I said, well, let me talk to the scout master. And I talked to the scout master, I said, "Why aren't there more kids of other nationalities, more races? Because the world is made up of different ethnicities, why all Black?" And he said, "Well you know, to be honest with you, I don't think you're going to find a Boy Scout troop out there that has a multi-racial group of kids. They're all either all Japanese, all white, or all Black."

Pamela: But that's okay too.

Woman #10: Well, I let my son join, not because it was what he wanted to do and I couldn't stop him anyway. I let him in because of the scout master. I liked the way he talked. There was just something about him that struck me as being very sound.

Man #3: I coach a soccer team and it's under twelve, it's that age when they start coming into their own. There are three homeschoolers on the team and there's only one person that isn't white. I coach because I didn't want my son to feel pressure from schooled parents. Because school is innately cruel. School children are cruel, they do come after the other kids. And you see that the ethnic—the boy of color—he's Hispanic, he's the only person who's not white on the team; it's a small town. He's even more of a minority than the homeschoolers, and I think homeschoolers....

Woman #2: Right, well he is definitely more of a minority.

Man #3: Yes, he's on his own and they do kind of chase him. Just to follow on what you were saying, Reed, along economic diversity differences is there....I don't have a *sense* of what the economic diversity is among homeschoolers, but I would guess that it's people with resources, a lot of people with resources that have thought about the educational system. Is there much organizing—do people go out and figure out how to reach other people in different economic levels? Or is it primarily people doing this in isolation?

Woman #2: Most homeschoolers where I come from make under $30,000 a year, and I know of welfare moms who homeschool throughout the country. And they are definitely in isolation because they think that....

Pamela: They're more fearful.

Woman #6: And they have reason to be.

Man #3: You say the majority of homeschoolers in your state—the family income is less than $30,000?

Woman #2: Less than $30,000.

Woman #14: It's not a lot of money.

Woman #12: Most of us barely make our rent.

Man #1: It strikes me that it's bipolar. You've got rich ones and poor ones.

Lenore: Before we go, before we close this up, we've got sample issues here from both the *Drinking Gourd* and *Umoja*. [*Umoja* was a newsletter for homeschoolers of color, now discontinued.]

Woman #15: I just wanted to thank you for putting this together; I think it was quite valuable.

Lenore: Maybe we can do it again next year. ❖

HOW TO START HOMESCHOOLING

Find out the legal requirements in your state. You can request a copy of the actual statutes from a legislator or directly from your state department of education. (Any reference librarian can get you their address or phone number.) It's usually best not to ask school administrators about homeschooling legalities, as they are often misinformed, ignorant, or hostile.

Members of local homeschooling support groups are often eager to offer help and advice, and may be your best source of guidance, especially at first. They can also help you understand what the law actually means, in practice. (It may be rarely enforced, or loosely interpreted.) There are all kinds of groups, so don't give up if you don't feel comfortable with the first one you try. Some exclude non-Christians; some include everyone; some emphasize child-led "unschooling;" a few are all African American. Holt Associates regularly updates their excellent list of groups nationwide—see Appendix III.

You may want to read other books on homeschooling, or attend conferences or workshops. If you want to stay informed about events or organizations especially for homeschoolers of color, subscribe to *The Drinking Gourd* (see Appendix II). If you get on the mailing list of your state's larger homeschooling organizations (using the Holt Associates list), you'll receive information about local events.

But remember that ultimately homeschooling is about trusting yourself and your children to figure out what works for you. Don't let people push methodologies or expensive curriculums down your throat. If you really *want* a prepackaged curriculum, fine—many people do, especially at first, to ease the transition. But you might be happier and wealthier, and your kids happier and smarter, if you pull your own curriculum together. Draw from library books, apprenticeships or volunteer work (museums, veterinarians, food co-ops, and libraries frequently take homeschooled volunteers), perhaps a math textbook, an occasional foreign language or art class, independent projects of any sort, plenty of time to just *think*, and whatever else makes sense to you.

For many families, the most difficult part of homeschooling is the first few months. It's often important to give kids a vacation from school to heal, rest, and let off steam, before they're expected to start doing academic work. Without this relaxed transition time, it's hard for many kids to make a complete break from school and reclaim their natural love of learning. Again and again, homeschooling parents report a similar pattern. They nervously bite their lips for weeks while their kids stare out the window or read romance novels or sleep all day. Then, amazingly, their innate human curiosity resurfaces, and they are truly motivated to learn and grow from within. The boy who stares out windows begins to notice birds, and ultimately ends up carrying out a serious project for the department of wildlife, documenting birds seen in a particular habitat. The girl who reads romance novels shifts to historical novels, and then to U.S. history and to memorizing the U.S. constitution word for word.

As you can tell from reading the essays in this book, there are a vast number of ways to learn outside of school. Don't worry if you're unsure which homeschooling style would be right for your family. Just start out with whatever feels comfortable, and then make it a point to stay flexible so you can adapt later in response to your own growing confidence and your kids' growing interests.

Even if you experiment with homeschooling for only one year, you will probably find that from that point forward, your children can take greater control over their educations—even if they choose to return to school. Furthermore, this increased independence and responsibility often carries over into college, into adult work, and into all of life. ❖

RESOURCES FOR HOMESCHOOLERS AND OTHER INDEPENDENT LEARNERS

BOOKS ON HOMESCHOOLING & RELATED ISSUES
There are dozens in print now. Among the best-loved and most helpful:

David and Micki Colfax, *Homeschooling for Excellence* (Warner, 1988) and *Hard Times in Paradise* (Warner, 1992). The Colfax boys spent their childhoods and adolescences immersed in good books and various agricultural projects on their California homestead, and when they grew up, one after another was admitted to Harvard. These books are their parents' explanation of how it all unfolded. One reason the Colfaxes are so important to the homeschooling movement is their lack of snobbery and anxiety. They did not homeschool with the ivy league in mind; rather, they understood that the best way to *live* includes freedom and self-directed learning. That freedom naturally led to excellence...and then to Harvard. *Homeschooling for Excellence* is short and focuses quite directly on homeschooling issues; *Hard Times* is longer and broader, a wonderfully detailed narrative of life on the homestead. See Reed Colfax's comments in Appendix I. From *Homeschooling for Excellence*:

> Parents would do better, it appears, not to concern themselves with the acquisition of reading skills, but to endeavor to provide their children with an *appreciation for reading.* The child who is exposed to books at an early age, who sees his or her parents reading, who is read to, and who is encouraged to spend time with picture books, will all but certainly become a reader in due course. How and when this occurs will vary from child to child and from family to family. Some children, sometimes to the distress of their parents, will be happy to be read to and to look at picture books well past the point at which they would "normally" be reading. Grant, our oldest son, was a late reader. We had moved to the country at about the time when, if in school, he would have been taught to read, and it was a great adventure. Learning to read simply wasn't important. Not until he was nine, and found that his desire to know more about the Pomo Indians who once camped on our ridge required that he learn to read, did he bother to do so. Thus motivated, he was reading college-level anthropology monographs within a year, and was writing short stories based upon his reading.

From *Hard Times in Paradise*:

> When they were young, our efforts to restore the land, to plant gardens, and to improve our livestock stimulated the boys' interests in biology, chemistry, and nature in general, and we were always on the lookout for books and materials that would encourage them to widen and develop these interests. We'd virtually plunder the county library on our weekly trips to Ukiah for feed and building materials and spend whatever little cash we were able to generate on educational materials that ranged from chemistry laboratory equipment to movie reference books. From the outset it was apparent that the boys' natural curiosity provided the motivation to learn and that our job was to be there to provide support, materials, and, when it was requested, direction. We seldom *taught* the boys in the conventional sense of the term. We learned together, and we *talked*—about politics, literature, religion, and economics, about breeds of cattle and brands of feeds, about arts and crafts. Initially, when they were younger, they relied upon us for information and direction, but as they grew older they'd turn more and more to each other as they carved out their different areas of special competence, Grant becoming our livestock expert, Drew the botanist and astronomer, Reed the athlete and musician, and Garth the naturalist-artist.

John Taylor Gatto, *Dumbing Us Down: The Hidden Curriculum of Compulsory Schooling* (New Society Publishers, 1992). If you have any doubts as to what school is doing to the minds and souls of your children, this book will clear those doubts right up. Gatto taught school for twenty-six years, winning awards like New York State Teacher of the Year. Powerful and uncompromising, this book lays down the truth.

> The third lesson I teach is indifference. I teach children not to care too much about anything, though they want to make it appear that they do. How I do this is very subtle. I do it by demanding that they become totally involved in my lessons, jumping up and down in their seats with anticipation, competing vigorously with each other for my favor. It's heartwarming when they do that; it impresses everyone, even me. When I'm at my best I plan lessons very carefully in order to produce this show of enthusiasm. But when the bell rings I insist they drop whatever it is we have been doing and proceed quickly to the next work station. They must turn on and off like a light switch. Nothing important is ever finished in my class nor in any class I know of. Students never have a complete experience except on the installment plan.—"The Seven Lesson Schoolteacher"

Daniel Greenberg, *Free at Last: The Sudbury Valley School* (Sudbury Valley School Press, 1991). This description of a radically free alternative school beautifully illuminates the way people can develop in uncoercive, supportive environments.

> I guess it's worth repeating. At Sudbury Valley, not one child has ever been forced, pushed, urged, cajoled, or bribed into learning how to read. We

have had no dyslexia. None of our graduates are real or functional illiterates. Some eight-year-olds are, some ten-year-olds are, even an occasional twelve-year-old. But by the time they leave, they are indistinguishable. No one who meets our older students could ever guess the age at which they first learned to read or write.

Ronald Gross, *The Independent Scholar's Handbook: The Indispensable Guide for the Stubborn Intelligence* (Ten Speed, 1994). This book can help older children or adults become a true expert in any subject, without being controlled by a university or any other institution. Among the many independent scholars who have used this approach are Charles Darwin, Albert Einstein, and Betty Friedan.

> Major intellectual journeys quite often begin with browsing. As a teenager, Joel Cohen was browsing at his local bookstore in Battle Creek, Michigan, some years ago. He began leafing through the pages of *Elements of Physical Biology* by Alfred J. Lotka. "Here's a guy who thinks the way I do," he recalls exclaiming to himself. "Mathematics might be a useful way to make some sense of life." Cohen had been amazed to learn that the degree to which an earthworm turns its head in the direction of light is directly proportional to the logarithm of the intensity of the light. "I had just learned about logarithms in school. This simple organism was behaving in a mathematically lawful way, and it knew logarithms without school! It seemed to me I had better learn some math." Another book, Abraham Moles's *Information Theory and Esthetic Perception*, so captivated the youngster that he wrote the author in France, asking permission to translate the book into English and enclosing his version of the first chapter as a sample. Moles granted the request and Cohen then wrote to the University of Illinois Press, which subsequently published the translation. Neither author nor publisher knew that their translator was sixteen years old. Twenty-five years later, Cohen conducted his research in "biology by the numbers" as head of the laboratory of populations at The Rockefeller University.

David Guterson, *Family Matters: Why Homeschooling Makes Sense* (Harcourt Brace, 1993). Guterson is a public high school English teacher who homeschools his own four children. In *Family Matters,* he thoughtfully examines the homeschooling movement of the 1990's, considering questions such as: Are homeschoolers elitist, isolationist, un-American? What is the real difference between the ways "schoolers" and homeschoolers are socialized? Would our national economy suffer if more parents arranged their careers in order to be able to homeschool their children? How can homeschooling give more meaning to our communities, to our extended families, and to adults' working lives? How can homeschoolers and schools cooperate for the benefit of both? Guterson is provocative and insightful whether discussing homeschooling in terms of educational theorists or comparing two vastly different situations in his own life: teaching in school vs. teaching at home.

....While I might already have described myself as a walking contradiction—a homeschooling parent and a public educator—I see no real conflict in what I am doing and remain committed to both worlds. At school I come to admire many of my students, to like them so well that I am sad to see them go; at school there are moments in which I am gratified, even moved, by a sentence a student has written in an essay, by a question somebody asks. Yet for all this, for all the quiet joys of the classroom, I am forever aware of some amorphous dissatisfaction, some inkling that things might be better. It seems to me that many of my students should simply be elsewhere, that they would be better served by a different sort of education, that their society would be better served by it too. I believe this education is one their parents can help provide and that their parents should expect schools to assist them in providing it, should help create a community that nurtures learning. They love their children with a depth I can't match, finally; and finally teaching is an act of love before it is anything else.

Mark and Helen Hegener, editors, *Alternatives in Education* (Home Education Press, 1992). I am shamelessly opinionated and think that most kids who really want to be alive would be best off unschooling. But there are other options, too, for people who have had enough of public school. This book is a straightforward and insightful guide to different types of alternative schools, to the Waldorf and Montessori methods, and also to homeschooling/unschooling and compatible activities, like apprenticeships, tutoring, etc. It also contains a revealing section of interviews and essays on the politics of education and on alternative educational theories. Not a directory, but a thorough and intelligent overview of philosophies and methods.

I find that when there are those who oppose home educating—and there still are, sad to say—they do so from two directions. They do so because they feel it's a threat to their jobs. If, in fact, home education is successful, then we won't need as many administrators in schools, the school population will decline, I'll be without a job if I'm a truant officer or a principal or a superintendent or whatever. So money is what it boils down to. Fear for themselves and fear for their kind. The other aspect that they come from is power. Unfortunately, they are of the mind that they own students and families. Unfortunately, there is a proprietary attitude on the part of school people far too often toward those they serve. They are of the mistaken mind that kids exist for the school instead of the other way around. So it's from this position of having been given too much power by us that they say, "Well, wait a minute, you can't do this, I'm the professional, you don't know what you're doing, you don't even have a certificate." —Pat Montgomery, director of Clonlara Home Based Education Program

Matt Hern, editor, *Deschooling Our Lives* (New Society, 1995). An outstanding, radically sane collection of short writings, ranging from early ideas and influences (Tolstoy, Ivan Illich) to practical twentieth-century issues like single-parent homeschooling. The most thorough and provocative homeschooling "reader" in print.

John Holt, numerous books. Holt was *the* visionary pioneer of the unschooling movement. After decades of trying to improve schools by working as a teacher and urging educational reform, he turned his energy instead toward encouraging families to leave the system altogether, and toward supporting them in their efforts. He started *Growing Without Schooling* magazine, described below, and wrote many books. He observes young people from a profoundly fresh, honest, and unassuming perspective. You may want to keep at least one of his many books around for moral support and a wise, logical, and moving reminder of why your kids should be out of school. Some of his best include the following.

Freedom and Beyond (New edition: Boynton-Cook/Heinemann, 1995). In this book, Holt started questioning whether we needed schools. Throughout, he writes about freedom, choice, authority, and discipline. Several excellent chapters examine the relationship between schools and poverty.

> In short, I don't think the schools are or can be made into a kind of springboard or ladder to help poor kids rise in the world. Instead, I think that schools and schooling, by their very nature, purposes, structure, and ways of working are, and are meant to be, an obstacle to poor kids, designed and built not to move them up in the world but to keep them at the bottom of it and *to make them think it is their own fault*. The odds against not just all poor kids but any poor kid being helped rather than hurt by school are enormous. For the parents of poor kids to put all their hopes into getting good schooling for their kids seems to me to have about as much chance of paying off as putting all their money into sweepstakes. They would almost certainly be wiser to put their time, energy, and political muscle into getting the obstacle of schooling out of the way of their kids, instead of trying to turn it into what it was never meant to be and with the best intentions in the world never can be.

How Children Fail, new revised edition (Addison-Wesley, 1995). Astute, specific observations of children in school and other situations. One of the main catalysts of the school reform movement of the sixties and seventies.

> What this means in the field of numbers and math is simply this: The more we can make it possible for children to see how we use numbers, *and to use them as we use them*, the better.
>
> What do we adults do with numbers? We measure things with them, a huge variety of things in the real world around us. Why? So that we can think better about them and make better use of them. We measure, among a host of other reasons, to find out whether we are sick or well; to find out whether we are doing something better than we did before; to find out which of several ways of doing this is better; to find out how strong we have to make things in order to make them stand up; to find out where we are, or where we're going; to find out, if we do a certain thing, what other things are likely to happen as a result. And so on. We don't measure things out of

idle curiosity. We measure them *so that we can decide things about them and do things with them.*

Since all this is inherently interesting and important to us, it will also interest children.

So we should introduce children to numbers by giving them or making available to them as many measuring instruments as possible - rulers, measuring tapes (in both feet and meters), scales,. watches and stopwatches, thermometers, metronomes, barometers, light meters, decibel meters, scales, and so on. Whatever we measure in our lives and work, we should try to measure so that children can see us doing it, and we should try to make it possible for them to measure the same things, and let them know how we are thinking about the things we have measured.

How Children Learn, new revised edition (Addison-Wesley, 1995). A powerful testimony to children's ability and desire to make sense of the world.

> Not long ago, the mother of a seven-year-old child who was not yet reading told me that he had asked her, "Why should I learn to read; I can tell what all my books are about just by looking at the pictures." Books for little children, beginning readers, have so few words and so many pictures that many children may not be sure where the story is coming from. They may think that it is in the picture, and that in reading we are just telling a story about the picture. When I was little, children's books contained mostly words and very few pictures. We knew that if we wanted to find out the story, we had to learn to read the words. Remembering this, I one day took into a classroom of three-year-olds a book with no pictures in it at all, sat down in a corner, and in a quiet voice began to read it aloud. After a while, some of the children began to notice, and listen. One by one, they came over to see what I was reading. When they looked in the book, and saw no pictures, they were at first surprised. Then, after more watching and listening, quite a number of them would point to a word on the page and ask, "What does that say?" I would tell them. None of them stayed for long —it wasn't a very interesting book. But they all grasped the vital idea, new to many of them, that in some way those black marks on the page *said* something.

Instead of Education (Holt Associates, 1976). This book builds on the concept that meaningful learning and doing are inseparable, and that you can't have one without the other. It gives many ideas for ways to improve and change communities so people have more opportunities to learn outside of school.

> To be peaceful and stable, every society organized into winners and losers must persuade the losers that this state of affairs is necessary, and that its way of picking winners and losers is just, that the losers *deserve* to lose. At one time, winners and losers were picked by the accident of birth. Modern societies do this more and more with the schools. But the people who control society naturally want the schools to pick winners in such a way that *the existing social order is not changed*—in short, so that most of the winners are the children of winners, and the losers the children of losers.

The schools, then, must run a race which mostly rich kids will win but which most poor people will accept as fair. On the whole they have done this very well.

Learning All the Time (Addison-Wesley, 1989). Anecdotes and detailed observations that show how young children learn a variety of things such as phonics, handwriting, fractions, music.

> I can sum up in five to seven words what I eventually learned as a teacher. The seven-word version is: Learning is not the product of teaching. the five-word version is: Teaching does not make learning. As I mentioned before, organized education operates on the assumption that children learn only when and only what and only because we tech them. this is not true. It is very close to one hundred percent false.
>
> Learners make learning. Learners create learning. The reason that this has been forgotten is that the activity of learning has been made into a product called "education," just as the activity, the discipline, of caring for one's health has become the product of "medical care," and the activity of inquiring into the world has become the product of "science," a specialized thing presumably done only by people with billions of dollars of complicated apparatus. But health is not a product and science is something you and I do every day of our lives.

Teach Your Own (Dell, 1981). Currently out of print but available in libraries, and John Holt's Book and Music Store catalog sometimes has copies of the British edition. This remains the best overall guide for parents taking younger children out of school. Despite the title, the book does not really advocate that parents *teach* in the strict sense; rather, it encourages them to support their kids' learning, which often means staying out of their way. Holt talks a lot here about the way people learn basic math, reading, and writing skills, and offers solid thought on legal strategies, on good work situations for unschoolers, on the philosophy of unschooling, and other topics. A chapter called "Common Objections to Home Schooling" helps readers clarify their own positions.

> People are best able, and perhaps only able, to cross the many barriers of race, class, custom, and belief that divide them when they are able to share experiences *that make them feel good*. Only from these do they get a stronger sense of their own, and therefore other people's, uniqueness, dignity, and worth. But as long as schools have their present social tasks, they will not be able to give such experiences to most children. In fact, most of what happens in school makes children feel the exact opposite—stupid, incompetent, ashamed. Distrusting and despising themselves, they then try to make themselves feel a little better by finding others whom they can look down on *even more*—poorer children, children from other races, children who do less well in school.

Grace Llewellyn, ed., *Real Lives: eleven teenagers who don't go to school* (Lowry House, 1993). These kids tell—in-depth—what it's like to be responsible for their own educations. They learn the "basics" and much more from biking alone through Colombia and Ecuador, publishing a newsletter on peace issues, volunteering at a marine science center, writing to over fifty pen-pals worldwide, performing with a violin quintet, working at a shelter for homeless people, raising honeybees, compiling portfolios of writing and artwork (to prepare for a career in video game design), talking with people all over the world on ham radio, building houses with Habitat for Humanity, working through the mail with a writing mentor, playing banjo in bluegrass jam sessions, answering the phone at a crisis line, and helping midwives at births. They also discuss issues such as socialization and finding work, and answer the question, "Do you have to be a genius to unschool?" From an essay by Ayanna Williams:

> I have a pen-pal in South Africa in his forties who teaches people about my age. He writes long interesting letters and illustrates them. I have another pen-pal who is a native of Ghana, went to school for a year in Cuba, and now works in Libya. In Nigeria I have many pen-pals, one of whom is an eighteen-year-old Igbo:
>
> *The Christmas celebration was very dull this year in Enugu state. The reason was that many people moved out of the state since the creation of new states recently. During Christmas day everywhere was so dull that it looked like a ghost town. The masquerades that usually chase people around were nowhere to be seen. I went out that afternoon with my brother in our car. We drove to some of the places that are usually congested with people and masquerades, but no one was seen. Only a few people loitering around. Back home we celebrated happily with our family. After prayers, we dined on rice cooked with coconut juice, stew with chicken, and goat meat and some drinks. Celebrating Christmas in Enugu state is usually very enjoyable, especially when watching different masquerades passing by, sometimes chasing people around.*
> —Chionye Alisigwe, Nigeria, 1/20/92

Grace Llewellyn, *The Teenage Liberation Handbook: how to quit school and get a real life and education* (Lowry House, 1991). This is the first and only complete guide to self-directed education for teenagers. Many adults use it also, either in connection with homeschooling their children or teenagers, or to continue their own independent learning. It covers broad areas like legal issues and unschooling philosophy, and also gives very specific information to help anyone teach themselves anything, with thorough chapters on each major academic subject. There is a large section on learning through work (volunteering, apprenticing, starting a business, etc.), and over a hundred real-life examples of self-taught kids.

> Good grades are often equally dangerous. They encourage you to forsake everything worthwhile that you might love, just to keep getting them. When schoolpeople give you good grades, you give them your unquestioning loyalty in return. It makes me think of the Algonkian Indians who gave

Manhattan Island to the Dutch in exchange for six dollars' worth of trinkets. We are not talking here about fair bargains; we are talking about manipulation and colossal rip-off.

Good grades, moreover, are addictive. You start to depend on them for your sense of self-worth, and then it becomes nearly impossible to do anything that will jeopardize them. When you have good grades, you have something to lose, and so you stop taking risks. The best things in life come from taking risks.

Mary Pride, *The Big Book of Home Learning*, volumes 1-4 (Crossway Books, 1991). A widely used Christian homeschooling resource books. Pride is lively and opinionated yet well-informed, and these four books are friendly guides to the plethora of curricular materials available to homeschoolers. A valuable, though brief, component of the books is Pride's introduction to each subject area, where she does a remarkable job of explaining its fundamental perspectives. From Volume II, *Preschool and Elementary:*

> The most painless way to teach history to young children is through stories. Our kids love to hear their birth stories, and stories about the funny things Mom, Dad, Grandma, and Grandpa did when we were younger. Such simple stories give kids a sense of *past*, *present*, and *future*, and show them where they fit into the general scheme of things. You can then follow this up with simple historical tales, either from your own memory or from the library. Once a child learns to read well, the library is full of historical biographies he will enjoy....Good historical fiction serves much the same purpose in giving kids a taste of life in different time periods. Then wrap it all together with a time line, and your preteens will know as much about history as you can decently expect!

Barbara Sher, *Wishcraft: How to Get What You Really Want* (Viking, 1979). Although not specifically for homeschoolers, this is a powerful resource for anyone, of any age, who wants to design and carry out rewarding projects that further her or his most passionate interests....and that's the heart of what homeschooling is about for many happy kids. This book can help your children change their lives, especially if they're unmotivated and not really excited about anything. (This is a common temporary problem for new homeschoolers, who haven't yet unlearned the school lesson that Other People Run Our Lives.) Also excellent for adults who wish they had been homeschoolers—it's not too late!

> It's true that original achievements, great works of art, and the kinds of lives that are works of art almost always have their roots in childhood. Ask any famous woman or man, and you will probably find that they remember having a very clear sense of what they were meant to do at a very early age. A *Redbook* magazine article about singer Linda Ronstadt say that "Her first memory is of saying to her parents, 'Play me some music.' . . .She was four years old and singing with them one evening when she began to harmonize. Her father said, 'You aren't singing the melody.' She said, 'I know.' " And the sculptor Louise Nevelson, in her memoir *Dawns & Dusks*, remembers,

"From earliest, earliest childhood I knew I was going to be an artist. I *felt* like an artist. . . I drew in childhood, and went on painting daily. . . .As a young child I could go into a room and remember everything I saw. I'd take one glance and know everything I saw. That's a visual mind."

The only real difference between these people and you is that there is an unbroken continuity between the children they were and the adults they have become. We're going to go to work to reestablish that continuity for you. But first we need to know: who was that child? What did she or he love? The design of your life path is right there in miniature, like the genes in a seed that say it's going to become a tomato plant, a palm tree, or a rose. So I'd like you to think back to your childhood, and see how much you can remember that might point to your own special kind of genius.

Nancy Wallace, *Better Than School: One Family's Declaration of Independence* (Larson, 1983) and *Child's Work: Taking Children's Choices Seriously* (Holt Associates, 1990). An early pioneer of the movement, Wallace unschooled her son and daughter and watched them grow with tremendous insight. *Better than School* is a detailed account of the way she learned through experience to trust her young children, and of how she learned to deal with prejudiced school officials. *Child's Work* traces her children's development through adolescence, discussing the relationships between play, work, and education. From *Better Than School*:

> I wasn't the only person learning how to do less teaching—Bob had his little troubles too. Ishmael wanted to learn about electricity, so Bob went out and bought a bunch of electrical equipment and suggested that they begin by building an electric motor together. Bob had meant to let Ishmael do all the work, of course; but, in the typical adult manner, he began giving more advice, and then more advice, and finally, without even realizing it, he began to do all the work himself. Soon, out of sheer boredom, Ishmael slunk away and started reading. Naturally enough, Bob felt rotten. That afternoon Ishmael spent hours secretively building something in his room. When he emerged, we were amazed. Eyes glowing, and overflowing with pride, he showed us his new invention: an electric car, similar to one he had seen at Dilly's house, made out of a flashlight battery, tinker toys, and rubber bands! Ishmael wanted to learn about electricity but, once again, in a way that made sense to him.

From *Child's Work*:

> Children lose interest in us as teachers as soon as we make ourselves mere passive conveyors of knowledge, like most teachers in school, who try *not* to reveal their own personal biases and passions for fear of unduly influencing their students and preventing them from learning to think objectively. But children *want* us to reveal ourselves to them. Just as important, they want and need to be able to reveal their own feelings, ideas, and personal biases to us. Just as when we invite children to share in our pleasures and enthusiasms, so we play an important role as their teachers when we listen to them and take their ideas seriously. Only then can they actively test out

their ideas against honest and thoughtful responses. Children need us, as their teachers, to "push against," as Susannah once put it.

Carter G. Woodson, *The Mis-Education of the Negro* (Africa World Press, 1990). First published in 1933, this time-tested classic explores the history of African American education and the reasons it fails African American people. Offers ideas for solutions, specific to the difficulties African Americans face. A resource for justifying homeschooling to school officials and relatives. (Description adapted from *The Drinking Gourd* catalog, see below.)

> With "mis-educated Negroes" in control themselves, however, it is doubtful that the system would be very much different from what it is or that it would rapidly undergo change. The Negroes thus placed in charge would be the products of the same system and would show no more conception of the task at hand than do the whites who have educated them and shaped their minds as they would have them function. Negro educators of today may have more sympathy and interest in the race than the whites now exploiting Negro institutions as educators, but the former have no more vision than their competitors. Taught from books of the same bias, trained by Caucasians of the same prejudices or by Negroes of enslaved minds, one generation of Negro teachers after another have served for no higher purpose than to do what they are told to do. In other words, a Negro teacher instructing Negro children is in many respects a white teacher thus engaged, for the program in each case is about the same.

RECOMMENDED HOMESCHOOLING MAGAZINES

The Drinking Gourd Multicultural Home-Education Magazine, $15/year (six issues), $4 single issue, from The Drinking Gourd, PO Box 2557, Redmond, WA 98073, (800) TDG-5487. Edited by Donna Nichols-White. (Her essay in this book was actually culled from several pieces previously published in *The Drinking Gourd*.) Donna's witty, opinionated commentaries are definitely the highlight of this encouraging magazine, but it has helpful information contributed by other families too. Many ethnicities are represented, and a multicultural perspective is encouraged. From a piece by Donna:

> But then there are the surprises. One day you realize that you haven't done school in at least two weeks, because you've been too busy shopping for food, cooking meals, running after your toddler, visiting other homeschool families, and reading books. As you wallow in your guilt, you'll hear a strange sound emanating from somewhere in the house. You'll wonder, "What is that noise? It sounds vaguely familiar." It'll take a moment, but you'll eventually realize the sound is laughter. Squeals of delight are ringing through the house. Your children are actually playing—and playing well. For the first time in years, siblings are enjoying each other. Blocks, Legos and puzzles are actually being played with. You'll realize that some of the old problems like bed wetting, headaches, temper tantrums, and teeth

grinding, are no longer problems. And, most important, no one is asking you to entertain them. The child you sent to school for "x" number of years has returned, and the thrill of homeschooling has begun.

As the months go by, you'll realize that if you just answer 80% of your child's questions, she will be well educated. This is the essence of child led learning.

Growing Without Schooling magazine, bimonthly, $25/year from Holt Associates, 2269 Massachusetts Avenue, Cambridge, MA 02140, 617-864-3100. Current issue $6. The nation's oldest homeschooling magazine is wonderfully reassuring, comprehensive, and honest; many families say it's their single most important resource. *GWS* is full of detailed letters from parents and kids, which explore every conceivable subject related to homeschooling, from young children's play to teenagers working on archaeological digs to parents who disagree with each other about educational choices. *GWS* also prints short essays, articles, book reviews, legal news, and excellent interviews with people working on the cutting edge of education. For an unparalleled encyclopedia on homeschooling, buy the whole set of over 105 back issues and index for approximately $180. (Or share a set with other families or convince your support group library to buy them.) Subscribers can also ask Holt Associates to choose single back issues for them which focus on particular concerns, such as learning science, single-parent homeschooling, etc. From a mother's letter:

> Between August and mid-October of this year my ten-year-old daughter Morgan and I were one of nine volunteer teams doing water quality monitoring for the Nashua River Watershed Association. Every other Monday, we went to three sites along the Squannacook River and collected water samples in various containers. We then rushed our samples to the watershed treatment plant in the next town where the samples were tested. The man who runs the treatment plant was kind and patient enough to teach Morgan to run the tests herself. She learned to do the titration and calculations for dissolved oxygen, run the pH machine, and set up the incubation dishes for the fecal coliform tests. Morgan also came to meetings with me where we discussed and compared our results with each other. This was a terrific opportunity for Morgan to see how scientific data are gathered, analyzed and put into documentation form.

Home Education Magazine, bimonthly, currently $24/year from Home Education Magazine, P.O. Box 1083, Tonasket, WA 98855, phone (509) 486-1351. Current issue $4.50. Another excellent magazine which includes letters and good information about resources and legal issues, but the best attributes of this magazine are its thoughtful essays, its well-researched articles, and its regular columnists. (Very different from *GWS*—not in attitude but in format. These two magazines complement each other well.)

> Ahh, but real life isn't like that, you say? We all have to do things we don't want to do. Well, of course. Devon has chores that he needs to do, whether he is enthusiastic about them or not. And he knows that if he wants to

program computer games, he's going to have to sludge through some pretty dense material before he gets to the exciting parts. But if there's a reason, wading through difficult material becomes not only palatable, but interesting —as I found out then I became fascinated by the internet and decided to learn everything I could about it—which necessitated my reading some pretty technical computer books. But guess what? Suddenly bytes and bits were fascinating—because I had a valid, real life need to know.

What do your kids want to know about? What do they need to know to make their dreams come true? There's your curriculum—the real one. The one that you and your family create every day. Throw away those lesson plans and curriculum guides and spend some time talking—and listening— to your kids.

Homeschoolers for Peace and Justice, $15 for 5 issues from HFP&J, P.O. Box 74, Midpines, CA 95345, (209) 742-6802. Sample issue $3; enclose SASE with all other inquiries. All checks should be payable to Serena Gingold. Many homeschooling families publish newsletters and zines; this is one of the best and most enduring. It's written by and for homeschoolers ages twelve to eighteen who care about peace, justice, and environmental issues. Members use the newsletter as a forum for sharing their thoughts and to make friends with other like-minded homeschoolers. It's filled with articles, book reviews, and original artwork and poetry. Over the years HFP&J has devoted issues to subjects like Black History, the Power of Song, Native American Treaty Rights, the Struggle in South Africa, and Trailblazers of Peace and Justice.

MAIL ORDER SUPPLIERS.

Many catalogs now reach out to homeschoolers. A few stand out:

The Drinking Gourd catalog, free from The Drinking Gourd, PO Box 2557, Redmond, WA 98073, (800) TDG-5487. Produced by Donna Nichols-White (see her essay in this book). Donna and her friends and family have done some very serious research in putting together this unique catalog, which emphasizes materials for independent learning. It offers
- carefully chosen and tested multicultural biographies, literature, and interesting books about history (not history *textbooks*, which are usually dull and skewed).
- a variety of inexpensive curriculum materials in phonics, spelling, grammar, etc., and math and science materials from elementary through college level.
- educational software (including foreign language).
- laboratory equipment.
- books on homeschooling.

Product descriptions are interspersed with Donna's insightful comments and suggestions. **All the book descriptions in this bibliography followed by *DG* were taken from *The Drinking Gourd* catalog.**

Genius Tribe catalog, free from Genius Tribe, P.O. Box 1014, Eugene, OR 97440, (503) 686-2315. An offshoot of Lowry House Publishers, which brings you the book in your hand. Many little-known, inexpensive, valuable resources for unschoolers.

John Holt's Book and Music Store, free catalog from Holt Associates, 2269 Massachusetts Avenue, Cambridge, MA 02140, (617) 864-3100. This longtime national favorite (produced by the publishers of *Growing Without Schooling*) sells wonderful resources, all carefully chosen, kid-tested, and clearly described. No hype, no rip-offs.

Recycled Resources, trial issue $2.50 from P.O. Box 533, Red Feather Lakes, CO 80545, (970) 482-6755. Not exactly a catalog, but a nationwide want ad paper dedicated to homeschoolers who want to buy, sell, or trade used materials. As this book goes to press, *Recycled Resources* is so new that the first issue hasn't quite been printed yet, but the idea is timely and Michelle Foster, the editor and a homeschooling mother, is enthusiastic and committed. The first issue's ads will include a BBC German language course, a complete Cuisenaire math program, etc.—at very substantial savings. In addition to want ads, *Recycled Resources* will also run photos, articles, crafts ideas, pen-pal listings, profiles of homeschooling families, and other features.

OUTSTANDING BOOKS FOR REFERENCE AND FOR GENERAL LEARNING AND KNOWLEDGE

Richard Fobes, *The Creative Problem Solver's Toolbox: A Complete Course in the Art of Creating Solutions to Problems of Any Kind* (Solutions Through Innovation, 1993). One of the best books, if not *the* best book, on thinking skills. Unlike most other creative problem solving books, this one deals with solving real-life problems of every conceivable kind, rather than with made-up riddles or brain teasers. Zillions of strategies you can use to subdue all kinds of problems—the hunger of homeless people in your community, a friend's offensive jokes, the challenge of finding a great summer job, an ugly, cramped bedroom, the toxic waste in the air you breathe.

> A very useful way to create new ideas is to create new *combinations* of existing ideas. A simple form of combining ideas consists of combining existing objects to create a useful new object. For example, the clock radio was invented by combining a radio with an alarm clock. Notice that the

resulting combination offers an advantage—namely the clock can turn on the radio—that isn't available if a radio and alarm clock are simply placed side-by-side.

E.D. Hirsch, editor, *What Your First Grader* Needs to Know: Fundamentals of a Good First Grade Education* (Bantam Doubleday Dell, 1991). (*Also 2nd, 3rd, 4th, 5th, 6th.) Actually, I really hate these titles, the editor's purpose in creating the series, and the way the publisher promotes them. The arrogant phrase in the title, ":needs to know" says it all—as if almighty Hirsch is qualified to designate, from the vast array of human knowledge and experience, exactly which bits of data should be memorized by millions of unique children, simply because they have reached a particular age!

However, many homeschooling families do feel more *secure* if they know what their kids' peers are supposed to be learning in school, so they can at least expose their children to similar material. For this purpose, these books are excellent, and they're designed to be read to or by children themselves. Another good feature is that they pack a lot into a few words, yet manage to stay fairly interesting. Therefore, they don't need to dominate your homeschooling—they can provide quick access to the proverbial "well-rounded" education, while your kids spend the bulk of their time getting on with things that really matter—making compost, playing chess, building robots, painting walls, whatever. Each book clearly presents key concepts and information in language arts, social sciences, music, math, fine arts, and the natural sciences.

Howard Rheingold, editor, *The Millennium Whole Earth Catalog* (HarperSanFrancisco, 1994). Certainly one of the best friends any independent learner can have. This huge, intoxicating, masterfully designed book opens up hundreds of options you and your kids never knew existed, by describing and quoting from the best books (and other resources) in every imaginable category, from the Internet to Community Gardening, from Garage Robotics to Wildlife Care, from Understanding Corporations to Doing More With Less. Also see the earlier out of print (very useful) versions: *The Whole Earth Catalog, The Last Whole Earth Catalog, The Next Whole Earth Catalog,* often available in libraries and used book stores. You can learn an immense amount from reading these fun reference books alone, or you can follow up by going to the library or a store to track down some of the books, software, and other resources they recommend.

> Overspecialized education is the problem. This Catalog is intended to be part of the solution. We've intentionally arranged it to make obvious that everything really is connected to everything else....Consider it to be an introduction to the missing parts of a more formal education, with a bit of humor and delight thrown into the brew for seasoning.

Rebecca Rupp, *Good Stuff: Learning Tools for All Ages* (Home Education Press, 1993). Written by a longtime homeschooling mother, this is an excellent listing of great resources to help children and teenagers (and adults too) learn science, math, reading, writing, history, geography, foreign languages, art, music, creative thinking, and life skills. Thorough descriptions of books, magazines, catalogs, audio and video programs, equipment, games, educational toys, organizations—and of simple do-it-yourself ideas tested by the author, like making an "Imagination Box for Writers." Many of these resources are inexpensive, free, or widely available in libraries.

Edmund Scientific Company

The Edmund Scientific Company has been selling high-quality technical equipment for over half a century now. The company is particularly noted for their optical instruments; Edmund Scientific is thus an excellent source for those in the market for good-quality student microscopes. The catalog also offers a large and fascinating assortment of scientific kits, toys, gadgets, and books, targeted at junior scientists. Edmund Scientific sells Sea Monkeys, Magic Rocks, gyroscopes, and optical illusions cards - and model steam engines, molecular model building kits, and, for $19.95, miniature cloud chambers. For those on a budget, Edmund Scientific carries the "Shoe Box Science" kits, covering eight different topics: Magnets, Prisms, Mirrors, Weather, Illusions, Color, Bi-Metal Discs, and Science Oddities. Each kit costs $3.99 and contains an informational background booklet, suggestions for experimental investigations, and the necessary equipment and materials. And we've all got our eyes on Edmund's "Edible Optics" kit, with which kids cast lenses out of Jello, using as assortment of petri dishes and watch glasses. Students then measure the curvature of their gelatin lenses, and determine refractive indices. For a free 100+-page catalog, contact Edmund Scientific Company, 101 East Gloucester Pike, Barrington, NJ 08007-1380; (609) 573-6260 (customer service) or (609) 547-8880 (orders).

BOOKS FOR LEARNING ACADEMIC SUBJECTS

When creating a learning plan for yourself or your children, remember that everyone learns differently. And one of the most effective, joyful, and rewarding ways to learn is to devotedly pursue one or two of your greatest interests. For these reasons, there are no absolutely "best" resources for any of the academic subject areas. Help your children discover their own favorite books in libraries and stores, and recognize that their best learning aids might not be books at all, but perhaps relatives, parks, computer programs, shops, museums, hobbies, friends, ditches, family vacations.

That said, I'll go ahead and point out a few excellent subject-area books just to give you àn idea of what's available and what sort of books many homeschoolers use. Most of those listed below cost under fifteen dollars and are available from at least one of the catalogs above. Libraries and good bookstores can provide many of them too. Some of the following books emphasize African American history and achievements, to help balance the skewed Eurocentric worldview that children pick up from even a few years of school or from TV. **All descriptions followed by *DG* are adapted from Donna Nichols-White's *Drinking Gourd* catalog, described above.**

Biography/History/Social Sciences

Linda Brent, *Incidents in the Life of a Slave Girl* (Harvest, 1973). An inspiring autobiography. Born a slave, Linda spent years in hiding in order to keep her children (who were slaves) from harm. Her determination to be free and to free her children from slavery is inspirational. Ages ten and up. *DG*

John Carey, editor, *Eyewitness to History* (Avon, 1987). A lively history book, almost impossible to put down, but not for the squeamish. It's all written by eyewitnesses: Pliny the Younger describes Mt. Vesuvius erupting and burying Pompeii on August 24, AD 79. Bartolome de Las Casas describes Spanish invaders torturing natives of the West Indies in the 1500's. An American news reporter witnesses the execution of Nazi war criminals. Tales of death and destruction are, thankfully, interspersed with happier accounts like Neil Armstrong's description of his first moments on the moon.

Burke Davis, *Black Heroes of the American Revolution* (HarBrace, 1976). Accounts of Black people who fought, worked, sacrificed and died in the struggle for America's independence. Grade levels five and up. *DG*

Frederick Douglass, *Narrative of the Life of Frederick Douglass, An American Slave* (Penguin, 1982). The eloquent and dramatic autobiography of his early life, first published in 1845. Ages ten through adult. *DG*

Marie E. Lyons, *Deep Blues: Bill Traylor, Self-Taught Artist* (Scribner/Macmillan, 1994). The story of Bill Traylor, who was born a slave and became a self-taught, famous artist. His life spanned the Civil War, Reconstruction, and both World Wars. Illustrated with full-color and black and white photos. Ages eight to eleven. *DG*

Marie E. Lyons, *Master of Mahogany: Tom Day, Free-Black Cabinetmaker* (Macmillan, 1994). The biography of Tom Day, a free, literate African American master craftsman, whose cradles, beds, and tables graced many southern homes, including the governor's mansion. Rarely is a book published that depicts the lives of free Black people during slavery. An excellent example of self-teaching and self-determination. Twenty full-color photographs and ten black-and-white photographs. Ages eight to eleven. *DG*

Milton Meltzer, *The Black Americans: A History in their Own Words* (Crowell Jr. Books/HarperCollins, 1984). A condensation of his three volume *In Their Own Words* series, covering three and a half centuries of Black life in the United States. Letters, speeches, newspaper articles, and book excerpts. Junior High level and up. *DG*

Walter Dean Myers, *Now is Your Time! The African American Struggle for Freedom* (Trophy/HarperCollins, 1992). An exploration of the African American experience from slavery through the civil rights movement to contemporary times. Winner of the 1992 Coretta Scott King Author Award. Grades five and up. *DG*

Ann Petry, *Harriet Tubman: Conductor on the Underground Railroad* (Marshall Cavendish, 1991). A well written and moving story of the life of Harriet Tubman, who led over three hundred Black people from slavery to freedom in the north. Ages eight to eleven. *DG*

Steven Vanderstay, *Street Lives: an oral history of homeless Americans* (New Society). Over thirty diverse homeless people share their stories and circumstances. Runaway and homeless teenagers, veterans, homeless families, and people with mental illnesses. A moving, disturbing book.

On Black America Collectors Cards. A series of cards that highlight the contributions made by African Americans to American history. Each set contains thirty-five cards and a teaching guide; accompanying cassette tapes and quiz sheet available too. *Vol. 1, The Civil Rights Movement*: The people, places, and events which helped shape American society during the struggle for equality. *Vol. II, They Fought For America*: African American soldiers' service in defense of America from the Revolutionary War to Desert Storm. *Vol. III, Science and Discovery*: scientists and discoverers in the fields of engineering, science, medicine. *DG*

The Timetables Series (Simon and Schuster). When the review copy of *The Timetables of African American History* arrived, I [Donna Nichols-White] was thrilled. Finally, an accurate time line of the history of African Americans! I was so impressed I decided to include it and its predecessors in The Drinking Gourd Book Co. line. Remarkably informative, this series of books presents major events in history, science, religion, the arts, publications, laws and legal actions, sports, medicine and more. Each book is an in-depth time line of people, events and discoveries. Written for adults, the ten-year-old who reads well should be able to understand, utilize, and enjoy this series. One note: Many homeschoolers enjoy unit studies. *The Timetables* are written in chronological order with subject titles (General History, Education, Religion,

Science, etc.) consistently categorized. A time period can easily be referred to, and the information offered will supply an excellent framework for your unit study. Series includes *The Timetables of African American History*, *The Timetables of American History*, *The Timetables of Jewish History*, *The Timetables of Women's History*, and *The Timetables of Science*. **DG**

Foreign Language

Barry Farber, *How to Learn any Language: Quickly, Easily, Inexpensively, Enjoyably, and On Your Own* (Citadel, 1991). Empowerment at its best. The revolutionary common sense here will forever rid you of the silly idea that you have to go to school to learn German or Arabic or Hausa or Portuguese. The author, who proves that "aptitude is less important than appetite," has used the methods in this book to learn more than seventeen languages. Wonderful strategies for learning both at home and abroad, by drawing from numerous resources including books, tapes, native speakers, and clubs.

> Most phrase books offer too few of these "crutch" phrases. When you meet your first encounter, pull out pen and pad and fatten your crutch collection. Learn how to say things such as, "I'm only a beginner in your language but I'm determined to become fluent," "Do you have enough patience to talk with a foreigner who's trying to learn your language?" "I wonder if I'll ever be as fluent in your language as you are in English," "I wish your language were as easy as your people are polite," and "Where in your country do you think your language is spoken the best?" Roll your own alternatives. You'll soon find yourself developing what comedians call a "routine," a pattern of conversation that actually gives you a feeling of fluency along with the inspiration to nurture that feeling into fruition.

Language Arts

Kathy Henderson, *Market Guide for Young Writers* (Writer's Digest, updated frequently). A comprehensive, serious guide for writers eighteen and younger. Henderson gives general advice on getting published, and extensive lists of contests, awards, and places that encourage submissions. She profiles editors and young writers who have been published, and answers common questions—"What is a query letter?" "Why should I bother sending material to a publication that doesn't pay for it?"

James Weldon Johnson, editor, *The Book of American Negro Poetry* (Harvest Books/HarBrace, 1969). This anthology includes Langston Hughes, Countee Cullen, Paul Lawrence Dunbar, Leslie Pinckney Hill, Georgia Douglass Johnson, and others. Ages twelve and up. **DG**

Clarence Major, editor, *Calling the Wind: Twentieth-Century African American Short Stories* (HarperCollins, 1993). An anthology which includes short stories from the Reconstruction, World Wars I and II, The Harlem Renaissance, and The Civil Rights Movement. Ages twelve through adult. *DG*

Robin Moore, *Awakening the Hidden Storyteller: How to Build a Storytelling Tradition in Your Family* (Shambhala, 1991). An outstanding and empowering guide written by a professional storyteller. Full of creative exercises, activities, examples, and advice, this book helps children and adults deepen their imaginations, grow closer to one another, and develop a wide range of language skills. Straightforward and fun to read, yet wonderfully detailed. Moore clearly recognizes that learning, loving, and living all unfold best when not separated from each other.

> As our ancestors knew very well, storytelling adds a layer of richness to everyday life. Stories become real for us, and simple objects—trees or candles or racks—take on special meanings because we have encountered them in our stories. When I tell my kids a story like "Silver Lake Trout," they know that some of it really happened and some of it didn't. They know that a story doesn't have to be true in the literal sense. They also know that I am not trying to deceive them or trick them. What we seek in storytelling is mythic truth. A myth is, as the mythologist Jean Houston says, "something that never happened but is going on all the time." The Jungian analyst Robert Johnson points out, "A myth is something that is true on the inside but not on the outside." Although the story of the walking fish is not factually true, it is an accurate reflection of how I felt about my grandfather and our summers at Silver Lake. When my kids hear this story, they get a glimpse into a time before they were born, a time they somehow come out of. This story gives them a link to me and to their great-grandfather, who died before they were born. Storytelling, creating an imaginative world and investing it with meaning, has added a great strength and joy to our family's life.

Peter Stillman, *Families Writing* (Writer's Digest, 1989). This book truly answers the question, "Why write?" Write to strengthen connections between you and the people you love. The author clearly gives many detailed (but not restrictive) ideas for shared journals, unique letters, words as gifts, stories tailored for particular people, etc. Inspiring examples by writers of all ages get the point across vividly. I wish there were more books like this one and *Awakening the Hidden Storyteller*: books that help people both develop their own skills *and* at the same time get better bonded to families and friends.

> At least once a week plan a journal read-around. There are no rules to guide this practice beyond everyone's listening attentively to whatever the reader has chosen to share and nobody's being critical of subject matter, style, and most especially mechanical errors. For that matter, families should make an enduring habit of weekly readings-aloud of anything, journal extracts to be

included, but just as appropriately five minutes' worth of Charles Dickens or Garrison Keillor, a letter written by an ancestor or a current family member, an editorial, brief article, poem, song lyric, short-short story—whatever amuses, engages, instructs. Do encourage pre-readers to participate. *Three-year-olds don't know that they can't read and write.* So ask them to read the stories they make with cryptic crayon scrawls, even if you can't...

Science

Gail L. Grand, *Student Science Opportunities* (Wiley, 1994). Do environmental research on an Alaskan ice field, traveling between base and field camps by cross-country skis and dog sleds. Work on a physics research team. Study monkeys in the Kenyan rain forest. This is an enticing directory of opportunities available to teenagers. (A few are open to younger and older people also.) Mostly, these are summer programs and internships lasting from one to eight weeks. Also contests, awards, enrichment classes and programs, scholarships, and listings especially for women and minorities. **Many are free** except for transportation to and from the site; some even *pay* you to go.

Louis Haber, *Black Pioneers of Science and Invention* (HarBrace, 1970). This book highlights twelve scientists and inventors, including Garret E. Morgan, inventor of the traffic light, and Daniel Hale Williams, who performed the first open heart surgery. Ages ten and up. *DG*

Jearl Walker, *The Flying Circus of Physics With Answers* (Wiley, 1977). "What I mainly want to show here," writes the author, "Is that physics is not something that has to be done in a physics building. Physics and physics problems are in the real, everyday world that we live, work, love, and die in." Difficult and challenging, to be sure, but you can work/play with this book whether you've had zero physics classes or ten years of physics classes. Basically, it's a heap of questions. Choose one, think and dream on it for a few hours or a few years, and then when you've had enough of that, turn to the back and read a brief explanatory answer. The author also lists reference articles and books that can take you deeper into each question/answer. A sample question:

> If you've ever taped your own voice, you were probably surprised by how thin it sounded when you played it back. Other people recorded their voice and their playbacks sounded fine to you. But yours...it just wasn't right. What was wrong?

Math

Ron Van Der Meer and Bob Gardner, *The Math Kit, A Three-Dimensional Tour Through Mathematics* (Macmillan, 1994). An extraordinary collection of mathematical pop-ups, interactive mechanics, pullouts and more. Explores the beauty, the power, and the fun of mathematics. Unlike any book or game ever created it covers a wide range of mathematical subjects from basic arithmetic, to plane geometry, to trigonometry to simple calculus.

Designed for everyone from the math illiterate to the most gifted mathematical prodigy, this is an excellent resource that eliminates math anxiety. I've shown this kit to friends who, by their own admission, do not even attempt to teach their children basic math. To their surprise they quickly became comfortable with *The Math Kit* and were enjoying mathematics within minutes. Your children will not view *The Math Kit* as curriculum and they shouldn't, for it was designed for fun mathematical exploration and understanding. *DG*

Saxon textbooks (from kindergarten math through calculus and physics, free placement tests available). The Saxons are becoming famous among homeschoolers (and in many schools also) for two reasons. First, except for the kindergarten through third grade sets, they are intelligently designed to be used independently. Most kids find that they can understand the clear explanations, and complete the work without a parent's help. Second, the Saxon method stresses review, so people who use them usually retain the material far better than their peers who use other textbooks. Like most textbooks, Saxons are expensive, with prices ranging from approximately $45 to $90. However, you may be able to find them used locally or through Recycled Resources, and you will probably sell them easily when you're finished. Request a free Home Study Catalog from Saxon Publishers, Inc., 1320 West Lindsey, Norman, OK 73069, (800) 284-284-7019.

MISCELLANEOUS RESOURCES

Johna Bergstrom and Craig Bergstrom, *All the Best Contests for Kids* (Ten Speed Press, frequently revised). If your kids enjoy competition (fine if they don't, of course), this book can make it more fun and meaningful than just competing for A's given by a confused teacher in a class graded by the bell curve. Some of these contests are only open to people twelve and under, while many have divisions for teenagers also, and some for adults. Over a hundred contests for sand castle builders, poets, horse essayists, spellers, gardeners, photographers, computer programmers, and just about everyone else.

Judith B. Erickson, *Directory of American Youth Organizations* (Free Spirit Publishing, updated frequently). Many unschooled kids find social and educational fulfillment *without* joining organizations of any kind. But some families seek out youth organizations to provide their kids with the experience of working with a peer group. While 4-H, Scout troops, and performing arts groups are very popular among homeschoolers, there are also hundreds of other little-known national organizations with chapters across the country. This comprehensive guidebook describes over five hundred national adult-sponsored clubs, groups, teams, etc. for children and teenagers—ranging from math to sports to religion to environmental activities to career education. Some examples: The U.S. Youth Soccer Organization, Fellowship of Christian Athletes, Rotary International Youth Exchange Program, National Student Campaign Against Hunger and Homelessness, National Double Dutch League (for jump-ropers), Young Actors' Guild, Students for the Development and Exploration of Space.

Martin Kimeldorf, *Creating Portfolios: For Success in School, Work, and Life* (Free Spirit Publishing, 1994). A portfolio is like a serious scrapbook, which might contain essays, photographs, artwork, award, computer printouts, videos, recipes, brochures, letters, quotes, songs, poems, formulas, newsletters, reviews, or maps. It's an excellent—and *fun*—way for homeschoolers to organize and present their work and talents. Portfolios can help tremendously with college or work applications, and in some states, portfolios help homeschoolers satisfy legal requirements. This workbook holds your hand as you choose what kind of a portfolio to make, what to put in it, and how to organize it for maximum style and impact. Simply written, but thorough, useful, and unique.

> Once you've selected and organized your samples, it's time to give each one a title and description. Without this important information, your audience might not understand why you included a particular sample.
>
> For instance, a letter of reference or award certificate might explain itself. But what about a union card, a student ID card, or a copy of your driver's license? Perhaps the union card shows your ability to assume an adult role in the work world, where you earned union membership by working in a factory or hospital. A student ID card might be used to tell the story of your participation in fundraising, student committees, or outstanding attendance. Maybe you've given up driving a car and now ride a bike to help reduce pollution and that's why you put a copy of your driver's license in your portfolio. In other words, you have excellent reasons for selecting these samples, but your audience won't know your reasons unless you include them in your descriptions.

A Homeschoolers' Consulting Service is now offered by the oldest and (many people say) best homeschooling organization. Holt Associates always welcomes calls or letters requesting general information or advice about homeschooling, and generously provides such information and advice at no charge. If you want to discuss issues or questions in greater depth, 45-minute private phone consultations are available. For rates and more information, call 617-864-3100 or write Holt Associates, 2269 Mass. Ave, Cambridge, MA 02140.

Homeschooling Resource List (Holt Associates, updated frequently). Available for $4 from Holt Associates, 2269 Massachusetts Avenue, Cambridge, MA 02140 (617) 864-3100. Extensive list of nationwide homeschooling organizations and support groups—use it to get in touch with homeschoolers near you. Also: hundreds of schools that work with homeschoolers, correspondence schools, suppliers, etc.

HOMESCHOOLING RESOURCES IN CYBERSPACE

Undoubtedly, many more will appear as rapidly as everything else on the internet. As of August, 1995, each of the major commercial providers (Compuserve, Prodigy, America On-Line, etc.) has some type of homeschooling forum or bulletin board. In addition, several of the most important homeschooling magazines and other resources now have sites on the World Wide Web or on one of the commercial providers. Here are a few:

Growing Without Schooling/Holt Associates has a section on Compuserve. Enter GO EDLINE at any Compuserve "!" prompt, and you'll find information about products in their catalog, on-line support for unschooling, libraries of speeches, articles, book reviews and references, and the opportunity to chat electronically with the *GWS* staff and other homeschoolers.

Home Education Magazine has a forum on America Online, which provides an opportunity to interact with the people who produce and write for the megazine. The forum includes a message board, a library, articles and columns, resources, and a weekly two-hour chat session. Find it in the larger Homeschooling Forum, which is in the Parents Information Network. Keywords are "Homeschool" and "HEM."

Donna Nichols-White and *The Drinking Gourd* have a section within the *Home Education Magazine* forum.

Cheríe Pogue (see her essay in this book) is willing to discuss homeschooling on-line. As this book goes to press, her e-mail address is qmfv00@prodigy.com. Hopefully it will remain a little more constant than her *home* address! ❖

INDEX

about the editor

Grace Llewellyn worked for three years as a school teacher before leaving to unschool herself and to spread the word about self-directed education. She wrote *The Teenage Liberation Handbook: how to quit school and get a real life and education*, edited *Real Lives: eleven teenagers who don't go to school*, and founded Genius Tribe, an unschooling resource center in Eugene, Oregon. She enjoys speaking at conferences, colleges, and special events. Also, she teaches and performs Middle Eastern dance, and lives happily with her husband Skip. They plan to have children and, of course, to unschool them!

tell your story

The experts on homeschooling are not scholars, authors, or superintendents, but rather individual families who have learned through trial and error what works. The homeschooling movement thrives largely because these experts share their experiences, which inspire and help others. Lowry House Publishers may later publish an updated, expanded version of this book, so please contact us by mail if you are interested in telling your story. And consider contributing to *Growing Without Schooling* magazine, *Home Education Magazine*, or *The Drinking Gourd*--all are eager to hear from homeschoolers of color.

spread the word

Would you like to sell copies of this book or *The Teenage Liberation Handbook* or *Real Lives* at a festival, conference, party, fundraiser, or other event? We offer discounts for large orders. **Option #1**: Order fifteen or more copies (can be mixed between the three titles) and receive a 30% discount--TLH/RL $10.95 each, *Freedom Challenge* $12.35 each. Prices include shipping. **Option #2**: Order a full case of any book (36-48 copies) and get a 40% discount--phone for details. **No returns** on large orders except by special arrangement. **Payment:** U.S. funds only: check, MO, or Visa/MC (include card #, expiration date, and signature). Phone us at 503-686-2315, fax to 503-342-7236. or mail to Lowry House Publishers, P.O. Box 1014, Eugene, OR 97440-1014. Thanks!

ALSO FROM LOWRY HOUSE PUBLISHERS

Erin's favorite teacher is her horse, who's blind in one eye. Kyla flew to South America--alone, except for a bike. Jeremiah and Serena publish a newsletter on peace issues. Ayanna keeps pace with 50 pen-pals--mostly in Africa--while Kevin talks with people worldwide through ham radio. Amanda performs with a violin quintet and works through the mail with her writing mentor. Vallie answers questions at a marine science center; Tabitha answers the phone at a crisis line...and helps midwives at births...

REAL LIVES: eleven teenagers who don't go to school

edited & with an introduction by Grace Llewellyn

Nominee, Best Books for Young Adults 1994 (American Library Association)

Buy this book! ...It may stun some teens--more likely their parents and their teachers-- but it is a mind-expanding experience... Eleven "unschooled" teens write about...how they learn, socialize, study, and especially how their special interests and loves have directed their unconventional educations.... These autodidacts' days embrace a challenging freedom unimagined by those of us bound by the limits and assumptions of the classroom....For those teens who...travel to the beat of a different drummer, this fascinating book may point the way to a viable alternative....a consciousness-raising journey of a special kind. --Kliatt Young Adult Paperback Book Guide

A wonderful book, a revolutionary book like Uncle Tom's Cabin, *a book to set people free.* --John Taylor Gatto, author of *Dumbing Us Down* and *The Exhausted School.*

Compelling stories....Don't be fooled by your personal memories of teenage writing. This is NOT a stack of high school English essays waiting to be graded. Instead it is a fascinating study in self-teaching....Each essay is unique, both in style and content. --The Oregon Home Education Network Network News

[The profiles] are nicely varied and each student's personal voice shines through as he or she explains why traditional education was abandoned and what has replaced it.... --American Library Association Booklist

These kids give me hope for a brighter future. Highly inspirational--Living Free Newsletter

Rich in-depth biographical and philosophical essays solicited from 11 teens who tell why they made the decision (with the help of their families) not to be "tamed" or stifled by traditional schooling methodologies and regulations. The essays shed light on what happens during a typical day in the lives of homeschooled individuals, how the teens became as educated (and self-confident) as they appear to be, what motivates them to learn, their views on homeschooling versus traditional education, hopes for the future, etc. Many misconceptions about homeschooling are debunked...--Library Journal

THE TEENAGE LIBERATION HANDBOOK: how to quit school and get a real life and education
by Grace Llewellyn

This is a very dangerous book. It contradicts all the conventional wisdom about dropouts and the importance of a formal education. It is funny and inspiring. Do not, under any circumstances, share this book with a bright, frustrated high-schooler being ground into mind fudge by the school system. [I] cannot be responsible for the happiness and sense of personal responsibility that might come from reading this book.--Bloomsbury Review

Packed with information for young people who want more than schools can offer....an invaluable and unique resource....Llewellyn knows how to speak directly and persuasively to young readers, and even those who do not decide to leave school after reading her book will have a hard time viewing formal education in quite the same way again....A fascinating, frightening, and exhilarating book sure to prove controversial among parents and teachers. At the very least it will open eyes and minds. At the most it might open whole new worlds of possibilities for its young readers.--Voice of Youth Advocates (VOYA)

Sooner or later you're going to realize that you've been cheated out of a real life by missing a real education--when that time comes Grace Llewellyn's Handbook will save you a thousand hours of frustration, false starts and missed opportunities. Anyone who follows this clear blueprint is certain to meet the future with courage, enthusiasm, resourcefulness and the abundant love of life that the author has. She demonstrates brilliantly that school and education are two very different things, defining the latter precisely and with such a wonderful zest the reader is left dazzled with his own rich possibilities. Get this book now so it will be on hand for the great emergency when you wake up. --John Taylor Gatto, former New York State Teacher of the Year

I've just finished reading The Teenage Liberation Handbook and I can't find words to tell you how helpful it was to me. You've just dredged all my fears and hassles out, looked at them, and waved them goodbye. Thank you!!!. The Handbook gave me back my faith [in my kids] and made me look at them again. I saw that to take their freedom, inventiveness, curiosity, energy, and joy and bury them in a classroom would be a terrible waste of vital life. Thank you for giving me back that confidence. Thanks for your enthusiasm and trust and love in these kids.....--Terri Shoosmith, Ireland

Thank you for your Teenage Liberation Handbook. I purchased it last weekend and read it at one sitting. I am a credentialed home school instructor working for a County Office of Education Home School Program. I am recommending to all my families that they read your book, as it has profoundly affected me at an age and point in my life where I certainly didn't expect it! I want to try to express to you the support, excitement, freedom and regrets for missed opportunities that I feel from reading your book. But what I really want to thank you for is my own liberation. After reading your book, I have felt the renewed excitement and energy of learning again for myself, my way, without having to make excuses, apologize for it or wrap it up in an acceptable facade--acts that have wasted too much of my energy. I have visited schools in about 30 countries, looking for ideas, methods, trends and patterns that connect learning and growing with life and the community in hopes of being able to help my students do the same. Your book was the quickest (and cheapest) of those journeys I have yet made.
--R. Francesca De Lorme, California

GENIUS TRIBE MAIL-ORDER BOOKS

Genius Tribe mail order is an offshoot of Lowry House Publishers, and also of the Genius Tribe resource center for unschoolers in Eugene, Oregon. All these books are described in Appendix III. Prices may change. If you're not happy with your books, return them. We'll refund your money (except shipping costs) immediately and cheerfully.

TITLE	EACH	#	PRICE
Freedom Challenge	16.95		
The Teenage Liberation Handbook	14.95		
Real Lives: eleven teenagers who don't go to school	14.95		
Alternatives in Education	16.75		
Awakening the Hidden Storyteller	18.00		
Creating Portfolios	11.95		
The Creative Problem Solver's Toolbox	17.75		
Directory of American Youth Organizations	18.95		
Dumbing Us Down	9.95		
Eyewitness to History	12.00		
Good Stuff: Learning Tools for All Ages	14.75		
How to Learn Any Language	9.95		
The Independent Scholar's Handbook	14.95		
The Millenium Whole Earth Catalog	30.00		
Student Science Opportunities	14.95		
Genius Tribe catalog of books for unschoolers	FREE		
SUBTOTAL			
SHIPPING (see below)			
TOTAL (no sales tax!)			

SHIPPING: **U.S.**: $3 for the 1st book, $1 for each additional book to the same address, maximum $6, free if your order is over $100. No U.S. shipping charge for catalog. **Canada/World**: $4 1st item, $1 each additional item, $15 maximum. Pay in U.S. funds: check, M.O., or Visa/MC. Make checks to Lowry House.

Visa/MC #: _____ exp. date _____

Authorized signature _____

your
name:_____phone_____

street
address:_____

City/State/Zip:_____

PHONE? 503-686-2315. (If you call and get the voice-mail, please leave your order and also your phone number.) FAX? 503-342-7236. MAIL? Box 1014, Eugene, OR 97440.